"Pomp & Circumstance *is a ...... gers and cynics who want to write Britain off that they do so at their peril."*
JONATHAN ASHWORTH, LABOUR TOGETHER

"*This book is the antidote to Britain's crisis of confidence. Our traditions and values help us face the future and they should be celebrated.*"
IAIN DALE, LBC

"*An important and absorbing reminder of the importance of those colourful, deep-rooted rituals that have shaped Britain's soul – and why we meddle with them at our peril.*"
ROBERT HARDMAN, DAILY MAIL AND AUTHOR
OF CHARLES III: THE INSIDE STORY

"*A wonderful examination of the UK's customs and a celebration of those who created them. Guaranteed to cheer you up.*"
ALISTER JACK, BARON JACK OF COURANCE

"Pomp & Circumstance *is quietly subversive and challenges readers of all parties, and none, to reflect on how best to learn from our island's past.*"
PETER KELLNER, FORMER PRESIDENT OF YOUGOV

"*Egalitarianism resents colour and custom because they mark difference and stir emotions that cannot be tamed by officialdom. Tradition liberates us from fashion and its transitory tyrants. You'd never have found Karl Marx at a morris dance.*"
QUENTIN LETTS, DAILY MAIL

"*There's no one better placed to tell this important story about Britain's traditions.*"
CATHY NEWMAN, CHANNEL 4 NEWS

DAME PENNY MORDAUNT & CHRIS LEWIS

POMP & CIRCUMSTANCE
WHY BRITAIN'S TRADITIONS MATTER

Biteback Publishing

First published in Great Britain in 2025 by
Biteback Publishing Ltd, London
Copyright © Penny Mordaunt and Chris Lewis 2025

Penny Mordaunt and Chris Lewis have asserted their rights under the Copyright, Designs
and Patents Act 1988 to be identified as the authors of this work.

Extracts from Noël Coward's *This Happy Breed* reproduced by permission of Alan Brodie
Representation Ltd, www.alanbrodie.com

Extract from Chris Lewis and Pippa Malmgren's *The Leadership Lab* reproduced by permission
of Kogan Page Ltd, copyright © Chris Lewis and Pippa Malmgren 2019

Second and third stanzas from 'For Johnny' from *For Johnny: Poems of World War II* by John
Pudney © John Pudney, 1976, published by Shepheard-Walwyn (Publishers) Ltd, reproduced by
permission of David Higham Associates

Every reasonable effort has been made to trace copyright holders of material reproduced in this
book, but if any have been inadvertently overlooked the publisher would be glad to hear from them.

ISBN 978-1-78590-994-8

10 9 8 7 6 5 4 3 2 1

A CIP catalogue record for this book is available from the British Library.

Set in Minion Pro and Montserrat

Printed and bound in Great Britain by
CPI Group (UK) Ltd, Croydon CR0 4YY

To Frank & Ethel

CONTENTS

PREFACE

Being part of the coronation of HM King Charles III on Saturday 6 May 2023 changed my life in ways I didn't expect. My first inkling of this was just after the ceremony. I got changed, packed my kit into my car and drove from Westminster back to Portsmouth. Until that moment, I'd simply been focused on doing my job. I was just relieved that it had all gone well and I hadn't let anyone down. I hadn't tripped up. I hadn't dropped the Sword of State. I'd resisted looking over my shoulder at the head of the procession. This was mainly because we'd trained and rehearsed over and over again with military precision.

In the following weeks, I was sent hundreds of pictures of me carrying the Sword of State that had been drawn by children, together with hopes for their own futures and good wishes for their new King and their country. Others wrote letters about their pride. I received more letters about the coronation than I did votes at any election. I realised that the spectacle was a manifestation of all they held in their hearts about our country. We'd all been through so much with Covid and the death of Her Majesty. I knew it really mattered to so many.

Some were overwhelmed, perhaps by the emotion of the time, but so many wrote to me to thank me for my role on the day, saying how they really felt about the country. There were so many questions about how I managed to carry the weight of the sword. I hadn't really given it much thought. Frankly, I was too busy concentrating.

Looking back, though, the ancient tradition of the coronation did something unusual. No one forgot their sadness about Her Majesty

Queen Elizabeth II, but it made them think about the future that was vested in His Majesty the King. The tradition helped us through the transition. It helped us all see a bigger picture.

It was the composer Gustav Mahler who said: 'Tradition is not the worship of ashes, but the preservation of fire.'

There are times when it feels like we've lost our appetite for the future. The coronation, though, seemed to reignite the nation's appreciation for the things that had stayed constant, despite everything changing. It taught me something that I knew but had not fully understood until then. Right from the moment I delivered the Accession Council at St James's Palace to the moment I carried His Majesty's regalia at Westminster Abbey, something became clear. The ceremony and tradition brought together the many elements of what forms the constitution, the monarchy, the judiciary, the executive, the civic, the national, the local and the individual. It did what it was designed to do. It brought us together. It helped us through uncertain times. It reassured us during a time of loss. It helped us to process the past, understand its importance and prepare us for the future.

This is true of all traditions, whether they be national, local, formal or frivolous. These traditions become more important in rapidly changing times.

This book looks at the dramatic events of the last twenty-five years and at our current mood. It asks what challenges we face and how we might tackle them. It catalogues royal, military and state traditions and asks what is quintessentially British and why. There is a particular focus on the royal and the military because these are our most ancient and vivid traditions.

Finally, it draws conclusions and asks how our traditions prepare us for the future. It finishes with a UK-wide calendar of local customs and additional national events organised by season.

If you look through this calendar of events, it won't escape you that whether national or local, ancient or modern, they have much in common. They venerate royalty of all sorts – Pearly Kings are important, as are carnival queens. They pillory politicians of all levels. They celebrate identity and character. They cherish the next generation. They honour sacrifice and the selfless. They mostly involve dressing up, behaving unusually, banging a drum, marching around, drinking heavily, risking life and limb and, above all, laughing.

Our sense of humour seems to be the only thing we take really seriously and with good reason. It tells us about someone's timing, judgement, attitude and even terms of reference. It tells us how well they will bear stress and maybe even how much fun they might be. It also tells us about their humanity. After all, bureaucracy seldom has a sense of humour. It was Charlie Chaplin, a south London boy, who looked at Adolf Hitler and decided that the best response to unimaginable evil was to mock it in *The Great Dictator*.

So, if you're wondering why I'm writing a book about the monarchy, the military or morris dancers in the Midlands when the world seems to have gone mad, it's because there's something in our traditions that has become more important recently, given the increasing volatility.

Many feel these traditions are under threat and need to be defended. I agree. In a time of rapid change, they mean a lot to us. Our character is deeply ingrained in our culture, history and many of these ancient rituals, both national and local.

If ever a lesson needs to be learned, it's now. All politics is local. A wave of nationalism is being felt in many countries. This is not new in history. It's often felt in hard or uncertain times. It ends up with a retreat to national borders and a turning inward. That would be a disaster for Britain economically, socially and culturally, given our international trading past. This is where our history comes in. Because we've seen it before, we've learned. We're uniquely positioned to adapt.

I believe that localism is the antidote to nationalism. It's precisely the fear of losing our national priorities that's driving nationalism – the notion that globalism, left unchecked, will rob us of our high streets, churches, pubs and our identity.

One person we hear a lot from these days is the cynic. They are so certain about us and our country. They'll write it off. They'll say it's finished. That everything in Britain is broken or second-rate. But all that does is undermine morale and confidence. Since when did anyone improve with constant criticism? Our military, our schools, our charities, our universities, our police, our hospitals, our businesses, our emergency services are full of hard-working, dedicated people who love this country. They are not lazy, greedy, feckless or stupid. And if you condemn them, how would that make them less so? Leadership is about getting people to be the best they can, not sticking a label on them. The public knows this and remains sceptical of those that have done nothing to help and who have no real feeling for who we are.

These cynics say they know our country, but if they really did, they'd know that you can never write us off. We've heard these voices so many times before. We've been written off when facing the French at Agincourt. Written off by Europe when embracing religious reform and becoming a Protestant country. Written off when facing the Spanish Armada. Written off against Napoleon. Written off when facing the Nazis alone. Written off after Dunkirk, when Churchill came to power. Written off when Margaret Thatcher came to office. Written off when facing the Argentinians. Written off when taking on the trade unions. Written off again when Margaret Thatcher left office. Written off before the 2012 Olympics. Written off after Brexit. Written off after having five Prime Ministers in six years. This attitude was satirised by Noël Coward in 1952.

THERE ARE BAD TIMES JUST AROUND THE CORNER

https://www.youtube.com/watch?v=tSA5C8mQcLQ

There can only be one provenance of this sort of miserabilist certainty – mediocrity. You never really know how things might turn out. In all human endeavour, belief is important. If you believe you can succeed, then there's more chance you will. Imagination and innovation grow from a sense of hope, not hopelessness. Our democratic and capital systems also run on this belief. The investor has faith that they might get a better return in the long run. The student believes if they are educated, they might be more successful. The doctor knows that patients that want to get well, often do better than those who have given up. It's a bit like Tinker Bell's light in *Peter Pan*. Brains are important, but belief matters more. Belief and pride is to nations what self-respect is to individuals – a necessary condition for self-improvement.[1]

The only truly predictable indicator of the future is our character and culture – and ours is good. It is stubborn, sceptical, industrious, funny, practical, level-headed and fair. No matter what the world has thrown at us, we've always surprised it with our adaptability. We're able to do this because we know who we are. So, if the present doesn't make much sense, then we often take a step back into our traditions and their enduring values.

Our identity matters, because character is destiny.

Penny Mordaunt
October 2025

SOME NOTES

MAKING SENSE OF IT ALL

There are many types of customs and traditions in the UK. Some are regular or recurring as part of daily life and others are specific events according to a calendar. Others are organised for an event e.g. a wedding, death or anniversary. Where the customs happen according to a calendar, they have been incorporated into the Calendar of Our Customs at the back of this book. Where they occur by event, we've grouped them by their type, e.g. military or royal, or both.

MAGPIES AND WELLY WANGERS

In our research, we came across so many customs and traditions, we couldn't include them all. We have therefore not included simple sayings and family traditions such as saluting single magpies and asking: 'Where's your wife?' This would no doubt get us accused of various gender- or religious-based assumptions. If you get upset by misgendering Corvids, then this book is definitely not for you. Similarly, if your welly wanging contest has been excluded, then apologies. We've tried to include a mix of the ancient and modern, the significant and the silly. Similarly, there are many sporting events without unusual or surprising traditions, so we've also excluded those. Nor have we included every book, animal, cultural, religious, music, arts and craft and entertainment festival or show. We earnestly hope that this in no way discourages a future invitation to the Dunn-by-Badley Donkey Derby.

NEW TECHNOLOGY BAFFLES...

The traditions are bewildering in their diversity and scope. They only really come to life when you can see them happening. To address this, we've incorporated QR codes that link to videos. You simply point your mobile phone camera at the code to see the link. There are only so many things you can do in words to describe the mad spectacle of Cooper's Hill Cheese Rolling or the Maldon Mud Race.

HEROES

There have been a huge number of people who have helped with this book. Thanks are due to James Stephens, Mark Wallace and Lord Ashcroft at Biteback Publishing, without whom neither this nor our previous book *Greater: Britain After the Storm* would ever have been completed.

My special thanks go to my co-author Chris Lewis. Although the book is written in my voice, he has helped enormously in writing, researching and shaping the ideas. I am indebted to his tolerance of my mangled spelling. My dyslexia was first diagnosed in 2020 and without help, this book would not have seen the light of day.

Thanks also to the brilliant Eliot Wilson of *The Spectator*, Sarah Aitchison for her patience and proofreading, Umang Dokey for his illustration and design and Simon Billington for the creative supervision. Thanks also to Air Vice-Marshal Simon Edwards CB and Lieutenant Commander Hugo Mitchell-Heggs RN for their expertise and guidance on military tradition.

Most of all, I want to thank all those who have invented, revived, preserved, organised (and been hospitalised) while cherishing and creating the traditions this book celebrates.

CHAPTER ONE

THE END OF AN ERA

———————◆———————

This chapter details the many reasons why the Conservative government lost power in 2024. Why did it demonstrate such a lack of understanding of the British people? This chapter also records my role in the coronation the previous year and the effect it had on me. Why did I want to write a book about British traditions and the importance they have at the centre of British life? How did they influence my community? How do traditions help us cope with change? What happens when they are ignored or forgotten?

———————◆———————

Ethel Gibbons: It's wrong, isn't it? All this 'down with everything' business?
Frank Gibbons: Well, there's something to be said for it. There's always something to be said for everything. But where they go wrong is trying to get things done too quickly. We don't like doing things quickly in this country.
NOËL COWARD, *THIS HAPPY BREED*[1]

Let's turn the clock back to 5 July 2024, around 3.30 a.m. The Returning Officer for Portsmouth North has just confirmed that I have lost my seat in the general election. Nationally, it was the Conservative Party's worst defeat in its parliamentary history. It was not difficult to work out why. From 2016 to 2024, we'd had five Prime Ministers in six years and the country didn't like that.

Portsmouth North is usually the colour of government, so I was not surprised by the result. It was an 18 per cent swing against the Conservative Party. In any case, I felt I'd lost the seat a hundred times previously. This was just the final time. It was lost when we failed to listen to businesses. Lost again when we failed to protect our borders. Lost when we failed to act after accessible healthcare drifted further away from the needs of patients. Lost when we forgot the fundamental nature of the British people. This is what I said when the result was announced:

> Tonight, the Conservative Party has taken a battering because it failed to honour the trust that people had placed in it. You can speak all you like of security and freedom, but you can't have either if you are afraid. Afraid of the cost of living or accessing healthcare or whether the responsibility you shoulder will be recognised and rewarded. That fear steals the future and it only makes the present matter. That is why we lost. Our renewal as a party and a country will not be achieved by us talking to an ever-smaller slice of ourselves but by being guided by the people of this country, and if we want again to be the natural party of government then our values must be the people's.

We didn't lose to the overwhelming love of our opponents. We lost to a well-deserved contempt for our offer. The irony was that most of our MPs and our party membership knew it and felt the same way. There were so many leadership contests appealing to an ever-narrower slice of the party that we ended up talking to ourselves. It was time for a change.

The inflection moment in my personal campaign was not about policy or economics. It was the decision by the Prime Minister to leave the D-Day commemorations early. At the start of the campaign, polls showed a 5 per cent lead in Portsmouth North. His decision baffled veterans and colleagues alike and was the end of any chance we had of retaining the seat.

Even in the aftermath and following his explanation, many of his aides still did not get it.

Why was this so difficult to understand? Our history is there for everyone to see. We have a martial tradition and we should be proud of it. Proud of Trafalgar and Waterloo. Proud of the Battle of Britain and certainly proud of our D-Day veterans. Proud of our history in general. If not, which country would you rather trade our history with?

In my own patch, we're proud of Portsmouth's role in launching the liberation of Europe. Proud of our role in the Cold War. Proud of the Falklands. Proud of the Royal Navy. And proud of those who still sacrifice and serve. They don't do it for money or medals. They do it for duty – another thing that seems to have fallen out of fashion. How have we forgotten that? Every town, every village, every city in this country has a memorial to those who did their duty.

Whoever occupies Downing Street, it really matters that they respect, honour and make time for our values and traditions. If you are in a position of leadership, you represent all of us no matter what you do. If you are absent, so are we.

In any case, it should be the sort of thing politicians should want to do. God knows we're associated with enough that goes wrong. It makes a nice change to celebrate success. Maybe some consider they are somehow above these humble values. It is not the government or the civil service that provides continuity in Britain. The electorate's views may change, but collectively, we still hold some immovable beliefs. We want our nation to be fair, effective and capable. We admire people who get things done, who build things, who create opportunity. We value service, compassion and courage, in the many forms it takes. Our motivation is the love of family, of community and of country, irrespective of our political beliefs.

Go into any shop, pub, cafe, business, charity, church or sports hall and you'll see them. They're called volunteers. They are a great British resource and we produce them by the thousands. The greatest political lesson I ever learned was not from think tanks or Substacks or policy papers but from these volunteers. They do the hospital visits; they run the 'meals on wheels' delivery services and the youth clubs.

When I was selected to give the Loyal Address in Parliament, it was not for my overwhelming intellect. It may surprise you to learn that I was not cultured and crafted in the Oxford Debating Society. I got the job because I was 'Pompey Pen', the Portsmouth girl from the factories and pubs. I didn't stamp my political beliefs on my constituents. They stamped theirs on me. It's been said of Portsmouth people that they have no need of flags. They wear their patriotism on their sleeves. To know Portsmouth is to know British people. They don't want politics. They want practicality. And that has been my experience as well.

When my mother died, I was fifteen. I'd been a child carer from thirteen. I did what my mother and her generation of volunteers had taught me. I got on with it. They say love comes in many forms, but I honestly wasn't thinking about that. I did not begrudge the daily chores. They're not an expression of love and duty. I didn't even think about them. You don't when you're coping. It wasn't until much later that I had any idea that this wasn't normal. It certainly wasn't unusual in my experience. I'm not from the millennial generation where everything is shared on social media. Even if it had existed then, I wouldn't have had the time to post things.

Real life isn't what gets played out on social media. When big things happened to people of my generation and background, there was enough drama. I knew how to do more with less. Trying to access government services can be complicated. When you're hard up, you don't have the time for this. These days, most of our politicians have degrees. They know the answers to the questions. They're book smart. You can read lots about lots of things in books, but experiencing them first-hand is different. I believe everyone in government should know what it is actually like to use government services. The queuing, the form filling, the duplication, the waste, the missed opportunities, the absence of excellence.

I just viewed my circumstances as tough luck. I also knew I needed to find a job that I could do while still at school. It's the lot of so many in our country. They just get on with it. So that's how I ended up as a magician's assistant. It was good money. I could do it in the evening. These days, people are amused by this. Why did you want to do that? Well, of course, a politician needs a serious career to fall back on… no, of course, I didn't want to do it. Would you enjoy being gawped at wearing a stupid outfit? It was a necessity. It was the most money I could make in the little time I had outside of school and caring. While my peers were out on Friday and Saturday nights, I was to be found in ballrooms, messes and hotels across the country. Sometimes three venues a night. With an incontinent rabbit.

My school didn't encourage me to apply to university. I don't blame them. I was often absent due to other responsibilities. But my city, the most entrepreneurial in the UK, taught me there was more than one way to get where you needed. I had no role models. No one thought I'd make anything of myself. There were no connections or experiences of the life I would go on to live. And that's where Portsmouth plays a role again.

There's something special about ports. They make you feel part of something bigger. They hint that there's something out there, just beyond the horizon. For generations, curiosity has propelled citizens over the horizon to seek new experiences, ideas and opportunities. When you leave a place, the memories of it somehow grow within you. You begin to learn more about yourself and the place you came from. Every departure is an arrival. It's why I love another old-fashioned writer – Rudyard Kipling.

Winds of the World, give answer! They are whimpering to and fro—
And what should they know of England who only England know?[2]

You only really understand something when you leave it.

Every port town is full of people on the lookout for what's next. I didn't know it at the time, but I was struggling. When you're young, though, you have more energy and you can cope with more. I got to know people during this time who have remained lifelong friends. I would see them on social occasions in the city at commemorative services, Royal Navy events or ships coming in or out. Because of my father's military service, I'd always been interested in that community. The Navy often held open days when you could get close to the ships, both foreign and British. By the time I was ten, I had already been on a submarine, could identify a Wasp, a Merlin and a Sea King helicopter and had witnessed *Hermes* taking the task force out of Portsmouth Harbour bound for the Falklands. I'll never forget it. I saw the looks of pride and fear on the faces of the crowd, watching their dad, brother or son going off to war – pride that they were doing their duty and the fear of what the cost of that duty might be. But the duty was unquestioned and automatic. I saw the looks on their faces when they came back – those that did come back. In combat, there are no ungrateful survivors. There are no atheists either.

Everywhere you go in Portsmouth you walk in the shadow of sacrifice and service. It's all around you in naval and commercial dockyards. History is a spur, but it can be uncomfortable, too. It can ask difficult questions such as 'In 2,000 years of history, do you really think war has finally come to an end?', 'What will you do if it comes again?', 'Will you be ready?' and, above all, 'How would you deal with it?'

That's one of the reasons why I joined the Conservative Party. I had a gut feeling for these unspoken feelings. It was proud of our history. It didn't seek to judge, revise or rewrite it. It also fit who I was. The party was primarily practical rather than political. It rewarded independence. It was patriotic. It was the party of defence and law and order. It also had a generation of giants – local legends like Frank Jonas, the docker turned Lord Mayor – who were as famous locally as Margaret

Thatcher was nationally. They were common sense personified. They were a breed apart.

To get a measure of him, here's Frank's party political broadcast at the 2024 general election.

https://x.com/PennyMordaunt/status/1802993879077052483?lang=en

People like Frank don't talk about the struggle between the bourgeoisie and the proletariat or ownership of the means of production. They understand that we don't start from a theoretical place. We deal with imperatives and practicalities.

Thatcher knew this, too. She was a conviction politician, quick to recognise that real people care about their history, cultures and traditions. They couldn't care less about political ideology. They're too busy for that. Her politics and beliefs were not rooted in essays and books but in her experiences of family and life, having been brought up in a grocer's shop. She witnessed a father's determination to provide and do his duty. Yes, she read Hayek and understood Friedman, but after all the theory, she was focused on practical things. She wanted the nation to be capable, powerful and respected. That pride gave her the confidence needed to take risks. That comes from knowing who you are and what you represent.

I got on well with her. You can just tell sometimes how someone looks at you. I felt comfortable with someone who knew what real life was like. I think she also knew the insecurities felt by women in politics and the necessity of encouragement. She undoubtedly faced huge obstacles throughout her career. But she had been blessed with people, family, friends and colleagues who gave her support. She was generous in this regard to others. Especially those, I believe, who were the outsiders. Women and men who had fought their way up. That is how she was with me. She was frequently present at meetings to encourage and support candidates. I treasure two letters from her in particular. One was written when I had first run and failed to get in: 'You must keep going, we need you to get in. Work hard and it will come good.' Then I received one again congratulating me when I won my seat in 2010. She noticed and took care of the small details.

The image sometimes painted of her being unfeeling does not square with that. The late Sir Tim Bell, who had been her advertising man, told me she was the only one of her political generation that didn't 'treat him like trade'. She'd have him round for supper. She was grateful for his time and expertise. They were equals. No one else made him feel that way.

When I first worked in Westminster, I could deal with the snobbery I encountered because of the likes of her. In more recent years, that type of leadership has had long periods of absence in the party. There's been an over-reliance on the cool, the effortlessly superior and the overly confident. In the real world, leaders get perspiration, not condensation.

This is not about background or the school you attended. It's about having the imagination to see potential. Real leaders develop the aspirant. They don't sneer at them.

In those days, I was advised: 'Don't tell them which school you went to.' But it didn't frighten me. I was proud of where I was from. I knew that my party, its rank and file, was Maggie's. It didn't bother me that many of the elder statesmen spoke like Terry-Thomas and behaved like George Sanders.

I adapted quickly. I started working with many who would eventually become colleagues. In the post-Thatcher era, there were a lot of ladder climbers. Thatcherites were in the ascendancy. They recognised, admired and encouraged the wealth creators – the people that made it happen.

How is all this relevant today? Well, people talk as if this is the new age of uncertainty. But for many from my background, life was always uncertain. I found an antidote to this in the traditions of my family, community and in my time in the Royal Naval Reserve. For many, the traditions and rhythm of their communities serve as a consistent drumbeat to the fractured nature of their modern lives.

This is a key feature in what many are experiencing now. Latterly, so much has changed so quickly for so many. This is one of the reasons why the preservation of our traditions matter. In many lives, it's the only predictable thing that's left.

The Conservative Party used to understand the nature of Britain and its ancient patchwork of different customs, traditions and characters. It was tolerant of them all. The fundamental nature of Britain was cosmopolitan. Britain was America, before America. Everybody came through here – the Romans, the Danes, the Saxons, the Vikings, the French – and they were followed by different races, religions and refugees from political systems.

But they did so over hundreds of years, like waves breaking gently on our shoreline, gradually shaping the country. What happened in the last twenty years has been more like a storm, the shock of which has created anger and resentment. As Matthew Syed has pointed out:

> Things began to shift during the Blair/Brown years when net migration shot up to 247,000, rising to 318,000 under Cameron. Under Johnson … the figure soared to an average of more than 850,000 in his final two years, not far off the entire number between 1066 and 1945. It remains at 431,000 today.[3]

This does include figures for Ukrainian refugees and Hong Kong British nationals, but the point is made. The pace has been so violent as to discredit the very process of change itself. We now live in a present where the future is feared, partly because it feels like the politicians are either unwilling or unable to help. Of course, we can't uninvent the internet, the jet engine or global trade because they've brought unsurpassed opportunities for wealth creation. The pace of change, especially, the 'who' and 'how many come in', has resulted in a perceived loss of control and a feeling of impotent vulnerability.

Our unique ancient culture and identity is delicate and precious. We cannot allow it to be trampled by those who do not even see it, let alone respect or venerate it.

The fight back to defend traditions is underway. In April 2025, communities across the UK were told by the Department for Culture Media and Sport that they would soon be able to nominate their favourite traditions to be included within official inventories of our living heritage. Traditions that are central to the UK's many cultures and identities are among those expected to be put forward for a UK-wide official inventory.

This makes perfect sense. We would not allow any of our thirty-five UNESCO World Heritage Sites to be disrespected and destroyed. So why not protect and preserve the traditions of the people? Aren't they just as important?

This is not escapist whimsy. These are our roots – a confirmation and a preservation of who we are. Of course, to protect traditions you need more than a list. You need local people who want to participate and bring them to life.

As Simon Schama puts it in his series *The Romantics and Us*: 'The more modern we become, the more we need anchorage in memory, dreams, in ancestry, in myth, in the whole universe of our collective imagination.'

Schama points out that the Romantics were against the flattening of difference and wanted to provide a response to the anxieties of being modern and the rush into materialism and metropolitan uniformity.[4] That's just as true now as it was then.

This process was almost entirely reversed in the 1960s, when there was a desire to eradicate the past and create futurism. This was vested in the architectural style of the gigantic, the brutalist and the modern. The campus universities were the embodiment of yesterday's 'tomorrow', where the past was held as almost criminal. Yesterday's future is now long past and remains as testimony of how we almost tried to eradicate any vestige of idiosyncratic identity. The wheel turned. Walk around any big town or city and you'll see the buildings that look old, worn and out of place. They're the concrete giants of the 1960s.

A sense of place and history is embedded in our identity. It's in our accents, for instance, which change noticeably even over short distances. Manchester and Liverpool are thirty miles apart but have completely different accents. They define our place names, surnames and the football teams we support. If a place name ends in -caster or -chester (fort), then it's Roman. If it's -ton, -wick, -ley or -ham (a farmstead, village, or settlement) or -combe (a narrow valley or deep hollow), then it's Anglo-Saxon. If it's a -by ending (a farmstead, village or settlement), then it's Viking. If it's an Inver- or Aber- (mouth or estuary) or Dun- (fort), then it's Celtic or Gaelic.

There are fewer French place names because by the time they arrived, the naming was largely complete. They did however leave their mark on Rievaulx, a French version of Ryedale; Beaulieu, with 'Beau' meaning beautiful and 'lieu' meaning place; and Hainault, which was named after Philippa of Hainault, Queen of Edward III. There's also Ashby-de-la-Zouch ('de-la-Zouch' indicates the family who owned the land), Chester-le-Street ('Street' refers to the major Roman road running through the area) and Newton-le-Willows ('Newton' means new town and 'willows' indicates the presence of willow trees).

It's in our pets, too. Terriers (from the Norman French meaning earth) were working dogs, refined from older purpose-bred dogs. Some were crossed with fighting breeds to intensify tenacity and increase courage. The Kennel Club recognises thirty-three terrier breeds.

Popular breeds like Jack Russells, Staffies and West Highland Whites are among the types found in the UK.

Our places have been our places for hundreds of years. There are places in Europe where this is not the case. Alsace-Lorraine is a region on the border of France and Germany where residents have changed nationality three or four times in a century without ever moving home. Such is the interchangeability of European nationalities.

The only time anything even remotely like this happened in Britain was when some towns were moved from one country or county to another. It happened in Scotland and Northern Ireland and also in the north of England. Barnoldswick, along with several other Yorkshire villages, was transferred from the West Riding of Yorkshire to the Borough of Pendle, Lancashire, on 1 April 1974, following the Local Government Act 1972. Not only were proud Yorkshire people ceded to their arch-Lancastrian enemies, but a town with seven churches was transferred into a borough synonymous with witchcraft. Politicians being out of touch is no new thing.

If your surname is Archer, Arrowsmith, Bowman or Fletcher (from the French word *flèche*, meaning arrow), then somewhere in your family's past you will have been familiar with archery. If you are a Butcher, Baker, Cartwright, Cooper, Farmer, Painter, Tanner, Slater or Smith then you're from another trade background.

Our language and vocabulary represent history and the waves of migrants that broke over the British Isles. In chronological order, there was Latin, Anglo-Saxon, Norse and, more recently, French, but Latin was the accepted international language. For this reason, for every noun, there are plenty of alternatives. Royal is a French word. Regal is the Latin version. Kingly is the Anglo-Saxon. This makes the English language a living record of history and identity.

In John McWhorter's *The Language Hoax*, he puts it like this:

English got hit by a firehose spray of words from yet more languages. After the Norse came the French. The Normans – descended from the same Vikings, as it happens – conquered England, ruled for several centuries and, before long, English had picked up 10,000 new words. Then, starting in the sixteenth century, educated Anglophones developed a sense of English as a vehicle of sophisticated writing and so it became fashionable to cherry-pick words from Latin to lend the language a more elevated tone.[5]

These languages sometimes survive in songs and custom. Hickory, dickory, dock or hovera, dovera, dick, were eight, nine and ten in Celtic counting. In northern England, you can still occasionally hear people counting in Yan Tan Tethera.

Yan	Tan	Tethera	Methera	Pimp
Sethera	Lethera	Hovera	Dovera	Dik
Yan-a-dik	Tan-a-dik	Tethera-dik	Methera-dik	Bumfit
Yan-a-bumfit	Tan-a-bumfit	Tethera-bumfit	Methera-bumfit	Jigget

Source: TEAM LEWIS

This was a system traditionally used by shepherds for sheep counting, especially in the fells of the Lake District, and for counting stitches in knitting until the Industrial Revolution. Though most of these number systems fell out of use by the turn of the twentieth century, some are still with us. There's an explanation here:

https://www.youtube.com/shorts/Y9I3E79RLyw

So, who cares about these ancient stories? The pressures of an economically interconnected world might try to undermine our history, but we are not just economic units, driven by logical or mechanical reason. We are not animals to be herded from one location to another to consume (or be consumed). We have identities, attitudes and beliefs, however irrational. We have heroes who we admire or aspire to be. We hold them to be representative of our greatest values. Our places, our customs and our traditions are special to us. Success is not about having the best of everything. It's about making the best of what we have. That's different. It is not about us being all-conquering. It's about us being proud of who we are and where we come from.

Our communities are essential to our democracy. We give a mandate to those who we hope will represent our values. Most political discussion revolves around whether our representatives appear to do this. The concept of tribe is shot through politics and sometimes it suffers from the narcissism of small differences. This is at its most apparent in the extremist wings and this is why these movements are often doomed to failure. There will always be those who aspire to the ultimate purity of being utterly unelectable. Only the irrelevant can be truly pure.

The love for our place of birth and our nation does not confine us to the parochial. It should not facilitate xenophobia. Our communities sustain us because they are unified around common laws, beliefs and behaviours. Traditions matter because they are about the preservation of the community. This is not just about the present or the future. Identity is always a past participle. All else is mere aspiration.

When politicians forget our culture and traditions, they might be forgiven. By and large, the public will forgive an honest mistake. After all, what could be more representative than human fallibility? The problem, though, is worse than that. Some politicians are in danger of not having even learned the country's values, let alone forgetting them.

My focus has always been on responsibility. Taking it, rewarding it, inspiring it. My opponents on the extremes want to strip people of it. They're currently doing things which are utterly irresponsible. They make unrealistic claims and put forward unsustainable plans. They're not motivated by service or being in a position to actually deliver. They only criticise and disrupt. Harry Enfield's sketch 'You don't want to do it like that' always springs to my mind whenever they clear their throat.[6] They're the cowboy builders who shake their heads and ask who did the most recent work but are never seen again when you need a solution. Their passion is to preach rather than be pragmatic. Britain is not a place to perform some sort of unplanned experimental exercise. It has to work and it can only do so when a problem is understood and responsibility is taken. Understanding our values is the beginning of this.

In my community, if you were out of work, you took it upon yourself to find some. If you were unwell, you'd exhaust the contents of the bathroom cabinet before troubling a doctor. My community avoided handouts and they always found time to raise money for local causes. Portsmouthians are remarkably tolerant towards others – unless you're from Southampton.

My community knew those who had fallen foul of the law and suffered divorce, death and misfortune. Those down on their luck. Those broken by war. They didn't judge.

MY CONCESSION SPEECH

https://www.youtube.com/watch?v=CjwYd8E65tE

I fought Portsmouth North seven times and lost twice. It is a truly wonderful city, but it's always been the colour of government, which shows how representative of the wider country Portsmouth people are.

I'm no stranger to the unexpected. Like many things in my life, the fact that I played a role in the coronation was pure accident. People are surprised when I tell them I went to a comprehensive school. I was the first in my family to go to university. I've held the hands of elderly patients as a hospital visitor. I've dined with kings and queens. I've met some of the richest people in the world. I've sat on the board of the World Bank. The great myth is that those with money or status have no problems. It's not true. They have different problems.

In my final year as an MP, I found myself alongside hundreds of dignitaries in the coronation procession for King Charles III. If ever there was a danger of it all going to my head, I was brought back down to Earth when several members of the public pointed out that my demi-couture atelier embroidered gown was reminiscent of a budget Greek airline, an episode of *Star Trek* and/or something worn by Xena, Warrior Princess. It's exactly the sort of thing Portsmouth folk would say. Respectability and ridicule are neighbours in Britain.

There was nothing about the coronation that was ill thought out or irrelevant. Some looked on the ancient spectacle and questioned its relevance. Good. That's what we're trained to do. I'm a member of the British Astronomical Society. We question what we do not understand. All of our science and technology springs from this instinct. Logic has

16

its limits. Plato believed the first sign of wisdom is wonder, a sense of curiosity that leads to the pursuit of knowledge. Like Portsmouth, Athens is a port city too.

Most, though, did not think about the coronation too deeply. Many were just proud because it reflected their values. We all bore witness to a service of duty and love. It was an antidote to a cynical world. It was a celebration of who we are and what unites us. Those who protect us. Those who serve us. Those that carried the regalia were connected to defence, justice, faith and representation.

The congregation was a testament to all the values our nation embodies: its charities, its creativity, its communities, its industry, those who step up and take responsibility. Britain's connectedness and esteem were evident. Crowned heads and world leaders were relegated to mere faces in the crowd. The past was present but so were the possibilities – the Commonwealth's newly joined members, Gabon, Togo, Rwanda and Mozambique, with no connection to the British Empire, had come for the future not the past.

I was privileged to be at the event in Westminster Abbey, but if I hadn't been there, I would've been at one of the hundreds of street parties. I have loved talking to people about what they were doing on that day. Some brought a family together. Others convened a whole street or entire village. On that day, all of us were playing our part, doing our bit.

The coronation itself featured lots of traditions that enshrine the legend of monarchy, but these should not obscure its real meaning. To serve as a monarch is a serious and onerous undertaking. It carries great responsibility. There is no role in the world like it. You have responsibility but strangely little direct authority. You don't get to choose what you do or when you do it. You spend the majority of your life preparing for it. Whether you like it or not, your children repeat the cycle. It requires great patience and sensitivity to do it well. It requires a great deal of courage, too. It is the ultimate test of character. History tells us that not everyone is suited to it. To be King is to be constrained by history and expectation, the ultimate incarnation of service and sacrifice.

The role of those in leadership is representation, even for the unelected. Too few give thought to what this means. Any position of prominence is a platform upon which hopes and fears are projected. At times of crisis or tragedy, it reflects the way the majority feel. It shows how we handle sadness or loss – with bravery, dignity and determination. We all feel fear. Each of us deals with events in different ways. This is the stuff of which our personal and public history is made.

Just as his late mother did before him, the King has navigated events. At times of worry, through the backdrop of war and the legacy of the pandemic, his careful consideration has been evident. It has been in the care he and Queen Camilla have taken to thank and acknowledge people and to bring people together for the benefit of all. There is no greater example of this than his determination, following his cancer diagnosis, to quietly carry on.

It is an approach our parents and grandparents would recognise. That's why the monarchy remains enduringly popular. It's a point of continuity. It represents something beyond the day to day, that celebrates the everyday. It is above politics. It represents something that binds us all together – hope. Our monarchy is both a family and an enterprise. It is the mirror for a thousand points of light in this country. It is founded on love, propelled by hope and it remains a source of strength for us all.

At the heart of our traditions are our values and representation. When values are forgotten or not respected, trouble is the result. There are many lessons to be learned from the coronation. Of course, any coronation is an event that marks a significant change as one monarch hands over to another, but this period was more turbulent than most. In the next chapter, we ask what caused it to be so and what effect did it have on Britain?

CHAPTER TWO

CHANGE AND DECAY

This chapter chronicles the rapid pace of change in the twenty-first century. Why did it change so fast and in what areas? It records the shock of the 9/11 terrorist attacks, the banking crisis, Brexit, Covid, the loss of Her Majesty Queen Elizabeth II and the cumulative effect of change on the British people. How did it leave the country feeling?

---

*I belong to generation of men, most of whom aren't here anymore.
And we all did the same thing for the same reason no matter what we
thought about politics. Now that's all over and done with and we're
carrying on, the best we can, just as though nothing had happened.
But as a matter of fact, several things happened and one of 'em was,
this country suddenly got tired. She's tired now. But the old lady's got
stamina, make no mistake about that and it's up to us ordinary people
to keep things steady. And that's your job and just you remember it.*

FRANK GIBBONS IN NOËL COWARD'S *THIS HAPPY BREED*

The first twenty-five years of this century brought profound change to the UK. Of course, there has been change before, but nothing quite like this. Everything accelerated – technology, culture, politics, society, globalisation and commercialisation.

Migration, for instance, became one of the largest political issues in the country. The populations of major cities like London changed dramatically. In 2023, 67 per cent of births in London were to parents of whom one or both were born outside the UK. This is the highest-ever percentage of births to non-UK-born parents in England and Wales.[1]

And then, out of the blue, came Covid, and the change went into overdrive. Families were separated, travel was restricted and stay-at-home policies were put in place. It was the largest curtailing of civil liberties since the Second World War. We're still dealing with the legacies of this period.

It's important that we understand the hallmarks of our time – unpredictability and fear. People can cope with change, but they ask questions about why we always seem to be so unprepared for events and so inconsiderate towards those most affected.

The twenty-first century had, in fact, started with people worrying about new technology. The so-called 'millennium bug' was based on what might happen when computer clocks ticked past 1999. There was speculation about aircraft crashing and nuclear power stations malfunctioning. In the end, it was actually old technology that turned out to be the real worry.

On 11 September 2001, nineteen terrorists smuggled box cutters aboard passenger aircraft and hijacked them. They didn't exploit new technology or new opportunities; they just looked at the world that existed and thought about it in a new and horrifying way. No one had thought this a risk because no one had thought hijackers would want to sacrifice themselves, despite numerous incidences of suicide bombings. On a clear and crisp autumn day, they flew the aircraft into the two tallest buildings in New York City. Then, 24-hour rolling news, an innovation of the First Gulf War, carried it all live.

The military interventions that followed became known as the war on terror, the Second Gulf War and a subsequent campaign in Afghanistan. The loss of life among British service personnel in this theatre became second only to Northern Ireland in our post-war history. These lives were given to make the West safer and for a while, they did – only to be undermined by the reversal of US policy in the region, accompanied by a chaotic withdrawal. The lasting legacy of the campaign was that a generation of Afghans experienced freedom and education for the first time.

The stock markets, already then experiencing a massive collapse from what was known as the dot-com crash, plummeted further. Governments responded and spent heavily to prop up their economies. Money flooded in and stock markets were brought back to life by ever-more exotic financial instruments. Some of these bundled up debt and processed it through ratings agencies for credibility.

These packages of mortgages, or collateralised debt obligations (CDOs) as they were known, sold well because in theory, they were underwritten by a tangible property asset. Some enterprising analysts looked into this and found that they were worthless because many loans had already foreclosed. There was so much cheap money in circulation that the mortgages had been given to people who simply couldn't afford them. The mortgage companies had also taken out insurance contracts to cover any loss, so these companies were in difficulty, too. It was like dominoes.

The problem was that many of the world's banks had already bought these complicated packages of debt and insurance in vast quantities as a way of spreading their risk. It did exactly the opposite. It deepened and concentrated it and triggered the largest financial crisis ever. The global banking system came close to complete failure in September 2008, when the US investment bank Lehman Brothers filed for bankruptcy, triggering widespread panic in financial markets worldwide and marking the peak of the crisis. Another massive government bailout was required.

Her late Majesty Queen Elizabeth II was touring the City of London and asked the question: 'Why did nobody notice it?' A group of eminent economists later wrote to her in a letter apologising for failing to predict the financial crisis. It was paraphrased by papers at the time as: 'Sorry Ma'am – we just didn't see it coming.'[2]

She was asking an important question – why, with all the wealth, all the data, all the experience and all the money, did they end up not foreseeing their own demise? The answer was shockingly simple – they just lacked the imagination to see it.

There's a consistent theme here – a willingness to believe that the most confident is also the most competent. It's rarely the case. It's one of the greatest arguments for diverse leadership teams. Someone who has all the answers hasn't asked all the questions. They will worry about a wider range of problems. You need two-ulcer leaders in two-ulcer jobs.

Apart from undermining confidence in leaders, the banking crisis ushered in a prolonged period of low economic growth and hardship. This, again, required massive public sector support, which saw incomes stagnate as national treasuries had to be rebuilt. During this time, immigration, which had been rising, became a torrent. In Europe, the recent accession of countries to the EU had brought a new wave of cheaper labour. The Polish plumber had arrived in Britain.

Polish migration has been one of the largest movements in Britain's post-war migration history. Since Poland joined the European Union in 2004 and Polish people had a legal right to come and live and work in the UK, over 800,000 Poles made the move. Annual net migration to the UK in 2010 was 252,000 – the highest calendar year figure on record at that point. It was to grow massively. According to recent data from the Office for National Statistics (ONS), the year ending June 2023 was the year with the highest net migration in Britain, with a record high of 906,000 people migrating to the UK.

Since 2000, there have been 11.4 million immigrants to the UK, with just under 7 million leaving. The total immigration-related population growth since 2000 is approximately 7 million when including the children of migrants – the largest influx Britain has ever seen. India,

Poland, Pakistan, Romania and Ireland were the most common countries of birth among UK migrants in 2021/22.

This wasn't just about cheap labour. For many farms and agricultural communities, it was about getting any labour at all. What would have been perfectly acceptable work for a previous generation had become unacceptable just one generation later. Over this time, the productivity of farms went up dramatically, while the workforce diminished in size.[3]

This influx of foreign labour flowed into a feeling shared by many that their governments were not sufficiently prioritising their own electorates or that their labour rates were being undercut deliberately. Polish labour was cheaper, often more reliable and contributed fresh family life to rural communities.[4]

When labour rates are being depressed as the cost of living rises, those at the bottom get squeezed disproportionately. On top of this, the number of illegal immigrants, or asylum seekers, began to rise, first with people stowing away on lorries going through Channel ports, then coming across the Channel in dinghies. I had worked for the Freight Transport Association and seen the plight of lorry drivers having to deal with stowaways in their vehicles, soiling their produce and in some cases threatening their lives.

Not being able to stop this also increased the terrorist threat. I had spent a lot of time in the Mediterranean, the Aegean, northern Libya, Iraq and other places, mapping migrant routes being used by terrorist organisations. The EU did a terrible job at protecting its borders. Biometric scanners that British taxpayers had paid for were left covered up and unused in the camps on Europe's southern borders. The worst failing was when the money given to Italy was used to pay people smugglers to take back people they had just ferried across the Mediterranean from northern Libya. Gangs made money by trafficking people to what they hoped would be a better life. Then they made money again from the Italian government taking them back again. And then got a third payoff by selling the same people into the slave trade.

In October 2024, a UK Parliament debate estimated that there were up to 745,000 illegal immigrants in the UK. This estimate includes foreign nationals who have overstayed their visas, failed asylum seekers who have disappeared and some immigrants who have crossed the Channel in small boats.[5]

Although a minority of the total, many communities saw undocumented migrants given free accommodation and prioritised for healthcare while local people were still waiting. They also saw billions spent on weapons and overseas aid to help other countries while oversubscribed infrastructure crumbled around them. They felt abandoned and they wanted someone to fight for them. They felt unheard.

This created the widespread perception that the problem was the open borders of Europe, which led to the 2016 United Kingdom European Union membership referendum. Of course, there were many issues raised by the referendum, but immigration was, and continues to be, a concern for so many. British people have a keen sense of fairness and they hated what they saw happening.

Many polls were certain about the result of the referendum. One of the problems was that by that last month of the campaign, a lot of people who couldn't digest the possibility of a Leave victory had a narrative that explained it all away with 'rogue' results. The problem was not that the evidence was absent but that it was being read with bias. The establishment got it wrong – a pattern we saw repeated many times subsequently. Remain voters were more comfortable expressing their views, partly because the government supported their position and it was also popular with younger and more voluble people. But younger voters are unreliable. The older Leave voters turned out en masse and the government lost the vote.

The murder of my friend Jo Cox happened during this campaign. She had been the first MP to be killed since Ian Gow was murdered by the IRA in 1990. It was a shockingly tragic event that haunts every MP to this day. She was not the last.

The ridicule that was heaped on Brexiteers by the media and government just stiffened their resolve. When the British are told what to do, insulted and patronised from home and abroad, it makes them all the more determined. We just don't like bullies. The government campaign in favour of Remain showed yet again that it didn't understand the British character.

The tone-deaf quality of the campaign was memorable. For instance, it helped Brexiteers enormously when the government lectured the country about the potential to lose its supply of fresh salad.

They even co-opted an American President to tell us that we'd be sent to the back of the queue for a trade deal, as if, somehow, the prospect of being at the back of a queue would be unfamiliar or scary to someone British. I remember walking past the queue for the local chippy one Friday just after these warnings were issued. The panic was palpable. They were almost out of battered sausage.

Later in 2016, there was another shock that defied the pollsters. In the American presidential elections in November, Donald Trump defeated former Secretary of State and former First Lady Hillary Clinton in much the same way as he would go on to dispatch Kamala Harris eight years later. It was considered one of the biggest-ever political upsets in American history. It was a complete shock because celebrities and politicians had been lining up to explain why it was impossible.

https://www.youtube.com/watch?v=G87UXIH8Lzo

As happened with the Brexit referendum, the experts were unwilling to look and listen honestly without preconceptions. They were so sure of their expertise that they only looked for signs that told them they were right.

Three years into the new presidency, there were reports coming from around the world of a new highly infectious strain of the coronavirus called Covid-19 (named for the year it first appeared). It was so virulent that there was no vaccine for it and all travel had therefore to be stopped. The result devastated family and community life. All of our traditions were either stopped or radically modified and supply chains were disrupted, as were working practices. Government spending plans around the world were suddenly upended again. It triggered the largest-ever transfer of wealth from public to private hands in human history as governments sought to subsidise industries and jobs. Central banks cut interest rates in response and again flooded their economies with cheap money to keep them buoyant.

At the same time, after a long struggle, Britain finally left the European Union on 31 January 2020, two months before Britain was plunged into a Covid lockdown.

The US alone dedicated 26 per cent of GDP to soften the effects of the pandemic in 2021. This translates into stimulus packages worth $5.54 trillion.[6] In the UK, there was the Covid furlough scheme, 'Eat Out to Help Out' and many other programmes that paid companies to keep employees on their payroll or stimulate spending. This was estimated by the UK Parliament as costing £372 billion.[7] The UK government's entire budget for the year was around £1,200 billion, so the stimulus was 30 per cent of the annual budget – by way of comparison, the UK's annual defence budget is around £54 billion. The pandemic spending from government drove Pfizer's 2022 revenue to a record $100 billion and other pharmaceutical companies had similar record gains. This alone would've been enough to create an inflationary boom, but there were two other major accelerants.

Interest rates had remained low since the 2008 financial crash, encouraging banks and other institutions to lend. The resulting inflationary wave was then hit by another event.

In the middle of this period (possibly in exploitation of it), on 24 February 2022, Russia invaded Ukraine in a major escalation of the Russo-Ukrainian War, which had begun in 2014. Russia had previously annexed Crimea in 2014, and other parts of eastern Ukraine, with little response save condemnation and sanctions. This grew into the largest and deadliest conflict in Europe since the Second World War, causing hundreds of thousands of military casualties on both sides and tens of thousands of Ukrainian civilian ones.

Russia may have felt the European Union and the world were distracted by Covid. In the panic, Europe had reverted to type and each state made its own policy, putting up borders against the next. The vaccine response was hence slow and badly coordinated, except in Britain, which was first to produce a vaccine and rolled it out quickly and efficiently. It was one of the first benefits of being outside the European regulatory system.

The war's effect on an already disrupted global supply chain was catastrophic. Ukraine is one of the world's largest producers of sunflower oil, wheat, corn (with more than one-third of its corn exports destined for China), barley, soya beans, rapeseed and sugar beet. Global economies boycotted Russian energy, thus injecting price inflation into global markets as supply was cut and the cost of living rose dramatically.

In spring 2023, interest rates were raised rapidly by the Federal Reserve to counter the inflationary wave. Overwhelmed with Covid cash coming in, the banks had put so much into low-risk, low-yield treasury stock. When the interest rates were increased rapidly, many couldn't make the margin calls. This triggered four out of five of the largest bank failures in history. It almost escaped notice, as major business stories often do, but it was another seismic event affecting banking confidence, the biggest since 2009.

The pandemic was a health event felt as an economic, social, cultural, political and geopolitical crisis. It changed everything. It was this generation's Second World War, with as many far-reaching consequences. The end of Covid, according to the US Center for Disease Control, wasn't until 11 May 2023. While the disease was under control largely thanks to vaccines, the war footing needed to catch up in non-Covid healthcare and dentistry never materialised. Politicians had already moved on.

The last time there had been a comparable global pandemic was the Spanish flu epidemic of 1918. It was called 'Spanish' because it was first recorded in Spain. (It wasn't actually that the disease started in Spain but that most European countries had strict wartime censorship in place, but Spain didn't and so it was freely reported there.) That pandemic infected more than 500 million and killed 10 per cent of them. It killed more people globally than all the wars that went before it. In the US, 675,000 people lost their lives. Again, this was more casualties than the First World War, the Second World War, the Korean War and the Vietnam War combined. In one year, the average life expectancy in the US dropped by twelve years.

The comparisons with the post-First World War era don't end there. There are many similarities between the 1920s and the 2020s. Rapid technology changes, the rise of new types of media, boom and bust, political extremism, the acceleration of global capitalism, intolerance, antisemitism, business people with political views, wars on the periphery of Europe, new types of military technology, underinvestment in our defences, the questions about whether the 'young' share our values, turbulence in the Royal Family and the feeling of national decline. Whether we are heading towards another global confrontation remains to be seen. Even if we are, it's unlikely to look like previous wars. Some argue that the data war is already underway and has been for some time.

The main economic effect of Covid was to deepen and widen any gaps that had been there before. If there were differences between rich and poor, men and women, urban and rural, those in authority and others, knowledge and manual workers, elderly and young, healthy and infirm, by the end of Covid, they were greater. It imposed physical barriers and stopped travel and trade, forcing nations back onto their own independent resources.

It made the rich richer.[8] It boosted the share of global wealth held by the super-rich while dramatically weakening the finances of nations.[9] The pandemic allowed more than 131 billionaires to double their net worth.

According to recent reports, the cost of living in the UK has risen around 40 per cent in the last four years, with a significant portion of this increase attributed to rising food prices. This is predicted to continue increasing, albeit at a lesser rate. This surge is considered a major factor in the ongoing cost-of-living crisis in the UK. We saw inflation peak at 11.1 per cent in October 2022, marking a 41-year high. While inflation has since eased, the overall cost of living is still considerably higher compared to 2021, with a total increase of around 20.8 per cent over the past three years as of May 2024, largely due to increased fuel costs and energy insecurity.[10]

If all of the above wasn't bad enough, in the middle of it all, on 8 September 2022, we heard the saddest news of all. Aged ninety-six, Her Majesty the Queen had died at Balmoral Castle. She had become the longest-reigning monarch in British history on 9 September 2015, when she surpassed the reign of her great-great-grandmother, Queen Victoria. She was the only monarch most of the country had ever known and was an enduring and reliable source of continuity in our lives.

This is what I said in tribute to the late Queen Elizabeth II at the time:

Just three weeks since we lost Her Majesty the Queen, as we face new challenges without her, we would do well to keep her in our thoughts. History, after all, is experience.

She became a Queen just seven years after the bloodiest conflict humanity had ever seen. We were a nation facing debt, hardship, rationing and the daunting task of modernising in the twilight of the empire. It was said of the King's death that Britain had lost its balance wheel, that part of a watch which moves the hands forward, which keeps the beat, which keeps things steady.

The world witnessed a young woman, pale with grief, pledge her whole life to our nation's service. Doubt and despair gave way to hope. Her pledge turned out to be a shining gift to the world. She saw us through change and challenge, constitutional crisis, conflict, Covid. Every time we battled, we had Her Majesty alongside us, advising us, guiding us, unifying us and reminding us of the challenges we face together in her long life, many much greater than we face now.

Her gift was calmness, confidence and courage. She enabled us to stay the course. She gave us a common bond and a common goal between us all, between nations, beyond politics, for prosperity, for security, for unity, for a United Kingdom.

No words of mine can do justice to the depths of her devotion to us. She sacrificed her time, her freedom, her private life. Her passing was felt deeply in every place on Earth because it reminded us of our own grief for loved ones we'd lost, because she had shared her family with us. You see, crowns are not made of precious metals and jewels alone. They are mostly made of duty and love.

So, when she died, we carried her on a river of love from Balmoral to her final resting place at Windsor. Its tributaries weren't just pageantry; they were personal. There were the guards of honour from tractor drivers and horse riders. There were the crayoned drawings attached to railings and carpets of flowers and an enormous amount of cling-wrapped marmalade sandwiches. And prayers and thanks from every place. And the ceremony of her church, the state and her armed forces. Vigils and silence in the fading autumn light.

Everyone played their part; everyone worked together. That unity, pride and dignity are things we will remember for the rest of our lives. It made us proud of our Queen and our country.

Her final gift to us was to show us the truth about her remarkable reign. The revelation was in her meticulously planned final appearance. You see, our late monarch did not stamp her personality on the nation. She was the one shaped by us. All of us, her people. The stoic, dignified, kind, patient, dutiful, queue-loving British people. That's why she was the best of us.

As we mourned, we leaned on our constitution, our traditions and our planning. We saw the pride in the people, causes and organisations she cherished and that this nation was the cradle for, many of which were represented in her funeral procession. And we saw the values that bind us because they were embodied in her.

And we calmly got on with it, cheerfully facing change and challenge. We coped really well and an entirely new government was formed. Strike action of both the rail dispute variety and the football variety was cancelled. The supply of arms and support for Ukraine never faltered. We kept calm and we carried on, because that is what great people and great nations do. We are not measured in triumph, we are measured in challenge and in that final journey she brought us together again. She made us realise that duty and sacrifice and tolerance and above all love are everything to the British way of life.

But above all, we were filled with good wishes for our new King. He bears the same cross that she did – the burden carried by all who wear the crown. He will be our new balance wheel, standing by our side as we face new challenges. And we will face them together.

We should not and we will not be daunted by them. We will remember our duty. We will continue to move things forward, to keep things steady, not to miss a beat and to bring hope.

Do not forget what she taught us. Do not forget what we must do. Do not forget who we are.

It's easy to forget that the British monarch is a truly international figure.

As President Emmanuel Macron said: 'To you, she was your Queen. To us, she was the Queen.'

She was much loved, as evidenced by the number of people who turned out to pay their last respects. An estimated 250,000 people filed past her catafalque during the four days of her lying-in-state at Westminster Hall. The queue was open twenty-four hours a day and reached ten miles in length. It was orderly, cheerful and good-natured. The only time the mood changed was when someone was perceived to have jumped the queue. We British know how to queue. The spectacle was very moving to those who witnessed it.

TRIBUTE TO THE QUEEN

https://www.youtube.com/watch?v=tbXEIQkOGJg

There was a period of grieving while plans were readied and put into place. Of course, HM the King was ready and has performed his duties admirably, even through his recent illness. In so many ways, he is ahead of his time. His embrace of organic farming, his critique of some modern architecture and his prescient concern on climate change, for instance. Around 80 per cent of people in the UK express some level of concern about this issue, with most reporting that they are at least somewhat worried about its effects.[11] Other global issues such as water distribution are also likely to become greater areas of tension and conflict. We have already seen the first sparks of this in Cameroon, Yemen and Somalia.

There is also concern about the rapid pace of technological change, particularly when it comes to uncensored social media masquerading as 'free speech' and its effect on news and the way people consume it. According to recent data from Ofcom, the under-forties consume significantly less TV news compared to older demographics and a majority of younger adults (particularly those aged 16–24) get their news primarily from online sources. They are far less likely to rely on traditional broadcast TV news sources such as the BBC, whose share of the market has been falling consistently.[12] According to Ofcom, as of 2024, around 10 per cent of UK adults used TikTok as a source of news, placing it on par with *The Guardian* and ahead of news sources like BBC Radio 1 and Channel 5. This was a significant increase from the 1 per cent reported in 2020. A quarter of Britons get their news on X (formerly Twitter), making it one of the top social media platforms for news consumption. Younger generations are more likely to use X in this context, with the highest usage among 16–24-year-olds. While X is a significant news source, platforms like Instagram, YouTube and Facebook still have a larger reach in the UK. This highlights the power of individuals like Elon Musk and Mark Zuckerberg in controlling the news agenda.

The fears don't end there, though. British people are worried about the potential for artificial intelligence (AI) to render their skills obsolete. Many Britons fear their abilities could become redundant by 2030 due to the speed of innovation. They worry about the impact on their job security and future employability. They also know there are massive potential benefits from AI, reducing the cost of the state and improving delivery of public services, for instance. But they don't hear their leaders talking about it with any sense of balance or insight – or about the pensions crisis caused by declining birth rates.

British politics was not a source of reassurance during this period. From 2000 to 2025, the rate of churn in political leadership accelerated: eight Prime Ministers served an average of three years each. Tony Blair was the longest-serving (ten years and two months) and Liz Truss was the shortest (forty-nine days). The time that ministers spend in government posts has fallen significantly – on average, it is under a year, a trend seen around the world in multiple elections, fuelled by the fact that people everywhere are fed up with 'the usual suspects'.[13]

The turbulence even affected sport. In the entire first year of the Premier League in 1992/93, there was one managerial sacking. By the 2023/24 season, there were fourteen.[14] [15]

Nothing seems to be planned, permanent or predictable anymore. We now live in a time when we're not even confident about the basics. In healthcare, although waiting times to see a GP are coming down, NHS waiting lists in England remain high, with many patients waiting longer than the target times. As of September 2023, 7.7 million people were waiting for hospital treatment. This includes 3.1 million patients who have been waiting over eighteen weeks and almost 235,000 who have been waiting over a year.[16]

Our access to property and the feeling of security it gives has changed hugely. The average house price in the UK increased from £181,364 in January 2007 to £288,533 by July 2024.[17] In 2024, the average full-time annual salary was £37,430. You don't need to be an economist to understand what the relationship between those figures means: home ownership, for many, has become an unachievable goal.

Turning to law and order, violent crime has increased every year in London for the last ten years.[18] This is despite London having one of the highest densities of CCTV cameras in the world, with seventy-three cameras per 1,000 citizens. It is second only to the Chinese city of Taiyuan, where there are 117 cameras per 1,000. Violent crime has actually dropped dramatically except in a handful of areas (all Labour-controlled).

Scotland's police performance in particular has been woeful. A long evolutionary tradition of local and accountable policing stretching back to 1789 was thrown away in 2013 with the establishment of Police Scotland by an SNP government that wanted a national force it could control.

You could blame politics for the changes. After all, that's what democracy is for. And that's what Britain did. The period from 2016 to 2024 culminated in the Labour landslide on 4 July 2024. It was the Conservative Party's worst general election performance ever. But it's not just Conservative politicians that have lost the faith of the public.

We discussed this in *Greater: Britain After the Storm*. The book explores how Britain can enhance its future by leveraging its historical strengths, cultural values and national character. It emphasised the importance of national pride, self-belief and self-awareness as essential components for achieving any goal. In Chapter Two of that book, we took a look at every set of indices on how the UK has performed against other nations across a whole range of criteria.

In the years since 2000, the internet brought us enhanced transparency. We can now see our leaders more clearly in every walk of life. This was a passage from *The Leadership Lab: Understanding leadership in the 21st century*:[19]

Since the turn of the century, we've learned that our leaders illegally avoided taxes,[20] rigged interest rates,[21] evaded taxes,[22] laundered drug money,[23] presided over an offshore banking system bigger than anyone thought possible,[24] forced good companies into closure[25] and destroyed pension funds as they themselves grew wealthier.[26] They oversaw an unprecedented destruction of wealth and the collapse of the financial system.[27] They watched as life savings placed into investment funds set up by leaders of previously unimpeachable integrity turned out to be Ponzi schemes.[28] They sold off reserves of gold to compensate for these exercises in corporate greed, while never once convicting any banker.[29] Our spiritual leaders covered up sex abuse in the Church.[30] Our charity leaders sexually abused the vulnerable.[31] Our child welfare leaders have permitted child abuse.[32]

Our politicians cheated on their expenses,[33] admitted sexually inappropriate behaviour,[34] started ruinously expensive unpopular wars[35] on the basis of false information[36] and were taken completely by surprise by the Brexit vote[37] then tried to avoid implementing it. Our education leaders presided over exam cheating[38] and sexual harassment.[39] Our defence industry leaders settled claims relating to the bribery of government officials.[40]

This was a passage from *Greater: Britain After the Storm*:

More CEOs are now being forced out of office for ethical lapse than for any other reason.[41] Leaders of the automotive industry[42] lied about emissions,[43] were imprisoned, broke out of jail and remain fugitives.[44] The leaders of our water utilities polluted rivers then tried to cover it up.[45] Global entertainment leaders have faced multiple allegations of sexual harassment and abuse.[46] Britain's leading broadcaster falsely accused political figures of being child abusers,[47] while allowing actual abusers to commit crimes on their premises.[48] Meanwhile, sporting leaders have been caught cheating and doping.[49] Our medical leaders have chronically mistreated patients.[50] Human rights lawyers have been struck off for misconduct and dishonesty.[51] In the US, many of the former President's political advisors have been jailed[52] and he has been subject to impeachment proceedings.

From the Mossack Fonseca and Paradise Papers revelations it's estimated[53] that $8.7 trillion, or 11 per cent, of global wealth resides in tax havens.[54] Large corporations are routinely shielding money which deprives world governments of approximately $170 billion per annum in tax revenue. This offshore tax operation was surprising even to people who were aware of the problem. This was thought to be a *fraction* of the UK economy. It turned out to be a *multiple* of it.

Much of what was revealed may have been going on before. Technology change was behind much of it. Communication enabled much of what happened because it enabled it to be visible for the first time. It became harder to hide secrets. Change had been piling up faster than the ability to assimilate it and the strains were already visible even before Covid.

These events sound almost unimaginable. If there were divisions before Covid, the pandemic deepened and widened them. It divided healthy and infirm, young and old, black and white, rich and poor, urban and rural, left and right, male and female. It was no surprise that politics should also become more polarised. There are too many who feel unheard and unseen by successive administrations.

Every one of these events changed the way we see the world. It also changed the balance of the workforce. Covid, in particular, accelerated the exodus of older generations and the induction of a younger cohort, Generation Z, born between 1997 and 2012.

Does it feel safe to bring children into our current world? Gen Z doesn't think so. They worry about bringing children into an uncertain and increasingly dystopian world. To this must be added the fact that couples are delaying having children until they have a foothold on the property ladder. The birth rates reflect this trend. Many Western populations are in decline and this gap is being taken up by immigration.[55] [56]

Could you argue that the past twenty-five years have seen just the normal amount of change? In previous years, there were wars in the Middle East. There were global financial crises such as the stagflation of the 1970s and '80s. There were global environmental scares – for instance, the hole in the ozone layer. There were global health scares like HIV/Aids, which prompted government intervention. There had been scares with SARS, bird flu and the Ebola virus. The difference in the last twenty-five years is that everything is more connected and interdependent and information is much more freely available and often of questionable integrity. Abundance devalues any commodity. Quantity is no substitute for quality.

These threads are being explored by what Anne Applebaum calls 'Autocracy Inc', a group of authoritarian and non-democratic nations against whom we compete. They seek to gain advantage and to undermine our way of life, confidence and trust in one another.

Not everything was bad. Some good things have happened. School standards have improved. Sadly, the reforms that delivered this are being unpicked despite being established on a cross-party consensus. As a result of Brexit, we have been able to sign new free trade agreements, and Britain acceded to the Comprehensive and Progressive Agreement for Trans-Pacific Partnership (CPTPP). This agreement, along with other trade and economic deals such as those signed with US states, are hugely positive for increasing UK market share but also for the creation of some thousands of high-wage jobs. And there is so much more we can still do.

The belief and confidence that leadership and its institutions once enjoyed is ebbing away, to be replaced by a corrosive cynicism. We have become much more atomised, isolated and polarised. The question is, what do we do now? The answer is that we need to come together again, something which is within our grasp, but first we need to recognise the barriers to doing this.

The last twenty-five years have seen an extraordinary level of unsettling change. So many unpredictable events have changed how we feel. As we go from one shock to another, we're now facing profound changes to the world order from new political movements, which will bring more unexpected changes. The mood in the country is as important as the facts. This is what we look at next.

CHAPTER THREE

THIS HAPPY BREED?

———◦—◦—✦—◦—◦———

This chapter looks at how the mood of the British people has changed. How has this changed politics? Is this still a happy breed? Does the instability encourage the 'strong man' model? Are we still proud of Britain? If so, are we still proud of the same things? What role have our traditions played in our recovery since Covid? Have they helped us deal with such difficult times?

———◦—◦—✦—◦—◦———

What works in other countries won't work in this one. We've got our own way of settling things. It may be a bit slow and it may be a bit dull... but it suits us all right and always will.

FRANK GIBBONS IN NOËL COWARD'S *THIS HAPPY BREED*

It would hardly be surprising if our recent history left British people feeling depressed, fearful and even cynical about the future. The public has been through a lot: Covid, the increasing cost of living, the deterioration of public services, the death of the Queen and the unprecedented political turmoil in the run-up to the last general election.

You'd think that the mood would be dark, but strangely it isn't. Britons are surprisingly resilient. An Ipsos poll in August 2022 found that we're still proud to be British. The NHS remains the number one source of that pride, despite losing some of the boost it had received after Britons' experiences of the Covid pandemic.[1]

Over half (55 per cent) of British citizens say that the NHS is what makes them proud to be British, down seven percentage points since April but still higher than the 50 per cent of 2016. A third (33 per cent) say British history makes them proud – particularly middle-aged or older people and Conservative and Leave voters – followed by the Royal Family (28 per cent) and the armed forces (24 per cent). These are followed by our culture (21 per cent) and our system of democracy (20 per cent).

What makes you proud to be British?

Which two or three of the following, if any, would you say makes you most proud to be British? Please select up to 3 options.

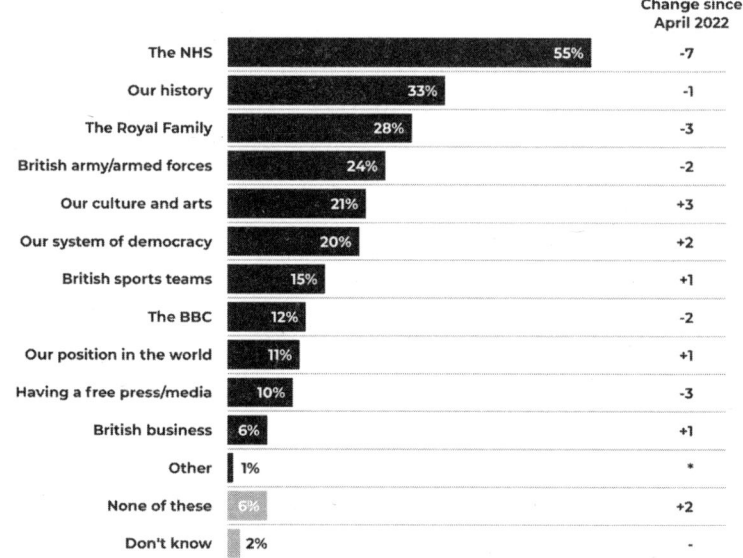

		Change since April 2022
The NHS	55%	-7
Our history	33%	-1
The Royal Family	28%	-3
British army/armed forces	24%	-2
Our culture and arts	21%	+3
Our system of democracy	20%	+2
British sports teams	15%	+1
The BBC	12%	-2
Our position in the world	11%	+1
Having a free press/media	10%	-3
British business	6%	+1
Other	1%	*
None of these	6%	+2
Don't know	2%	-

©IPSOS | August 2022

August 2022 Base: 1,661 Online GB Adults aged 18-75 who are British citizens, 3-4 August 2022
* Please note this option was not available when we asked this question previously

Source: Ipsos
Published on 15 August, 2022: https://www.ipsos.com/en-uk/what-makes-us-proud-be-british
from Ipsos Pride of Britain Polling, August 2022

We think our sense of humour is important and many identify good manners as one of our best characteristics. A growing number also think we are a friendly nation, up eight percentage points to 33 per cent (25 per cent in 2016). A quarter of Britons think that our hard-working attitude (26 per cent), tolerance of other sections of society (25 per cent) and patriotism (24 per cent) are the best attributes of the British. Only 18 per cent say one of the best characteristics is that we are law-abiding and 13 per cent say we keep to ourselves.

On the flip side, 41 per cent of British citizens say one of our worst characteristics is our ignorance of other cultures, little changed from 37 per cent in 2016. Our drinking culture is also seen to be one of our biggest negative attributes, with 35 per cent citing this, though this is down seven percentage points – and more likely to be mentioned as a negative by older rather than younger people (39 per cent of people aged 35–75 versus 24 per cent of people aged 18–24), while younger people are more likely to mention ignorance of other cultures.

Sometimes generations are talked about like they live in isolation. One of the strongest binding elements in any family is the sense of passing a tradition on to the next generation. This can be as much about, say, practical child-rearing techniques handed from grandparents to their children as it is about them learning them. Some figures have almost universal appeal across the generations. The Queen was one of those but there are others who have been elevated to the status of 'national treasure'.

More informal polls show that Brits admire Sir David Attenborough because he makes them 'glow with pride' (45 per cent), as does a well-risen Yorkshire pudding (43 per cent) and James Bond (42 per cent). Other icons include the London Eye (37 per cent), Sir Winston Churchill (34 per cent) and football (34 per cent).[2] It can seem like a random selection of people and things, but they accumulate and start to show us something a little more coherent.

Other polls show something similar. Since July 2019, YouGov has been tracking Britain's mood every week, asking the public which of a selection of moods best describes how they've felt over the previous seven days. The survey has tracked the ebbs and flows of national emotion, from the annual bump in happiness at Christmas, through the boredom, loneliness and fear of the Covid lockdowns, to the surges in sadness after the outbreak of war in Ukraine and Queen Elizabeth II's death.

The research reveals some reassurance. For example, happiness was the most common mood expressed by Britons over the past five years, though 'stressed' and 'frustrated' came second and third. It's no surprise that you're more likely to be happy if you're better off or older. Being optimistic also bucks the trend, though more in the form of a 'U' shape that dips in youth and rebounds from middle age. Women are more likely than men to have felt sad, stressed and scared over the last five years. Younger women, in particular, are more likely to have reported negative moods than men of the same age. Couples with children are reportedly happier, and no surprise again that Britons who regularly exercise are happier, less stressed and more energetic.[3]

But despite all this, other surveys reveal that anger remains a persistent problem. In so many areas of our lives, things have become easier, but when faced with administrative authority, we fare less well. According to the Gallup Global Emotions Report, anger has been rising since 2016, with 23 per cent of respondents now feeling angry on any given day. Additionally, according to research from the Institute of Customer Service, two-thirds of customer service workers have experienced hostility in the past year. Nearly half of those who faced abuse said callers were becoming more aggressive.[4][5]

The problem is that fear doesn't always reveal itself as fear; the more common expression is anger. The anger is in our public services, on social media and in the rise of physical violence and hatred. In London, the number of police-recorded knife or sharp instrument offences rose to nearly an all-time high from 2015/16 to 2023/24.[6]

Some of this violence has been convened online by conspiracy theories – for instance, in the case of the Southport murderer, Axel Rudakubana. He was not in fact an illegal immigrant, as some social media users had stated, but a British citizen born in Cardiff. In this respect, he was similar to the home-grown terrorists that perpetrated the 7/7 bombings in London.

In May 2023, the Mental Health Foundation produced a survey of the mental state of the UK. Entitled 'Uncertain Times: Anxiety in the UK and how to tackle it', the paper outlined the rising problem of fear and anxiety in the country. It identified several causes.

Polling found that nearly three-quarters of the population (73 per cent) had felt anxious at least sometimes in the previous two weeks. More than a quarter (26 per cent) felt anxious to the extent that it stopped them from doing what they'd planned. One in five people (20 per cent) felt anxious most or all of the time. This inability to plan is a key part of the loss of control that many felt – the loss of 'agency' or a chance to help sort it out on their own.

The poor mental health of large swathes of the nation can be seen in Britain's soaring welfare bill. According to the Centre for Mental Health, the overall costs of mental ill health equate to double the NHS's entire budget in England in 2022 (£153 billion). They are similar to the estimated impact of Covid on the UK economy in 2020 (£260 billion in 2020 prices) – comparable, economically, to having a pandemic every year.

Many people feel they can't look after themselves or their loved ones, they can't get a doctor's appointment and they can't control household costs. For example, even if they use no energy, they're still hit with massive standing charges. They can't get potholes fixed and they're not allowed to take matters into their own hands. It's as if, faced with these challenges, they are powerless.

Perhaps the biggest driver of this loss of agency is economic uncertainty. The country has faced a slump in productivity and stagnating wages. Brexit led to disruptions in trade and business operations. The pandemic had a profound impact on the economy, resulting in job losses, business closures and financial insecurity for many individuals and families. The rising cost of living, including housing, energy and food prices, has further exacerbated economic stress, leading to yet more frustration and anger.

Whether people love their country often comes down to two questions. Does my country matter to me? Do I matter to my country? Well, if your country seems to make you poorer and makes it harder for you to own a property or even get by, then you conclude accordingly. This is a telling statistic: 64 per cent say they are proud of Britain's history, a decrease from 86 per cent in 2013. This is almost exactly in line with the proportion of people who own their own homes. In the UK, approximately 64 per cent of households own their homes, with 34.8 per cent owning outright and 29.5 per cent owning with a mortgage. This is down from 73 per cent in 2007.[7]

It's clear the majority still love their country, but in many areas, it just doesn't love them back. People love the idea of the BBC, the NHS and the Post Office, but through many high-profile examples, these cherished institutions have all displayed contempt or mockery for the people they serve. The 'UK Theme' on BBC Radio 4 was a good example. We highlighted it in *Greater*:

> The BBC used to respect the union daily in its 'UK Theme', which was played on Radio 4 every morning between 23 November 1978 and 23 April 2006, immediately followed by the shipping forecast. The tune included excerpts from 'Danny Boy', 'What Shall We Do With The Drunken Sailor?', 'Scotland the Brave', 'Rule Britannia', 'Men of Harlech', 'Greensleeves', 'Londonderry Air' and 'Early One Morning'. It was an orchestral arrangement of traditional British and Irish airs. The five-minute theme was composed by a Jewish refugee, Fritz Spiegl, who came to the UK in 1939 after his family fled fascist persecution. It was a love song to

those that took him in. It was terminated by the BBC on St George's Day, 23 April 2006. It was a move designed by its timing to hurt. It did.

The decision to drop the theme was made by the controller of Radio 4 at the time, Mark Damazer, to make way for what he said would be a faster news briefing. He later admitted the mistake. He had misread a report and thought mere hundreds of people were listening at 5.30 a.m., rather than hundreds of thousands. Still, the decision was not reversed. Damazer later stood down after being in charge of Radio 4 to become head of a college at Oxford University.

THE UK THEME

https://www.youtube.com/watch?v=48YxyR-PSi8

These organisations are widely perceived as wasting large amounts of other people's money, often by paying themselves too much. They talk down to anyone who challenges them. They seem ashamed of the country's history. They hide behind lawyers.

The BBC, in particular, seems to prioritise the interests of its own reporters covering international news, politics and economics rather than a comprehensive perspective on British life and our interests. Less than 2 per cent of the electorate are members of a political party and yet, by some estimates, the percentage of BBC News devoted to these matters approaches a third of the airtime. Another example is international news, which made up over a quarter of airtime on *BBC News at Ten*.[8]

No political or economics programmes are in the top ten of the BBC audience figures. In a Barb 2023 report, the top-five most-watched programmes were the coronation, *Happy Valley*, the New Year's Eve fireworks, the *Eurovision Song Contest* and *I'm a Celebrity, Get Me Out of Here!*[9]

Sometimes, these publicly owned organisations and government agencies have CEOs who don't even live in the country they serve. In March 2025, it emerged that the chief inspector of UK Borders and Immigration was living in Finland. He was earning £130,000 a year. Some CEOs of local authorities do not live in the areas they manage either. The average salary for a local authority CEO in the UK is nearly £175,000; these are senior, well-paid roles, which rightly come with some responsibilities and expectations too.[10]

There is a pendulum here. For some time, it was common for government to shift responsibility away from elected officials to quangos (quasi-autonomous non-governmental organisations) or arm's-length bodies of various kinds. These include non-departmental public bodies, non-ministerial government departments and executive agencies. The best example of this was NHS England, an executive non-departmental body under the Department of Health and Social Care, the abolition of which was announced in the spring of 2025 by the Secretary of State Wes Streeting.

Police forces are another example where agency, the sense of getting stuck in and helping out where you can, is not encouraged. There are now fewer than 7,000 special constables spread across the forty-three territorial forces in England and Wales, the lowest in fifty years. Specials are required to complete sixteen hours of service a month and have the same powers as a regular officer but are largely unpaid apart from some expenses and allowances. They work on a volunteer basis.[11] There are various reasons given for this decline, including attrition during training and a lack of resources, leading to fewer volunteers.

This effect is felt at the local level, in hospitals, council services and police forces. The vast majority of us live, work, raise a family and die within twenty-five miles of our birthplace. A recent survey said that nearly half (48 per cent) of UK adults currently live locally, with the majority feeling content (49 per cent) and proud (26 per cent) about their decision to stay close to home. When asked why they were not tempted to move, reasons include proximity to family and friends (61 per cent), a sentimental attachment to the area (23 per cent), being close to green spaces (23 per cent), plus affordable housing (20 per cent).[12] It's very different in the US. In England, 100 miles is enormous and 100 years is nothing. In America, it's the other way around.

The public really cares about local matters. From around 2005, many local authorities used private finance initiatives (PFIs) to transfer everyday responsibility for road maintenance like potholes to private contractors, thus further distancing it from local elected officials. One of Reform UK's 2025 pledges was to rip up those contracts and return responsibility to elected officials. The last government announced an end to new PFI contracts in 2018, but many of the existing arrangements still have many years to run. The pothole has become the local metaphor for the failure to renew national infrastructure.[13]

This is perhaps why potholes and bin collections have become such big issues. For instance, a dispute between the council and unions representing refuse collectors brought the city of Birmingham to a halt in the spring of 2025, with tens of thousands of tons of rubbish piled uncollected in the streets. Responsibility is shirked. Those who might step up and seize it are discouraged.

This balance between local and national was explored by David Goodhart in his book *The Road to Somewhere*.[14] This is an investigation into the political fault lines that divide Brexit Britain and Donald Trump's America. He points out that mobility, economic and cultural openness have not benefited everyone equally. Among those who have been left behind, a populist politics of culture and identity has challenged the traditional politics of left and right, creating a new division: between the mobile 'achieved' identity of the people from Anywhere and the marginalised, roots-based identity of the people from Somewhere. This schism accounts for the Brexit vote, the election of Donald Trump, the decline of the centre-left and the rise of populism across Europe. The centre ground has given way. There's a saying in politics that the definition of a liberal is someone not yet affected – another reason why the 'left behind' are disillusioned.

The problem is that more and more people *are* affected, especially at the lower end of the income scale. They're more worried than ever before about falling standards of living, access to healthcare, law and order and the impact of mass migration. And there's your answer to why politics is now so divisive. More people are impacted and more have an opinion about the cause of it. What makes the frustration worse, is that politicians appear strangely either unwilling to see the problem or unable to do anything about it if they do.

What we're seeing in America is a backlash against the dominance of Anywhere interests, in everything from the curriculum in schools and higher education to mass immigration.

There's a feeling here that the global rulebook is out of date. There's no greater example of this than the refugee convention. Most nations have been generous and understand the importance of an asylum system. But legal frameworks have meant those same nations have found it hard to protect their borders. Ultimately, the state must be the arbiter of who is allowed to stay and be given shelter. Anything else results in a huge waste of resources.

In a similar way, Britain has always been a patchwork of distinct local identities that roll up into one. Like nature itself, these are delicate relationships that interweave from the capillary levels all the way up to the whole. This is a deeply conservative (small c) instinct. The global 'elites' or 'anywheres' are scarcely aware of this sense of place, but it is there nevertheless. This consciousness among the British people is profound. It's as deep as their sense of identity, history and belonging. This is not unique to Britain, but it's a phenomenon affecting it. The intricate traditions we see, therefore, are locally as much a matter of identity and belonging as they are pride. If you're not even aware of this history, how can you respect, let alone defend, it?

This book highlights so many voluntary, unpaid (and frequently unauthorised) groups who fight to preserve our traditions. What can our local government and politicians learn from them? Involve people, bring people together, allow them to participate and give them agency. And stop trying to shut them down.

You can only beat fear with fellowship. It speaks to the real human desire to come together around shared values and participate in their celebration and renewal. You can try all you like to offset this, but we each have loyalties, beliefs and identities. To deny it is utopian nonsense. To encourage it also has its dangers. But it must be understood because it is fundamental to our character.

President Trump is not only making changes quickly, but he's also using TV and social media every day to feed back to the public his version of his actions. No President has communicated so fully or frequently. He's using the media in a way that only a creator of media would know how. He looms larger and seems more effective because of this daily awareness.

The fact that a politician does what they said they would shouldn't be of note, but it is. Electorates have grown used to manifestos not being honoured and pledges being disregarded once in office. There are reasons why politicians can't achieve what they set out to, but no one wants to hear excuses. But this time, President Trump has planned much more thoroughly. He is delivering a significant change, which will not only change America but also the world's relationship with all elected representatives.

Some might say that the turbulence is counterproductive. This misses the point. He's having an impact. He's showing that the choice of politician really can change things. For the Conservative Party to return to power, it doesn't have to follow the same policies as President Trump, but it must follow at least one central principle – it must be able to deliver change. The Trump administration reminds us that the primary role of the elected institution is to protect and defend the values and beliefs of those who elected them as their number-one priority.

When institutions are perceived (rightly or not) as no longer in service of these values and beliefs, then expect disillusionment. The behaviour of politicians then looks disingenuous; hence the calls in America to 'drain the swamp'.

The frustration in the UK has been made much worse because the public has begun to realise that not even their elected representatives appear to have agency. They know the system is broken. They see their local politicians, who by and large they like, unable to have the slightest positive effect on their lives. When they promise things that they subsequently don't deliver but still retain the privileges of office, salaries and expenses, disappointment is the result. It becomes harder to convince the public that you understand their household budget concerns when someone else is buying your clothes, glasses and Sabrina Carpenter concert tickets.

This is felt most keenly at the lower income levels where many policies seem almost designed to deliberately impact those on low pay. For instance, on 1 April 2025, there were simultaneous increases in the BBC licence fee, broadband, mobile and TV bills, vehicle tax, council tax, energy bills and water bills. Of course, it's the beginning of the tax year, but the timing can look like a coordinated attack on those on lower incomes, especially when it affects so many services that are essential or mandatory.

None of these things can be changed by the individual. This is why so many local traditions are important. They are times when people can do something simple to raise money, support values, help out, feed back, wish good luck or even just talk to others who are experiencing the same frustrations. Local traditions are an example of popular, participative local government that doesn't exclude, demand money, chastise, patronise, lecture or proscribe. They are so often organised by those running local businesses, who are used to treating their community as regular, daily customers – not voters who they only need to deal with once every three to four years. Local businesses soon close down when they don't do what they promise. The most immediate universal franchise in the real world is thus not political, but economic.

This is why the return to power of President Donald Trump matters. Whether you agree with his policies or not, he is doing exactly what he said he would, perhaps more so than any politician in recent history. This is important because he is showing that the political franchise still works and that the levers of power are connected to something. So, for instance, when it comes to issues like illegal migration, people want to see the actions matching up with the words. Politicians are aware that people are disengaging, but the one way to get them back is to show them that they can have what they voted for, and this is exactly what the American President is doing.[15]

The lack of agency also extends into voluntary organisations that can't get local government funding. For this reason, many of the local traditions enshrine scepticism of the venality of authority (see the weighing of the mayor, explained later in the book). They also provide therapy for those exasperated by authority figures.

This sense of injustice is a source of resentment in the UK. Despite being one of the world's wealthiest nations, the UK has high levels of income inequality, with a widening gap between the rich and the poor. This disparity is evident in various aspects of life, including access to education, healthcare and employment opportunities. The perception that the system is rigged in favour of the wealthy and powerful has led to widespread frustration and resentment among those who feel left behind. The lack of social mobility and the persistence of poverty in certain communities further contribute to the sense of injustice and anger.

Political instability is another factor. The country has experienced a series of divisive leadership elections and referendums, for instance on Scottish independence in 2014. The lack of clear and consistent leadership has left many citizens feeling disillusioned and distrustful of mainstream politics. The polarisation of political views and the rise of populist movements have also fuelled anger and division as people struggle to find common ground and solutions.

The impact of hostility on social media fuels this, as people are exposed to a constant stream of negative news, inflammatory rhetoric and divisive content. The anonymity and immediacy of online interactions often lead to more extreme expressions of anger and frustration, which can spill over into real-life behaviour. The echo-chamber effect, where individuals are only exposed to information that reinforces their existing beliefs, further polarises opinions and intensifies anger.

Addressing the growing anger in the UK requires a multifaceted approach. Economic policies that promote stability and job creation and reward responsibility might help reduce economic inequality. Political leaders must work towards rebuilding trust and unity by engaging in transparent and inclusive decision-making processes. Efforts to address persistent social inequality, such as improving access to education and healthcare, can help create a more just and equitable society. Additionally, promoting digital literacy and encouraging responsible online behaviour might help mitigate the negative impact of social media on public discourse.

The increasing anger in the UK is a complex issue driven by many challenges such as political instability, social inequality and the influence of digital media. This is why our national and community traditions still play such an important role. They can be great levellers, oases of social interaction without the sharp edges of party politics and activism. No matter who you are, you can still enjoy a bonfire night, a beer festival, a royal wedding, a bank holiday, or a football or cricket match.

Although Covid accelerated and deepened fear of the unknown and the fear of isolation, there were also encouraging signs as many sought to volunteer and help. Look at the number that registered their name to help the NHS during Covid. The initial 250,000 target was smashed, with more than 750,000 volunteering.[16] One of the great disappointments post-pandemic was that this army of volunteers was just forgotten about. They could have been held together. A huge amount was needed after the pandemic in our communities and still is. Instead, things just went quiet, and they weren't even properly thanked. On the same day Labour unveiled its 'whole of society' approach to national resilience, the NHS disbanded this army of volunteers.

When people have a clear request made of them, whether it's managing a car park at a vaccination centre or helping Captain Tom reach his fundraising goal, they rally, they step up, they take responsibility. If people are allowed to, they get organised and have a natural ability to sort things out themselves. They don't want to leave it to others. It is gratifying and reassuring to be able to make a positive impact.

There's something here about a need to exert control. One of the ways to battle fear is to be doing something. In wartime diaries, fear was often reported as being at its greatest when waiting to go, rather than being in action. When people are busy, it's easier to keep their minds off the problem. Keep calm and carry on, if you like. This, alone, is a sign of the essentially good and pragmatic nature of the British people. It is a natural quality that government must not just allow for but should actively encourage. It represents personal responsibility, self-reliance and agency – what Scots and northerners would simply call gumption. Where people feel powerless, the knock-on effect on mental health and well-being is magnified.

We want to help. We want to belong to something bigger. Our

identity is as much about who we are as who we're not, and this is the great myth of social media. What was supposed to bring us together has often driven us apart. The internet is a poor substitute for physical proximity. Digital media cannot be overlooked when examining the rise of anger in the UK, but the anger itself also shows that some are challenging the idea that nothing can be done.

This sounds counterintuitive, but anger needn't be automatically a negative response. According to the science magazine *Greater Good*: 'Research overwhelmingly indicates that feeling angry increases optimism, creativity, effective performance – and research suggests that expressing anger can lead to more successful negotiations, in life or on the job.'[17] Maybe anger has a role, if people are prepared to express it politely and persistently.

You can see this trend in customer complaints about call centre outsourcing, for instance. Where a few years ago, people would end up getting frustrated with talking to a help desk in India, businesses responded by onshoring call centres and high street services. Mobile phone company EE, for example, created 260 new jobs at its North Tyneside and Darlington call centres.[18]

Despite anxiety being so common, stigma and shame play a part in how people deal with it, with almost half (45 per cent) of UK adults keeping it a secret. This suggests that although there has been progress in discussing mental health more openly in recent years, significant numbers of people are still not comfortable talking about their experiences.

It's clear that financial stress is giving rise to anxiety across the UK. The most commonly reported cause of anxiety was not being able to pay bills, reported by 32 per cent of respondents, while 40 per cent said that financial security would help prevent anxiety.

And this is just individuals. Businesses are also stressed. Since the change of President in the US, many have reported that the on/off tariffs have made companies much harder to run, especially those that have supply chains running across borders. This, accompanied by local tax changes, has meant a significant loss of confidence in the future of the UK economy.

But this is an area that is different – many of those business leaders, entrepreneurs and investors do have agency and they're using it.

Britain lost almost 11,000 millionaire families to migration last year, a 157 per cent increase compared with 2023.[19] This may not sound like a lot until you consider that the UBS Global Wealth Report for 2024 estimated that there were over 3 million dollar millionaires in the UK. The report forecasted a reduction to 2.5 million millionaires by 2028, a decrease of 17 per cent. Granted, many of these might have been made wealthy by property, but there's no doubt that losing high earners has a negative effect on tax revenues.

The top 1 per cent in the UK pays 30 per cent of all income tax revenues, a higher share than at any time in the past twenty years. In other words, three in every ten pounds that the government receives in income tax is paid by just over 300,000 people, and their families are much more mobile than most.[20]

As Daniel Daggers, founder and chief executive officer of property advisory DDRE Global put it:

These families aren't just numbers; they're a vital part of the ecosystem that fuels our economy. A survey by the analyst Oxford Economics showed that each non-dom paid an average of £800,000 of VAT in the last year and £890,000 in stamp duty over the previous five years … The trust the UK has earned over decades is being chiselled away by countries with low-tax environments, better weather and less bureaucracy. We can't do much about the weather, but the tax environment and the level of bureaucracy can, and should, be controlled much more effectively.

For businesses, the process of Brexit was a challenging one. For years, no one had any idea of what Brexit meant. The politicians on the winning side weren't the ones implementing the result. Businesses could adapt, find agents and build new IT systems but only if they knew what was going to be asked of them. They could prepare for any eventuality but not every eventuality. The same is true now with the pace and uncertainty in America over a retaliatory trade war on tariffs. Investment revenue is a bit like an in-flight beverage service. It tends to be suspended during turbulence.

For most people, the pandemic was the biggest shock of their lives. It sparked unprecedented fears for personal and family safety. This was accelerated by the physical isolation of people living in 'bubbles' that cut them off, in some cases physically, from family and friends. Life and death had to continue sometimes in different bubbles. For some, this created situations that will never be forgotten.

The pandemic has had a profound impact on mental health, too. 'Long Covid', in particular, is increasingly being recognised as a neuropsychiatric disorder. This means that the virus can affect the brain, leading to cognitive challenges such as brain fog, attention issues, memory problems and executive function difficulties. These cognitive impairments can contribute to heightened anxiety and fear, which are common in mental health disorders.

Millennials and Gen Z are more likely to experience mental health issues compared to other generations. This could be due to various factors, including economic uncertainty, social media influence and the prioritisation of purpose over salary. The pressure to find meaningful work and the fear of not achieving it can contribute to mental health struggles. Not for nothing has the bracket 16–24 been labelled the 'loneliest generation', living through the triple effects of social media, Covid isolation and the subsequent spread of working from home.[21]

Rebecca Munday is a talented Chelsea Art College painter of this period. Her paintings capture the zeitgeist and its effects on a generation. The lifeless eyes, the missing hands on the clock face and the sense of distance are all apparent in her work. If ever a generation's experience could be summarised in art, then it is here. It stands in comparison with the Weimar Republic paintings of Otto Dix and George Grosz.

THE PAINTINGS OF REBECCA MUNDAY

https://art.beopenfuture.com/rebecca-munday/

The necessary isolation from Covid created many knock-on effects. It's well-known in the military that isolation breaks people down, primarily due to the lack of human interaction. This leads to psychological distress, including anxiety, paranoia, hallucinations, depression and in extreme cases, thoughts of suicide. Essentially, it deprives individuals of the basic human need for social connection, which can significantly damage their mental health over time.[22] When isolation is combined with social deprivation, it doubles the suicide rate. People living in the most deprived areas of England have almost double the rate of suicide as those living in the least deprived areas.[23]

According to the Campaign to End Loneliness, loneliness is defined as:

A subjective, unwelcome feeling of lack or loss of companionship. It happens when there is a mismatch between the quantity and quality of the social relationships that we have and those that we want.[24]

It points out:

> Loneliness can affect anyone. Experiences of loneliness can vary, but its effects can be profound and wide-ranging. It is considered by many to be one of the largest public health challenges we face.

There are some profound misconceptions about loneliness and belonging – for instance, that it's mainly those of retirement age that are the most impacted. According to the Mental Health Foundation, 40 per cent of respondents aged 16–24 reported feeling lonely often or very often, while only 29 per cent of people aged 65–74 and 27 per cent of people aged over seventy-five said the same. This was data gathered in 2018, before Covid.[25]

In 2022, almost half of all adults (26 million people) in the UK reported feeling lonely occasionally. This has risen from 6 per cent (3.2 million) in 2020, indicating that there has not been a recovery since the pandemic came to an end. There is evidence that working-from-home culture has delayed the recovery.[26]

The latest facts and statistics about loneliness help us to understand more about the risk factors and the impact it can have on different areas of our lives.

For those particularly interested in how young people have fared in all this change and upheaval, *The Anxious Generation* by Jonathan Haidt is a collection of important insights into childhood. His proposition is that children should have less access to social media. He points out that many children are traumatised by experiences that thrill others and their fear is heightened by the rollercoaster of social media. Other research also shows the alarming statistic that boys are now more likely to have a smartphone than a dad at home.[27] They're dating at all-time record lows and teenage dating is rapidly disappearing as a part of the experience of growing up.[28] Children need strong role models. They must belong to something other than the internet.

JONATHAN HAIDT'S BOOK

https://www.amazon.co.uk/Anxious-Generation-Rewiring-Childhood-Epidemic-ebook/dp/BoCGWS3JQ6

It's clear that the economic fallout from the pandemic disproportionately affected certain groups, such as the young and women in low-wage, insecure jobs. Mental health problems affect twice as many women as men. (We ought to remember at the same time, however, that the suicide rate among men is more than three times that among women.)[29]

Nowhere in the world had ever seen lockdown and government curtailment of freedoms on the scale that began in 2020. This was born of a combination of factors: governments were desperate to introduce the most effective methods of controlling the spread of the virus and were willing to take drastic measures, even though the evidential basis was far from clear-cut (in some cases, understandably but with damaging consequences); scientific advice was accepted too readily and uncritically; and modern technology had also expanded the potential reach of the state so that it could enforce behaviour on the public in a way unimaginable only, say, twenty years before. To this end, lockdown was a giant experiment, the findings of which are only just now becoming clear.

Three of every four jobs lost during this period were lost by women, as women took on more of the childcare, elderly care, home education and domestic tasks. Jobs still have not recovered to pre-pandemic levels.[30] The economic instability has led to increased stress and fear about the future, contributing to changes in voting intentions. This was evidenced in the 2024 US election, where 45 per cent of women voted for Donald Trump.[31]

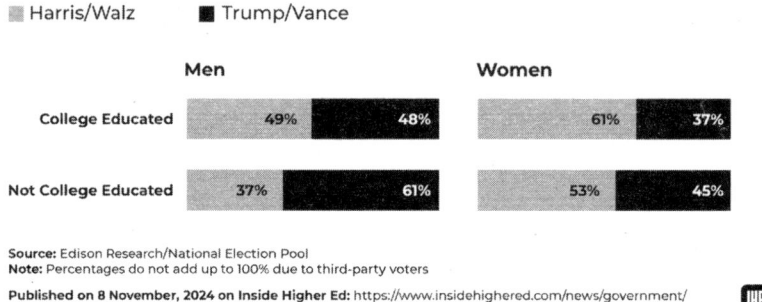

Educational Attainment by Gender

How men and women voted in the 2024 presidential election separated by education level.

■ Harris/Walz ■ Trump/Vance

	Men		Women	
College Educated	49%	48%	61%	37%
Not College Educated	37%	61%	53%	45%

Source: Edison Research/National Election Pool
Note: Percentages do not add up to 100% due to third-party voters

Published on 8 November, 2024 on Inside Higher Ed: https://www.insidehighered.com/news/government/politics-elections/2024/11/08/men-and-white-people-vote-differently-based-education

https://www.insidehighered.com/news/government/politics-elections/2024/11/08/men-and-white-people-vote-differently-based-education

Even the community organisations that were there to mitigate the effects were overwhelmed. Some 30 per cent of small charities lost more than half of their income during Covid.

The ongoing effect of globalisation is another factor. Some fear losing their identity. Some British people, for instance, think we're becoming too American. Some Americans believe they are losing their identity, too. Incidentally, there's a debate in Britain about us not wanting American food standards on, say, chlorinated chicken. Americans feel the same way. Import of haggis to the US has been banned since the US Department of Agriculture (USDA) prohibited the import of food containing sheep lungs in 1971. The reason for this is that the USDA believes that lungs should not be used as human food. The lungs of a sheep can contain bacteria, so the ban is in place with food safety in mind.

What's really happening is that everywhere is becoming a lot more like everywhere else – perhaps an inevitable effect of a global internet but with political consequences, nonetheless.

There's no doubt that some American traditions have been finding their way into the British way of life, like prom celebrations, trick or treating (although this was a North American evolution of the old

Scottish and Irish practice of 'guising') and commercial events like Black Friday. These are largely traditions that, hitherto, we did not have. We didn't have an event to mark the end of secondary school, for example. In any case, kiddies going around their neighbouring households to get sweets and toffee apples is arguably more wholesome than some of our homegrown traditions around Halloween, which can prompt uncomfortable questions about the process of being hanged, drawn and quartered or how the dead can be resurrected to walk the Earth.

Americanisation should come as no surprise. We shop in American-style supermarkets, wear American clothes, use American phones, listen to American music, watch American movies and TV and eat American food. There's plenty of evidence of reciprocation with this. For instance, the 'British Invasion' shook up American music in the 1960s. British bands like the Beatles and the Rolling Stones brought a fresh sound that captivated young audiences and challenged the status quo. This reshaped the music industry, influencing everything from fashion to recording techniques. More recently, British exports to America include tea, which is now the most popular beverage in the US and is more popular than coffee in thirty states; as nations, we seem to have moved on from the dispute that ended up with forty tons of tea sinking in Boston Harbor in 1773. That said, this newly popular tea may not be tea as most of us would know it: for example, matcha, iced and bubble teas.[32]

Despite this interplay, America and Britain remain two nations divided by weights and measures:

https://www.youtube.com/watch?v=JYqfVE-fykk

Other exports, though, are more conspicuous: the English Premier League, British films and TV like *Downton Abbey* and multiple Oscar-winning Aardman Animations films featuring Wallace and Gromit. There's even a 'Wizarding World of Harry Potter' at Universal Studios in California. This is being replicated with a new Universal Studios theme park and resort, the first in Europe, being built on a 476-acre former brickworks site near Bedford.

This is not to mention British cars and British fashion brands like Hunter, Barbour, Stella McCartney, Vivienne Westwood, Burberry and Alexander McQueen. There are royal events, too. The coronation drew 11.7 million viewers in US households, not far short of the peak viewing audience of 15 million viewers on BBC One, despite coverage beginning early in the day – 5 a.m. on the east coast of America.

Despite the ravages of Covid, the country is returning to pre-pandemic patterns in some areas. International traffic also increased significantly, with a 13.6 per cent rise compared to 2023. Some flights are important for these islands. The UK is home to the shortest commercial flight, lasting two minutes from Westray to Papa Westray in Scotland. Global air passenger demand reached an all-time record high in 2024, exceeding pre-pandemic levels, with total capacity up and a record load factor of 83.5 per cent.

There was a similar post-Covid effect on our festivals and local events. This was partly due to sheer relief at the pandemic having drawn to an end but also down to the reforms of temporary event licensing. Temporary event notices increased by 50 per cent when they were made easier to grant. These are events where alcohol may be sold and feature fewer than 500 participants.[33] This is welcome after one in six music festivals failed to return after Covid.[34] Notwithstanding, there are 482 festivals per year (2025) and over 192 music festivals in London alone.

Meanwhile, there's no doubt that some feel their identity is under threat when it comes to immigration and the ghettoisation of certain parts of our country. In some areas, this has become so pronounced that some communities seem unrecognisable.

In some areas, the figures are impossible to ignore. According to ONS census data, in central Bradford 43 per cent of people were born outside of the UK.[35] In central Luton, the figure is 38.4 per cent. As Robert Jenrick has said, this is unprecedented and unmandated.[36] He points out the wealthy reap the benefits of mass migration and can avoid the costs ordinary Brits face in their daily lives.

No one in mainstream politics thinks the separateness of these communities is a good idea. In pockets of the country, complacency or cowardliness has enabled a vacuum of British values. This can be seen in the tolerance of limiting the freedoms of women or the mistreatment and abuse of girls. Or in the fact that a nation of animal lovers permits over 30 million of them to be slaughtered without being stunned first.[37] Or in the consequences of generations of inter-marriage. What has caused this collective failure to recognise how far adrift we have become from the norms we would recognise as our national character? We could also apply this thinking to the vile extremities of social media content.

Some communities do have different values, many of which are unacceptable. Sometimes this involves women being stuck at home, not seen or recognised for their own talents. These communities are not the norm. We cannot simply look away because we find it too difficult to challenge such behaviour head-on.

There is, however, a valid question that needs to be asked: why do only 60 per cent with leave to remain here become citizens? Indefinite leave to remain allows permanent residency, but becoming a British citizen unlocks additional rights like voting and holding a British passport. The process of citizenship is different, with specific requirements including a language test and a 'Life in the UK' test.

In the year ending September 2024, there were 268,481 grants of British citizenship, a 44 per cent increase compared to the previous year, with 61,655 grants to EU nationals and 206,826 to non-EU nationals. Why does it not matter to those who will make their home here that they are part of our nation? Why would someone consider fighting for a foreign army and not the British Army?

There's a saying about change: if it isn't allowed to be a process, it eventually becomes an event. There has been so much change that it feels chaotic and out of control.

Speaking on BBC *Newsnight* in February 2025, former MI6 chief Sir Alex Younger said:

> We're in a new era where international relations aren't going to be determined by rules and multilateral institutions. They're going to be determined by strong men and deals. I think of the Yalta Treaty at the end of 1945. Three strong men as they were then, on behalf of the big countries the strong countries, decided the fate of small countries. I think that's Donald Trump's mindset. It's certainly Putin's mindset. It's Xi Jinping's mindset, but it's not Europe's mindset. That's the world we're going into for a whole set of reasons and I don't think we're going back to the old world.

The 'strong man' model has been seen from time to time in our history and it's usually accompanied by war. As former US Secretary of State Henry Kissinger said: 'There are only two ways to have stability – dominance or equilibrium.'

There's a danger here that after years of successive failures with centre-ground democracy, young people become more attracted to dictatorships that get things done.[38] They appear to deliver more stability and control.

There is nothing more attractive in polarised times than instant, straightforward solutions to complicated questions. Much of our political and social turmoil arises from the inclination to believe that overwhelming troubles can be resolved easily with sufficient determination. The strong-man principle reassures people who cannot figure out what to do and they seem to be relieved when a confident man tells them. Confidence, though, is not to be confused with competence. In an ambiguous world, it is easy to fall prey to almost any form of clarity.

There are people who describe President Trump's MAGA movement as deranged or unintelligent. We've heard this before. This sort of derision was heaped on the Brexit campaigners in the run-up to the referendum. Is it really so hard for Democrats to understand? Americans don't want to see their money being spent overseas when there are so many problems at home. They don't want their sons and daughters dying on faraway battlefields to protect other people's borders when they have problems at home protecting their own.

What the majority feel is understandable, logical and common sense and it was heard and acted upon. There was fear, which became the source of anger, which translated into voting momentum.

President Trump reflects something important in the history of America and the world – democracy still works. Anyone in British politics now seeking to regain the confidence of the electorate must recognise this in the same way. President Trump has co-opted people who he thinks can help him make it happen. He has cultivated extraordinary loyalty in those around him, his supporters in the new media and sometimes in both. It remains to be seen whether this will be enough to bring about the change he wants, or if those changes will even prove effective when so many are being unsettled by how they are being made. Recent British political history provides some unfortunate examples of those who tried to go too far, too fast. National political and economic systems are not laboratory experiments. They affect the lives of millions of people and the consequences of getting it wrong can be catastrophic.

Could this come to Britain? It could. Britain has occasionally ventured away from centrist politics, but it's less likely to happen because our political system doesn't have the same type of executive orders. Government needs a majority in Parliament to get legislation through. This requires experience, knowledge and the ability to compromise. It also needs a compliant House of Lords. You don't get this from extreme positions. The parliamentary system is designed to moderate, dilute and decelerate policy. Political power in the UK thus resides not with populism but with pragmatism. If you don't know how to get it done, then ultimately you can't deliver. Saying it doesn't make it happen.

Do the current structures of government work brilliantly well? They don't. They are too slow. They are far removed from excellence. They waste taxpayers' money and government bandwidth. They have little lasting impact. They cannot cope with the modern world. Pragmatism here doesn't mean compromising what needs to be done. It means being realistic about how you can achieve what the country needs. That needs a clear plan and it's always been the case.

The numbers are against you, however. In December 2024, the number employed in the public sector was over 6 million. The number of those elected is fewer than 20,000, a ratio of 300 to 1. It's like a mouse sitting on an elephant. Who is more likely to decide which way to go? Determination and planning can only achieve so much.

Furthermore, there are 650 MPs and the vast majority of the other elected office holders are local councillors. There are 17,000 of these in England. Almost half are retired graduates and describe their ethnic background as white. The majority hold other voluntary or unpaid positions, such as school governorships. These are unlikely to be the most radical or experimental of political zealots.[39]

If you want lasting change, you have to work with the grain of the people and stay close to them. You have to understand who they are and what they care about.

Are the British still a happy breed? The conclusion is yes, mainly. There is disappointment with political leadership, but this is showing itself more as KBO (Keep Buggering On) or as apathy rather than extremism. The 2024 electoral turnout was close to the lowest it has been in a hundred years.[40]

This apathetic mood indicates that some people think voting is a big waste of time. Some think that Britain is useless, and this really matters. Whether you think you can or whether you think you can't, you're probably right. Many feel that we're constantly letting ourselves down. The debacle at Heathrow Airport in March 2025 is a good example. The state of our armed forces is another. But there's not much you can do about cynicism, except to deliver against promises and encourage more responsibility, especially among those in office. There are many great people with huge talents who take responsibility.

There is also a perennial role for the language of optimism; not mindless assumptions that 'everything will be all right', or self-deception about the nature and depth of the challenges we face, but a calm, clear-eyed determination to make things better. But it can never be enough for leaders just to identify problems and agree how serious they are, maybe intractable. As Churchill told the annual Lord Mayor's Banquet in 1954, not long before he finally retired from office: 'For myself, I am an optimist – it does not seem to be much use being anything else.'

There are many examples of failure and dismay at the national level. The country, though, still has so much to offer, so much potential and it's still broadly proud of its history and achievements. This remains true, especially at the local level, where there is more participation, goodwill and optimism than we see in the bigger institutions.

Fear and anger have been prime movers in the changed priorities of politics. This is true not just in Britain but in many countries around the world. Large numbers of the electorate have turned away from mainstream politics because it feels ineffective. It does not address their priorities. In many instances, it seems totally ineffective. This view is being challenged by the 'strong man' model. It is forcing us to re-evaluate who we really are. So, let's find out.

CHAPTER FOUR

WHO WE ARE

––––––––––––––––––––––––✦––––––––––––––––––––––––

This chapter asks whether there is any such thing as the British character and, if so, how was it formed and where did it come from? What effect has the geography of our islands had on us? How has this been exported around the world for cultural and commercial gain and why does it remain important? Why did it matter that we were the first in so many fields of human endeavour?

––––––––––––––––––––––––✦––––––––––––––––––––––––

Somebody once said we was a nation of gardeners, you know they weren't far wrong. We like planting things and watching 'em grow, looking out for changes in the weather.

Frank Gibbons in Noël Coward's *This Happy Breed*

Our England is a garden and such gardens are not made
By singing, 'Oh, how beautiful!' and sitting in the shade,
'The Glory of the Garden', Rudyard Kipling

Let's start with what hasn't changed. I still love this country and its people. I love everything it stands for. For such a small country to have made such a big impact on the planet is unprecedented in human history. It's an extraordinary story. Even now, Britain still matters.

It matters not just because of what it does, but what it is and what it stands for.

It also laughs at angry extremists, which probably makes them even angrier.

JOHN CLEESE ON EXTREMISM

https://www.youtube.com/watch?v=HLNhPMQnWu4

Although Britain is not the biggest or the most powerful country, one of the surprises about it is how it still ranks so highly in so many areas. It's still the largest outside investor in America. It has one of the oldest, most stable monarchies. It still has the oldest continuous Parliament. It's not Westminster but the Tynwald in the Isle of Man. (Icelanders will tell you that the Althing is the oldest Parliament, which may well be true, but it was effectively non-existent from 1800 to 1844 and had lost its legislative power hundreds of years before that.)

It still has the largest theatre-going audience with the world's longest-running show – Dame Agatha Christie's *The Mousetrap*, which has been running since 1952. Shakespeare's *Macbeth* remains the most produced play ever written. On average, a performance is staged every four hours worldwide.

Britain leads the world in music. Only seven bands and artists have ever sold more than a quarter of a billion records. They are the Beatles, Elvis Presley, Michael Jackson, Madonna, Elton John, Led Zeppelin and Pink Floyd – four of these are from the UK. The Beatles song 'Yesterday' has the most covers worldwide, with 1,600 recorded versions. British TV exports are popular around the world and a real mix of programmes – *Peppa Pig, Doctor Who, Downton Abbey, Who Wants to Be a Millionaire?, Top Gear* and the *Great British Bake Off* – are sold or have their format licensed in a remarkable number of countries.

Incidentally, *Peppa Pig* is one of the few areas where the Foreign Office paid to protect intellectual property from the Chinese. *Peppa Pig* is, quite literally, a national treasure.

In literature, Britain dominates. Excluding religious and political books, only seven books have ever sold more than 100 million copies. Of those seven, five are from British authors: *The Hobbit* and the *Lord of the Rings* by J. R. R. Tolkien, J. K. Rowling's *Harry Potter and the Philosopher's Stone, Then There Were None* by Dame Agatha Christie and *She: A Story of Adventure* by the prolific Victorian novelist H. Rider Haggard. Further down the bestseller list, a few authors are strongly represented (such as Rowling and Christie) and British authors still dominate. This is particularly the case among children's books – it's not just Rowling, but also the Belfast-born academic and theologian C. S. Lewis, Enid Blyton and Beatrix Potter who have sold vast numbers of books. The British Library is one of the world's largest, second only to the Library of Congress, housing over 170 million items.

Before Labour came into office, UK manufacturing grew faster than Germany's. It outpaced most of the G7 economies last year, overtaking France. Exports to the EU were at their highest level since records began. The UK's trade balance with the EU had improved and we had the highest growth of any G7 nation.[1]

The UK was the fourth-biggest exporter in the world in 2022, behind China, the US, and Germany, and up from seventh in 2021, overtaking France, the Netherlands, and Japan. The UK is the second-biggest services exporter in the world, the second-largest exporter of financial services globally and the second-largest exporter of professional business services globally. It is the largest exporter of insurance and pension services globally and the largest exporter of telecommunications services globally.

We rank as a priority investment destination – second only to the US in Foreign Direct Investment (FDI). There is $2 trillion of investments in the UK. This metric refers to the total cumulative value of investments made by foreign companies. We are Europe's most attractive destination for financial services. We have a trillion-dollar tech economy and the largest life sciences, film and TV sectors in Europe. Britain is a global player in finance, investment and commerce.

Britain still has one of the top ten militaries anywhere in the world, ranking fifth or sixth. The British aerospace industry is the second or third largest in the world, including firms such as Rolls-Royce, the world's second-largest manufacturer of aircraft engines, a company that never gets the acclaim it deserves.

The UK space industry is ranked among the top three or four globally in terms of investment and market share. It is well placed to secure 25 per cent of the global satellite In-Orbit Servicing and Manufacturing market – estimated to be worth almost £11 billion by 2031. There are twenty-two active spaceports, including Cape Canaveral, Vandenberg, Kourou and Baikonur, as well as facilities in China, Russia, Japan and other countries. There are several spaceports in the UK, like SaxaVord and Sutherland, that are either actively developing or planning to host orbital launches. Few know about the space industry in the UK.

It's a similar situation with BAE Systems, the world's third-largest defence contractor. It should not be forgotten that 15 per cent of every Lockheed Martin F-35 is built by BAE. Britain also hosts the largest construction site in Europe. This is the Hinkley Point C nuclear power station in Somerset, England, which is building two new EPR-type nuclear reactors. Crossrail in London has added twenty-six miles of tunnel that connect forty-one stations. The Thames Tideway tunnel is now operating, as is London's new Silvertown Tunnel, which is a twin-bore tunnel nearly a mile long under the Thames that will alleviate congestion and improve public transport. In south London, there's a little-known National Grid project to dig a 37-mile circular tunnel underneath the capital. This will lay high-voltage cable well below the streets to ensure London has power for the next century. The tunnel has an average depth of thirty metres but sinks as low as forty-five metres in places – deeper than the Tube. Given the focus on resilience after the power outage in Spain, this is far-sighted.[2]

But we don't tend to talk about these successes. When trying to explain why, Aled Maclean-Jones said in *UnHerd*: 'The ability to build great things isn't something Britain has lost. It's something we've chosen to overlook.'

Maybe we just don't like to blow our own trumpet? The facts are clear. Britain has four of the top ten universities in the world. It's home to the second-highest number of Nobel laureates (142). The NHS, despite all its problems, is ranked fourth among eleven high-income countries. One of the world's leading artificial intelligence companies, Google DeepMind, is based in the UK. DeepMind was founded in 2010 by partners who met at University College London and was bought by Google in 2014 for $500 million. In terms of citations for research papers, the UK again comes second only to the US. It leads in offshore wind and renewable energy and in animal welfare standards. In the UK, all horses, donkeys and ponies must have a horse passport, even if they never leave their field.

Britain has thirty-five UNESCO Heritage Sites, placing it in the top ten globally. Stonehenge is one of the world's most famous prehistoric monuments and is older than the pyramids. The oldest home in the UK is about 6,000 years old and has stone furniture that is still intact today. This is at the Knap of Howar, a neolithic farmstead on the island of Papa Westray in Orkney, Scotland. College Garden at Westminster

Abbey is the oldest recorded garden in the UK, with a history spanning 900 years. It's believed to have been in constant use since the eleventh century, when the monastery was established.

Britain is still the home of motorsport. It is the home of seven of the ten current teams in Formula 1: McLaren, Williams, Aston Martin, Red Bull Racing, Mercedes, Alpine and Haas. It has the oldest currency still in use today. We invented postage stamps, meaning that the UK is the only country not required to name itself on its postage stamps. It is still the largest exporter of financial services. London has one of the most highly rated transport systems in the world. It is consistently voted as the best city in the world.[3] Chicken tikka masala is England's national dish and was almost certainly invented here. Britain still has more curry houses than Delhi and Mumbai combined. And the majority of Britons (67 per cent) still find time to volunteer or have given money for a good cause every year.[4]

STUFF WE'RE GOOD AT

In *Greater: Britain After the Storm*, we mapped how the UK stood on every international index. This video explains some of our achievements, one of which is 'drinking too much', according to the British Council.

https://www.dropbox.com/scl/fi/7mg9oitg2bh000a88mig/Innovation.mp4?rlkey=8d71026ankvpoyov8hy42717t&dl=0

Power can be measured in quantity, by dominion or geography, or in quality, by mindset, influence and attitude. Britain is internationalist, moderate and liberal (in the economic sense) and it respects the law (sometimes above its enforcement). The majority of British people still care more about their sports, pets or hobbies than they do about their politics. If there is any fanaticism, it confines itself to begonias and brassicas and the occasional backbencher.

Don't let anyone convince you otherwise. Britain remains a special place.

One hundred years ago, when it was at its most expansive, the British Empire was home to 412 million people, 23 per cent of the world population at the time, and 24 per cent of the Earth's total land area. As a result, its constitutional, legal, linguistic and cultural legacy is widespread. That does not disappear overnight. The new empires that replaced it are not just economic or geographic, they are philosophical, political and cultural, and they are ones in which Britain operates effectively, through organisations such as the Commonwealth.

English remains the most spoken language in the world, with about 1.5 billion native speakers (about 20 per cent of the world's population).[5] The US, India and Nigeria all have more English speakers than the UK. English is the primary language of politics, law and business. It's also the primary language of the world's free press, who are free to write or draw in cartoons that voice an alternative opinion or vision.

As complex as the British are, we are an understood people. English is one of six official languages of the UN. More often than not, it is the language in which international treaties are drafted. Over 5 billion people follow or play sports we invented, like football, cricket and rugby. The modern world started here.

The British influence is felt in other areas, too. There are at least 85 million members of the Anglican Communion in 165 countries, making it the third-largest Christian denomination in the world.[6] The Inter-Parliamentary Union is made up of 181 national parliaments and although it is based in Geneva, it was co-founded by a British Liberal Member of Parliament, Sir Randal Cremer, who went on to win the Nobel Peace Prize in 1903. Nearly every country in the world has some form of parliament. There are 190 national parliaments in the world, with 268 chambers and some 46,000 legislators. Around eighty countries have legal systems based on English common law.

And yet, for all of its influence and power, there was never an idea of any such nation as England. There was a plan for the UK, but there was never one for England. There is still no fully written constitution. More about this later.

As Harry Mount has pointed out in *How England Made the English*, we have a deep scepticism of grand plans and organisation. Britain has consistently extended and defended the rights of the individual against the system. Important principles have been handed down to us through Magna Carta – for instance, the defence of the rights of widows, the first foray into women's rights. Magna Carta enshrined a fair trial, habeas corpus, the limited rights of monarchs and the protection of property rights. It may have been a political agreement between King John and his barons, but the fact that it expressed the bare bones of an impartial legal and judicial system rejecting arbitrary rule by a hereditary sovereign 800 years ago is truly extraordinary.

Britons have been resistant to grand plans for a long time. That is why London streets look the way they do. We have always valued the rights of the individual, one of the reasons London never adopted Sir Christopher Wren's plan and big vision after the Great Fire in 1666. It went hand-in-hand with a quiet pragmatism: while the great and the good dreamed of streets, boulevards and palazzi that would transform the capital, Londoners, those for whom these surroundings were their lives and their livelihoods, got on and rebuilt. They couldn't wait.

We also have no history of fascism to create the grand Napoleonic boulevards of Paris (built wide and straight so cannons could disperse the mob) or Rome. There was no Haussmann, no Mussolini, no Hitler and no Franco to create a Valle de Cuelgamuros. This clash between the top-down planners and the local interest is still fought out today in local planning reviews.

We don't like those who try to organise us or boss us around too much. It's what you'd expect of a country that has a high tolerance for character and idiosyncrasy. As historian Dan Snow has said:

> There was no champagne smash on the bows of England. No proclamation brought it into existence. It was a generational project, forged in war. A combination of the vision of a few, the luck of battle, a fortuitous run of competent kings (and one particular queen) and demographics.[7]

He's right. But there's something else. There may have been luck and timing, but no other country has enjoyed anywhere near such a long run of fortune. There actually is something special here. Britain matters because it has stood the test of time. It has played such a prominent role in world history for the best part of 1,000 years. Some were surprised by Brexit, but why would a country with 1,000 years of history abandon itself to a superstate barely twenty-four years old? The Maastricht Treaty was signed in 1992, which opened up the single market, and the referendum in 2016 saw us vote to leave it.

King Charles III can trace his ancestry back almost 1,000 years to William the Conqueror. The year 1066 was the last time we were invaded. This has permitted long periods of predictability, continuity and stability. It allowed the law and the court systems to develop. Our legal system is very old and it has evolved and adapted rather than being torn up and rewritten. The oldest laws still in force today are four of the Statutes of Marlborough, which were passed by Parliament in 1267 and aimed at curbing the abuse of power by feudal lords.

Stability, trade and investment thrive under the law because it mitigates commercial risk. More than 750 years ago, the English Parliament was already making provision for negotiation, conciliation and the settlement of disputes through the courts, not by force of arms.

Our geography also matters. It's easier to defend an island. Attacking from the sea makes you vulnerable. You lack cover. Defenders on land can move troops faster than invading ones. You cannot approach Britain with a continental army. King Harold's army was defeated in large part because it fought two battles in quick succession – one in the north at Stamford Bridge and one in the south at Hastings.

Our natural infrastructure has been overlaid with a man-made one. The Romans realised that if you could move troops quickly, you needed less of them for the garrison. America took up this idea in the building of railways and freeways and the Panama Canal as strategic assets. Britain did similar with financing canals, railways, air and seaports.

The furthest you can live from the sea in Britain is seventy miles. It is, on average, a much lesser distance to the nearest navigable river. Our rivers and the sea were our internet before the internet. They were used for trade and communications. This enabled areas to specialise and therefore make our economy more efficient. Our unique geography of long internal rivers and deep harbours made us a trading nation. Our fundamental nature is to be commercial.

Incidentally, we admire commercial go-getters as long as they are held in balance with our aesthetic. You can see this in Piccadilly Circus. One side, owned commercially, is covered in advertising. The other is owned by the Crown Estate, which bans advertising, as does our national motorway network.

We developed the English common law to help with our trade and this became a global system. We set up some of the first stock markets, innovated in finance with pioneering joint-stock companies and the first life and property insurance schemes. We even placed the centre of the business day in London, through the Greenwich meridian at the Royal Observatory. So, we traded with our law, in our language, often in our currency and at times set by our calendar and our clock.

The City was, and continues to be, a set of major markets built on trust and tradition: the motto of the London Stock Exchange remains *Dictum Meum Pactum* (my word is my bond). This encapsulated one of the elements that kept our commercial heart beating. The world comes to London for financial services, insurance, investment management, private equity, banking, pensions, bonds, equities and, above all, regulation, the rule of law and trust.

This was famously satirised in *Yes Minister*:

SIR DESMOND GLAZEBROOK

https://www.youtube.com/watch?v=H2itKRPGFiE

Our skills in trade made us good negotiators, which made us good at diplomacy as well. We are good at coalitions and alliances, especially those to stop dictators. The UK is one of the most restrained and subtle diplomatic forces in the world. Britain has participated in approximately 15,000 global historical treaties, with details of these treaties available on the UK Treaties Online platform. The legacy of international law alone is massive.

Britain has been allied to the Germans and the Dutch against the French, to the French and Turks against the Russians, to the Canadians, French, Russians, Americans, Dutch and Poles against the Japanese, Germans and Italians, to the Americans and Europeans against China and North Korea and against the Iraqis and the Russians. It is a signatory to the longest-surviving treaty in history – the Anglo-Portuguese Treaty of Windsor between King Richard II of England and King John I of Portugal. It was ratified at Windsor on 9 May 1386 and is still in force today.

If you don't count the shortest war in history against the Sultanate of Zanzibar in 1896 (they surrendered after thirty-eight minutes), Britain has only fought one war on its own without allies, a brief, brave and successful campaign in the Falkland Islands in 1982 against Argentina.

In 200 years, Britain has never been on the losing side of a war. Many of our proudest moments have been when we've stood up to dictators. We look back on our history with pride and rightly so. Most other European nations don't have that relationship with their history. They want to forget it and put it behind them. This is hardly surprising, given that it often involves distress, disgrace and dishonour. We want to remember and study our history, understand and absorb it and draw lessons from it. After all, you can't learn lessons from the future. Our traditions are central to this remembering.

You don't have to pretend everything a country ever did was admirable or glorious to be proud of all of its history. Every nation has had moments of shame, infamy, cruelty and discredit. We learn from those too, but we take our inspiration from our ancestors when they were at their best. That's the source of strength and reassurance we can fall back on, the feats of which we can be proud and against which we can measure ourselves too.

Is our success down to luck or judgement? It could be geography. It could be trade. Countries tend not to kill their creditors. It could be a military investment. Britain is one of five powers that have an independent nuclear deterrent under treaty, the others being America, China, Russia and France. Of these, the only one that has consistently and significantly increased military expenditure in the last twenty years is China. Even Russia's recent expenditure doesn't come close to China's.[8]

One reason for our long-term success could be that we maintain close links with all our international partners and recognise the breadth of our relationships. It could also be because of the long-term stability and reliability of our monarchy, legal system and constitutional settlement. As any successful sports team knows, success is not an event; it's a habit or a routine. One thing's for sure – ours is not an accident.

Sometimes success can be in the way a story is told. For instance, no one would portray the British evacuation at Dunkirk in the Second World War as a victory. Even Churchill pointed this out:

> We must be very careful not to assign to this deliverance the attributes of a victory. Wars are not won by evacuations. But there was a victory inside this deliverance, which should be noted. It was gained by the Air Force. Many of our soldiers coming back have not seen the Air Force at work; they saw only the bombers which escaped its protective attack. They underrate its achievements.

We're good at history, partly because we've written so much of it. Britain doesn't just have a unique past. It accounts for so much of human history. The thing that makes us truly remarkable is that the ideas which have developed here have proved incredibly durable. Multiple layers of history are all around us. These are not times past. They contain ideas and experience. What part of our future cannot be better realised without ideas and experience?

Our parishes, villages, towns and cities reflect our individual identity, not some collective vision. Only very occasionally do you see something different with specific developments in, say, Edinburgh, Bath or the seafront at Brighton and Hove.

Freedom is not just about liberty. It's about rights. You cannot have a system of trade without secure personal ownership and inviolable property rights. Even more, it's about man's right to exert control over the vicissitudes of life. You can only truly learn responsibility when it is personal and not collective. The collective responsibility of the state is a poor substitute for personal responsibility.

Our proudest moments in history are when we have stood up to those who would threaten our rights and freedoms, the rule of law or break treaties. The revolt of the Iceni against the might of Rome, Elizabeth I against the Spanish Empire and Winston Churchill against Germany's Third Reich – within these moments of the greatest peril, there was a person in these isles prepared to risk everything. In fact, there was more than one.

There will be those who might point out a new truth – 'their truth', in modern parlance – that there are alternative historical facts that undermine a legend. For instance, as Steve Roud points out in *The English Year*, there is no actual evidence or record that any of our traditions are pagan or pre-Christian. This is because it was the Christians that were the original record-keepers, because they had a vested interest in bringing a new message and spreading the gospel. You need written records, a way to communicate and transmit faith. And, well, the pagans that built Stonehenge didn't leave an instruction manual.

Thank you for purchasing these bluestones from the Preseli Hills. Used in conjunction with approved Sarsens from the Marlborough Downs, they will give you years of trouble-free solstice spotting...

Our traditions are not all historical facts. They are legend. This doesn't make them necessarily true, but then they don't need to be. You don't need to believe that Wookies are real to enjoy *Star Wars*. You don't need to believe in hobbits or elves or orcs to enjoy *Lord of the Rings*. Our island story is just that. It's a story and you can choose to believe it or not.

Our stories and traditions are like clothes that we like to wear because they are comfortable. For instance, central to the Arthurian myth is the notion that he did not die but slumbers on, ready to awake in a moment of national peril. It's almost Micawberesque. No matter how bad, something will turn up. Mustn't grumble. Worse things happen at sea. There are characters who embody this spirit in literature and all of our lives. It's Joe Gargery and Herbert Pocket in *Great Expectations*. It's Jane Bennet in *Pride and Prejudice*. It's Charles in *Four Weddings and A Funeral*. It's Philip Henslowe in *Shakespeare in Love*. You can even see it in our children's characters like Alice, Mary Poppins, Mr Toad, Tigger and Paddington Bear.

So what? Who cares about fictional characters? Well, it matters because if there's one thing that defines Britain and the British, it's these fictional characters. They make us who we are. Yes, you can find the feckless, the lazy and the ignorant in Britain. That's not difficult. If you want a dose of reality, you can find them pretty much anywhere. But what other nation has a 1,000-year continuity of nationhood welded together by national institutions?

History is a narrative, not a series of unconnected facts. It's exactly how our laws work. It's dependent on precedence, behaviour and context. It makes us who we are. Our historical position has been one of independent strength but also skilled diplomacy and close cooperation with our closest friends and allies. America has the power, unquestionably, but Britain still has influence.

In Europe, Britain has historically been the largest contributor to NATO after America. If America's commitment to NATO is in doubt, Britain becomes much more important to European security. It may be that the realities of military imperatives change EU leaders' approach to Britain's economic and political participation in Europe and the way we cooperate with our neighbours and partners.

Britain is of course represented by its military, its musicians, its politicians, its citizens and its sportspeople, but no one comes close to the embodiment of Britain as the monarch. For three generations, there was only one queen, the Queen. She was the most recognised person on the planet and made an incalculable contribution to what being British still means today. Stoic, shy, subtle, funny, consistent, dedicated and determined. You do not have to mine for these qualities in Britain. They are found open cast.

How have we managed to defend ourselves for 1,000 years? Because the British are good at it. They know how to use what's around them to defend themselves. They are ingenious, resourceful and pugnacious. They have been at the forefront of technical development in communications, cryptography, missile, radar, satellite, drone, anti-tank weapons, aircraft, nuclear propulsion and even training techniques.

They have been especially skilled in submarine warfare. Two of the pioneers of submarine design, George Garrett and James Franklin Waddington, were Brits, as was Robert Whitehead, who developed the first effective torpedo. The Royal Navy's Astute Class will consist of seven nuclear-powered submarines: HMS *Astute, Ambush, Artful, Audacious* and *Anson* are all currently in active service and a further two boats, HMS *Achilles* and HMS *Agamemnon*, are under construction.[9]

The sea features prominently in our history. The vast majority of goods entering and leaving the UK are transported by sea under British insurance policies and British law. Even more importantly, so is most of our data. The chair of Parliament's Joint Committee on the National Security Strategy, Matt Western, said in January 2025:

> Our internet relies on undersea cables: around 99 per cent of our data goes through them, connecting the UK to the outside world.
>
> As the geopolitical environment worsens, foreign states are seeking asymmetric ways to hold us at risk. Our internet cable network looks like an increasingly vulnerable soft underbelly.
>
> There is no need for panic – we have a good degree of resilience and awareness of the challenge is growing. But we must be clear-eyed about the risks and consequences: an attack of this nature would hit us hard. Our inquiry will look at what's needed to defend our subsea cables and consider the UK's national resilience should our internet face major disruption.[10]

Global trade has driven the development of democracies around the world. It affords property rights to individuals, which allows them to exert control over their lives. This economic franchise is viewed by the West as linked to a political franchise. This is not the case in China, for instance. Many Chinese believe that the country's recent economic achievements have actually come about because of, not despite, China's authoritarian form of government. One thing is clear. Much of the technological progress has come from a highly innovative and well-funded military that has invested heavily in China's new industries. This exactly mirrors the role of US defence and intelligence spending in the development of Silicon Valley.

Democracies have their ups and downs. Their virtue lies not in the number of good leaders they throw up, but in their ability to get rid of the bad ones. Our democracy remains admired around the world, even if some of its leaders are forgotten. Other nations know rights are embedded here, no matter who leads. Yes, Britain doesn't have the military or economic might that America has. But what happens here still matters because if history is about anything, it is about the relationship of people with the structures that seek to organise and control them – the state, the monarchy, religion and other states and their philosophies.

This is why our traditions matter. Our constitutional settlement is not written in a single document but as a set of laws, conventions, practices and traditions that have evolved over time in much the same way as judicial precedent: trial by jury, Magna Carta, the Act of Supremacy, habeas corpus, the Bill of Rights, the Act of Settlement, the Acts of Union, the secret ballot, the Parliament Acts. Traditions are living and evolving. So much of how we live is 'custom and practice'. This is why Covid was so profoundly disrupting; it stopped our way of life. The way we live is not written down and nor are our customs, but they are broadly accepted, nothing more than people freely participating in a shared relationship with a set of values and an identity they wish to promote and extend.

Over time, traditions become codified and baked into rules and eventually pressed down like sedimentary rock to form our institutions.

Do our traditions make British people aloof or snobbish? The answer to this is that it depends on your point of view. Some dislike the etiquette of golf or professional clubs, which have strictly upheld standards of dress and behaviour. Members, though, can always vote to change.

There are so many aspects of British life that are touched by tradition. It's shot through so much of our daily lives, from language to sense of humour and behaviour. The belief that a cup of tea will make any situation better. The fact that almost everyone has a favourite local pub (whether they use it regularly or not). It's difficult not to feel like you are a part of a club.

Does it create a sense of superiority, of exclusivity? Certainly, to many experiencing it for the first time, it can be confusing and difficult to understand. Why do British people apologise and say please and thank you so much? Why is it hot milk in coffee but cold in tea? Why are *although* and *enough* pronounced differently? Why is a truck called a lorry and a shopping cart a shopping trolley? It's not surprising that some struggle with British idioms. How can you be on 'a sticky wicket' with a 'loose cannon'? Why does it matter if you 'spill the beans' and end up 'in a pickle'? When you wish someone to 'break a leg', when they'll be doing something that isn't necessarily a 'piece of cake'.

You see this everywhere in Britain, and you can see it all the way up from the smallest club to full-blown associations, with varying stages of development in between. We have specific regulations, language, behaviours and even clothing to signify our identity and belonging.

We are a densely populated, tribal country with fierce local loyalties and associations. These can be to clubs, counties, towns and, of course, political parties. Even football clubs. It's vivid and we like it that way. There are people who say our traditions are irrelevant, outdated, even barbaric. 'Who wants Latin mottos, ancient symbols, weird traditions and rivalries?' they ask. The answer is, actually, a lot more people than you think. Being British is a club, a brand, a look, and it is marketed as such by hundreds of modern companies.

Trade thrives on long-term predictability. This is why Britain needs a decade of reinvestment in its defence capabilities. The benefit of this would be massive growth in our research tech and manufacturing bases. This is an investment in hard power that could happen and needs to happen. But we also need to be aware that Britain has many soft-power assets that can also be marketed.

Look at the English Premier League. These are British local traditions and rivalries amplified, extended and marketed across the world. West Ham sings 'I'm Forever Blowing Bubbles'. Liverpool sings the Merseybeat song 'You'll Never Walk Alone'. Everton has someone throwing toffees into the crowd. Chelsea crowds have form when it comes to throwing vegetables, specifically celery. In 2002, five supporters were arrested for throwing the vegetable during a game against Aston Villa. In 2007, the club issued a statement warning fans they faced a lengthy ban from Stamford Bridge for taking celery into the stadium. Forget the Millwall Brick or 'my mate Stanley'. Chelsea fans come armed with *Apiaceae*.[11]

The Premier League is a major export success story, especially in the US. For many years, while the rest of the world had always loved football, America focused on baseball, basketball and American football. Over the last two decades, though, America's love for soccer has grown consistently and is now at an all-time high. British clubs have been bought by American private equity firms, even film stars. Most fans in the US are younger, 60 per cent of them aged between eighteen and twenty-four, and they love the authenticity, competitiveness, passion and cultural traditions.

The annual results show the global Premier League season-on-season audience has grown by 7 per cent, with the biggest growth of international markets in China (+373 per cent) and the US (+42 per cent), including what was at the time a record live audience in America of 2.3 million for Liverpool's game against Arsenal in December 2023.[12][13]

The Premier League's own figures bear this out. It is booming. Around 8 million watch Premier League football in the UK regularly. There are new stadiums being built all over the country. Stadiums have been 98.7 per cent full at Premier League matches in 2023/24, which equals the record figures set last season. Of the twenty clubs, eighteen have stadium utilisation of over 97 per cent.[14]

It shows that people come together to support something whole-heartedly. This was captured by the legendary Liverpool manager Bill Shankly, a tough, determined Scotsman from a hard upbringing in the Ayrshire coalfields: 'Some people believe football is a matter of life and death. I am very disappointed with that attitude. I can assure you it is much, much more important than that.'

Our history has many illustrations of these apparent contradictions and tensions: serious and frivolous, formal and casual, class and crass, structure and chaos, gentlemen amateurs who are brilliant high achievers. Rugby football is a game where players run forwards while throwing the ball backwards.

The Victorians advanced the boundaries of science, engineering, medicine and knowledge but were unsettled by the industrialisation and ugliness of their modern world. They were forever producing practical progress while reminiscing about the romantic. This explains their obsession with the perpendicular Gothic revival style. The Palace of Westminster (part of a UNESCO World Heritage Site since 1987) embodies this thinking. The exterior appears ancient. The interior (for the time) was full of innovation. Charles Barry was also careful to join the old to the new so that the surviving medieval buildings – Westminster Hall, the cloisters and chapter house of St Stephen's Chapel and the St Mary Undercroft Chapel – formed an integral part of the whole. You can see this contradiction in the Natural History Museum, the Albert Hall, the V&A and even Waterhouse's Manchester Town Hall.

Old and new. Ancient and modern. Myth and reality. Statute and precedent. This country is a pushmi-pullyu.[15] Towards the future, it is sceptical but hopeful. Towards the past, romantic, but clear-eyed. We have produced some of the best people in the history of humanity and still not yet one of its worst.

The British mentality is a strange paradox to people from the outside. They ask quite serious questions about how we can be so steeped in history and yet be so surprisingly modern. We're known in this country for being stubborn, dogmatic and loving our traditions, yet all the while at the forefront of fashion and culture. These characteristics live side by side without conflict here.

One of the most tolerant and liberal countries in Europe has, historically, also maintained one of the largest military budgets. This is no accident. Liberal, tolerant democracy goes hand-in-hand with military strength.* If we wish to preserve our public square, we need to be able to defend it both at home and abroad.

Someone who had thought a bit about the balance between liberalism and authoritarianism was George Orwell: 'People sleep soundly in their beds because rough men stand ready to do violence on their behalf.'[16]

Easy-going, disorganised, weak-minded people are not good at defence. Stubborn, energetic, inventive and proud people are. Especially those who know their history and the obligations that it places on them. We're at our best when it comes to innovation and ideas. We're good at it. There are some in this country who have never wanted to do anything else with their lives. They are drawn to it. They love to blow things up. I know from personal experience as Honorary Captain of the Royal Navy's 2nd Mine Countermeasures Squadron.

This is why we need a renewed relationship with the defence industries. Ask yourself, what shape would our defence industry be in had it been run solely by government? Don't answer that. Spare my blushes.

There are so many examples of technologies and defensive weapons that have been pioneered by brilliant individuals. Do you know how many have been created by government? That's right. None.

The relationship between the defence industry and government is

---

* Britain has only just recently been overtaken by Germany, despite it historically having the bigger economy by far.

a long one. There have been millions of words written about it and very dull they are. Defence contractors often wait for a brief before responding to it. Governments often wait to see what others are doing before drafting new requirements. The most common questions asked are who is waiting for whom? And where is the money?

Those are the wrong questions. We need to look a little wider for meaning and understanding and it comes down to who we are. We can moan about the changing nature of politics, or we can adapt and change and see opportunity.

No European government is going to commit to a supply chain if it threatens to become unreliable. They will be forced back upon their own resources to European defence contractors such as BAE, Dassault, Leonardo or Rheinmetall. This will be welcomed by national politicians because it will benefit European economies and their local standing but at the cost of something much greater.

The cohesive nature of NATO forces rests on the fact they all use a large amount of American equipment. This promotes interoperability and flexibility. This includes aircraft, armoured vehicles, air defences, small arms and ammunition. US contractors like Lockheed and Raytheon make excellent equipment, but if they are shut out from procurement, then the West loses its agility and massive economic scale.

We share innovations. We share intelligence. We train together. We exercise together. Training builds trust. This has been built up across lifetimes and careers. These are deep multigenerational bonds. We have similar cultures and we actually enjoy each other's company. NATO is an enduring defensive alliance because, although it's frequently deployed, Article 5 of the North Atlantic Treaty, which enshrines collective defence and security, has only ever been triggered once. On behalf of the US, in response to the 9/11 attacks, if you're wondering.

You cannot achieve greater rationalisation, cohesion and efficiency in defence procurement by restricting your choice of supplier. Yes, we can build our own equipment, but it's nothing without the national characteristics to back it up. The SA80 is a brilliant weapon, but it's nothing without a well-trained, disciplined British infantry soldier behind it, determined to close with and destroy the enemy. The Dreadnought-class submarine is a powerful weapon, but it's nothing without the willpower of its fighting crew and the logistics, facilities, families and communities behind them.

And this brings us to some big questions. Why do some nations rise and why do they collapse? Politics is not the only cause. Culture always precedes politics. President Trump may be a cause of rapid change, but he is also a symptom and an agent of it. Let me explain.

I mentioned easy-going, nice people. Don't get me wrong. You wouldn't see this at the weekend in any county town in Britain. British people are pretty reasonable unless they've had a beer or nine. Underneath it all, though, you might find something stronger. So strong, in fact, that it's one of the most powerful naturally occurring phenomena. Forget fossil fuels, dynamite or even atomic power. The most powerful thing is individual willpower. Unharnessed, this is merely wilful. Engineered to an objective, there is nothing stronger. It spans gorges, crosses oceans, heals the sick and makes space flight possible. It works with the biggest ideas and the smallest details. It's all around us, all of the time, and its enemy is government. Until government realises the only real power it has resides in understanding and convening the national mood, it will remain a mere bureaucracy destined for disappointment. This is why we lack a sovereign steel industry, inexpensive energy and the proper respect for our armed forces at the core of who we are.

Your willpower might have brought you here, via school, via university in some cases, via the military, via the relationships you formed. Let's ask some questions about your willpower. Are you an eight out of ten-willpower person? How would you rate, say, Chris Hoy, Mo Farah or Tanni Grey-Thompson? Ten? Twenty?

Despite all the batshit things I've seen in the Conservative Party, its abiding principle is that it places the freedom and potential of individuals above that of government. Of course, I believe in caring for others. If you believe in human potential and freedom, that's a pre-requisite. I just happen to believe that humans caring for humans is infinitely better than governments trying to do it. Governments make terrible substitutes for families and parents.

There are many people in Britain brimming with willpower. If you're one of them, my advice is to tell people what that will is. Dream it, discuss it, design it. Everything around you. Every piece of equipment. Everything you are wearing and carrying. It all had to be brought into existence by someone's will. When you decide to let your will dominate, the resources of the world come to your side.

You will find two types of people in your life – those who make you more like who you are and those who will make you less of the person you are. The thing is, being somebody else is not an option. All you can choose is to be more like who you are or less like who you are. British people are very similar. We'll never be more French than the French, nor should we attempt to be so. If we know who we are, then we will have a better understanding of how we fit into the future.

How do I know this? Because I've been at the top and the bottom. I've been close to senior politicians and business and military leaders. I've served on the board of the World Bank. I didn't meet anyone at the top of these institutions who was there by accident. None arrived without the willpower of knowing who they were. There were none that just happened to get there by accident, a stroke of luck, or happened to know a 'mate'.

Our history is filled with those who knew they'd never sit in the shade of trees they had planted. Their will, their vision, extended hundreds of years, thousands of miles, to millions of people as yet unborn and ultimately to the defence of democracy – the right of free individuals to determine their leaders and to reach their potential.

It is our willpower, not our skills alone, that will dictate what we achieve. It is our collective willpower that will dictate our industrial capability. Ultimately, it is our national willpower that will decide whether our democracy will survive.

For 1,000 years, we've defended this island. Every village, every town, every city has a memorial bearing a list of those with the ultimate willpower. We should always remember. We should never let them down. Those generations still speak to us, if we care to listen. When they went off to war, this is what they said: 'You want to invade us? Well, not on my watch you don't.' We should be inspired by their willpower and we should say the same.

This does not answer sharp-edged questions about immigration, the NHS or taxation. My message, though, is that these challenges are made more daunting by a loss of faith and a betrayal of trust. Cynicism is the parent of apathy. Maybe all the politicians are liars and grifters? If you believe that, then you're unlikely to solve any problems. It's easier to stay popular in politics if you don't trust anyone to solve problems. Better still, if you never hold office or have responsibility for change.

Our ancient rights are passed down with responsibilities: the duty to protect and preserve them and then hand them on. Too many seem to have forgotten this. They want to do what they want, when they want, and to hell with everyone else. This is not freedom. It is tyranny.

Civilisation must be defended. Not just with fine words, but actions. Conservatism, for instance, needs to become more muscular. You can see this instinct at work in new parties like Reform. I applaud the instinct, but novelty is not enough. Of course, they are popular because they repeat what obviously must be done. They work on the mistaken assumption that nobody else has spotted the problem. Doing something pragmatic about it is different, though. It requires compromise and cooperation. You can't do that from the extremes. You can't win trust from there. And trust is everything. It's where we came into this book. Hope is something permanent opposition parties deal in. Trust, though, is the currency of government.

Civilisation requires restraint – ideally imposed reflexively or by those close to us. In the last resort, it needs to be imposed by the state on the state if necessary. It needs to recognise that without a strong defence, there is no state, nothing to provide any welfare or healthcare. If our state is threatened, then everything within it is threatened too. The state needs to impose the discipline on itself.

The Royal Family provides that model. Members of the Royal Family are not free to do whatever they want. They have duties to perform. That's why I've always been a monarchist. You can't have my background and not be committed to the monarchy. This is why my involvement in the coronation, with all its significance, wasn't just an official duty; it was an immense personal honour.

This honour was not just for the historical context, but because the event was also personal for two people whose love had seen them through everything. There were no ashes being worshipped there. It was the rekindling of the royal, constitutional and national flame.

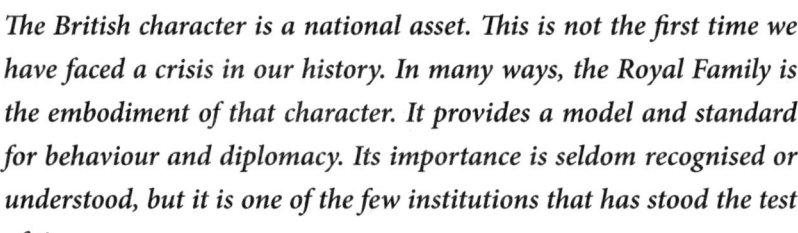

The British character is a national asset. This is not the first time we have faced a crisis in our history. In many ways, the Royal Family is the embodiment of that character. It provides a model and standard for behaviour and diplomacy. Its importance is seldom recognised or understood, but it is one of the few institutions that has stood the test of time.

CHAPTER FIVE

GOD SAVE THE KING!

———————————— ⟶⟡⟵ ————————————

This chapter asks how the monarchy and its traditions have contribut-
ed to our culture. How did the death of Queen Elizabeth II affect the
country? What were her lasting legacies? What are the practical ways
that our traditions help us to govern? How do they strike a balance
between change and stability? How do these work in practice? What
events enable the values of one generation to be passed to another?

———————————— ⟶⟡⟵ ————————————

I brought them here to see the glories of Empire and
all they think about is going on the dodgems...
Frank Gibbons in Noël Coward's *This Happy Breed*

At the time of Her Majesty Queen Elizabeth II's death, I had recently been appointed the Leader of the House of Commons and
Lord President of the Council. The latter role is the senior position of
the Privy Council, the formal body of advisers to the monarch. Privy
Councillors are typically senior politicians. They are appointed for life
on the advice of the Prime Minister.

It was my job to chair the Privy Council. Before each session, I
would have a private audience with His Majesty. The meetings happened every couple of weeks. However, during the political turmoil of

the transition from Johnson to Truss to Sunak, the council met much more frequently to swear in new ministers.

Secretaries of State needed to be sworn in and some needed to receive the seals of their office. This is normally an infrequent event, but during the turmoil of three Prime Ministers in one year, it had become rather more frequent. In less than four months we had as many Chancellors of the Exchequer. We had an Education Secretary who lasted in post a full two days. A moment of high farce came when Suella Braverman was fired from the post of Home Secretary by one Prime Minister, only to be rehired by a new Prime Minister in less than a week. If this chaos was lost on the King – and I suspect it was not – he could not have missed my embarrassment about it. At the end of each now almost daily Privy Council meeting, we would part company by saying: 'See you tomorrow.'

It was a busy time. Her Majesty passed away on Thursday 8 September 2022. On Monday that week, I was a trade minister. On Tuesday, I was promoted to Leader of the House and President of the Council. On Wednesday, we tried to hold a Privy Council to enable us to swear in the new Truss administration. I was so moved by that moment. I thought about my grandmother in the week before she passed away. How frail she was and how we wished to remove every pressure, so that her sole concern was her own comfort and peace. And here we were asking a 96-year-old woman, just twenty-four hours before her death, to hold a business meeting. That was the ultimate testament to her devotion to duty and her care for us. It was faithful to the oath she had taken seventy-five years earlier, which was fulfilled to her last day.

On Thursday, the sad news broke. Two days into the job, I was the late Queen's last Lord President and the King's first. On Friday, I discovered my duty was to chair the Accession Council in St James's Palace. This is only convened in the event of the monarch's passing and as soon as is practicable before Parliament meets after the death of the monarch. It is formed of certain Privy Councillors, Great Officers of

State, the Lord Mayor and High Sheriffs of the City of London, Realm High Commissioners and some senior civil servants.

There are two parts to the Privy Council business at the Accession Council. There's a part that formally announces the death of the monarch and proclaims the succession. It sets out how a proclamation will be delivered and makes the arrangements for it. The new sovereign is not present for this part, although members of the Royal Family are and bear witness.

The second part takes place with the new monarch, who undertakes a solemn declaration of their duty, which includes the preservation of the Church of Scotland. At a later date, they also take an oath to ensure the established Protestant succession, this being made before Parliament.

After the service, the first public proclamation of the new sovereign is read by the Garter King of Arms at St James's Palace in the presence of the Earl Marshal. Three cheers are then given to the King. After I'd overseen the Accession Council, I was listening to those proclamations and cheers for King Charles.

I had been apprehensive, not of the service but that the public might not accept the new King. It couldn't be taken for granted. There was a brief pause after the last cheer had been given from the assembled guard and then I heard it. A roar of approval from the many thousands of people that were lining the streets around St James's Palace, down The Mall and Pall Mall. Those scenes would be echoed in every city and town across the land. First in Edinburgh, with the proclamation read by the Lord Lyon King of Arms, and then in Belfast and Cardiff and the City of London. And then in every place. It wasn't just Privy Councillors who proclaimed who was King. It was all of us – local and national combined.

I have found in my career, that the Royal Family is more popular than ever. This is reflected in our traditions, too. The royals hold a special place in our hearts. In our local customs and traditions, while elected officials are frequently mocked, abused or pilloried, Kings and Queens are much more often revered. There are Snow Queens, Goose Queens, May Queens and Pearly Kings and Queens, a type of Cockney royalty. Pearly Kings and Queens evolved from the costermongers, market traders who sold fruit, vegetables, fish and other produce from a cart or stall on the street. They were said to have sewn mother-of-pearl buttons onto their clothes to set themselves apart. It is always an honour to be chosen. You represent your community. Monarchs in all walks of life are different to mere officials.

The monarchy is only ever unpopular when there is a perception that it has not done its duty. No one could accuse HM Queen Elizabeth II of that. Perhaps this explains the most demonstrable sense of loss when she died. It was palpable. She had seen so much change and continued to do her duty until the very end. It was a moment of peril for the nation, set against the backdrop of the turmoil caused by Covid. Tradition and established procedures provided the structure needed to navigate the shock of such a significant event. If it felt like a military operation, that's because in many ways, it was – actually, a sequence of them all interlocked.

Operation London Bridge was the code name for the ten days leading up to the Queen's funeral. This plan included succession rules and funeral arrangements. In addition, there was Operation Unicorn, the code name for the Queen's death in Scotland. This included ceremonial events in Edinburgh and the return of the coffin to London. Both of these plans formed part of Operation Lion, the overarching plan for any royal death. Operation Marquee was the plan for the Queen's four days of lying in state at Westminster Hall. This was augmented by Operation Feather, the plan for logistics outside Westminster Hall, including arrangements for the public. At the same time, Operation Golden Orb, the plan for the coronation of Charles, was underway. This was followed by Operation Spring Tide, the plan for Charles's first trip as King to Scotland, Wales and Northern Ireland. During this, I became aware of the late Queen's attention to detail in these plans and to other matters not covered by them. One of these aspects was the care she had taken over what would happen to her beloved animals. I made inquiries regarding their future due to the enormous number of letters I received from children asking what would happen to her corgis. They stayed as pets to other members of the family.

How can people function normally in such times of grief? The answer is simple. They focus on their duty. It's a very British trait. Of course, people feel the loss, but their duty comes first. This is embodied by poets such as John Pudney:

> Fetch out no shroud
> For Johnny-in-the-cloud;
> And keep your tears
> For him in after years.
>
> Better by far
> For Johnny-the-bright-star,
> To keep your head,
> And see his children fed.[1]

Many of these plans had been passed down from previous generations. The catafalque that so many walked past was historically consistent. It was the same tableau as when George V died in 1936. When we experience these moments of national trauma, all we have as a nation to guide us are our traditions. These were laid down by people that went through this previously and passed down their experience. The fascination with these traditions and the institution itself is not new.

Perhaps surprisingly, the monarchy is capable of swift reform and innovation. Providing continuity, above politics and economic turmoil, is a huge advantage for the nation. It is connected to every part of the UK and is one of the strongest links binding the Union. HM the King is there for all nations and all faiths.

This is the event that inspired the writing of this book. All we had during this period of shock and turmoil were our traditions. They were ready and waiting for this moment. That's the reason for all this pomp and circumstance. Our traditions bind the present and the past to the future. Never have they been more important to us. Our traditions give us more than an identity. We know where we are, who we are and what we're supposed to be doing and why. This allows us to move quickly and adapt without thinking too much about the enormity of it all. They give us the strength to carry on. The absence of tradition leaves people alone and without a plan at a critical time.

It's a notable feature that in any crisis, there will always be those who will carry on regardless. The courage to carry on is not a conscious decision. It is a discipline. It is a habit. It's why these traditions, these habits, make us what we are.

Why is this sort of dedication so important? Because representation is more than just doing your duty. It's not enough. Only unconditional love can release potential.

Love is a bit like water. It can appear in different forms. It can be steamy and powerful. It can be pressurised and used to drive action. It can be a fluid in a radiator that flows around. Or it can also be a solid like ice. In this form, it's cold and uncompromising. This is the form of unconditional love called duty. It powers our soldiers, sailors and airmen. People who are prepared to put others before them even if it costs the ultimate sacrifice.

This is nothing new. As Sir Water Scott said in 1810:

> In peace, Love tunes the shepherd's reed;
> In war, he mounts the warrior's steed;
> In halls, in gay attire is seen;

In hamlets, dances on the green.
Love rules the court, the camp, the grove,
And men below and saints above;
For love is heaven and heaven is love.[2]

Churchill said that courage was the parent of all virtues. It takes a great deal of courage to be a King. The pressures are unique. It is not courage but love which is the cardinal force, because it is based on duty and respect. The best policy is always to treat people with respect, even if it doesn't guarantee you get the best out of them.

What is respect? Put simply, it's a feeling of admiration for someone or something based on their abilities, qualities or achievements. This is how I feel about the Royal Family. They have done so much. They have stood for so much. And they still mean so much to so many. There are so many examples of love, duty and sacrifice. The King's grandfather, George VI, sacrificed greatly when his brother Edward VIII abdicated. He had never planned to be King, but he did his duty. After the Second World War started, the Queen (later Queen Elizabeth, the Queen Mother) was asked why she and the two young princesses didn't seek greater safety, perhaps in Canada. Her answer was simple: 'The children won't go without me. I won't leave the King. And the King will never leave.'

It cost him his health. It may have hastened his death. His daughter therefore had very little time for a normal life. She dedicated her entire life to her duty.

There are many of us in public life who have experienced the kind of commitment it takes in positions of authority and leadership. However, none of us have had to do this for our whole lives. I was moved to hear that part of the reason why the late Queen Elizabeth II loved Balmoral so much was that she got to sleep in the same bed for a whole six weeks. Among all the remarkable things she did and the extraordinary experiences she had, she cherished the night she and her sister slipped out of the palace to celebrate VE Day on the streets of London. It was her one 'normal' night out and it must have been an extraordinary one. Nothing can be private or personal. Not even grief at the loss of a parent. That must be shared with the nation. Not even your own death is private or personal.

In more recent times, the Royal Family have placed duty before their immediate personal happiness. Duty is not incompatible with personal happiness, but for the Royal Family, the latter must never trump the former. They have carried on through ill health. They have faced personal fears. They have risked a great deal.

The relationship between a monarch and a head of state is unique. The tenure of a monarch is incomparable with other leaders. It cannot be understood by those with a comparatively short term of office. Monarchs provide continuity and stability. The price is to shoulder responsibility and maintain continuity for longer than any elected official.

This is not about viewing our country through rose-tinted glasses. Belief in your country is not a romantic position. It is a pragmatic one. Suppose you despise everything we stand for? How does that help you or anyone else around you? It inevitably raises the question: what would you do to bring about change? Is there another country you hold in higher regard? Or one with a similar history? True authority to speak must be paired with the responsibility to act.

Britain has long been committed to the values of decency, discretion, fairness, justice and humanity, with a core rooted in generosity of spirit and tolerance – qualities that are often tested in challenging times. How we respond in moments of adversity truly matters, as we must live with the consequences when things eventually improve.

These values have often been ridiculed as mere evidence of naivety and good intentions. Even in wartime, they were satirised in Michael Powell and Emeric Pressburger's *The Life and Death of Colonel Blimp*. Colonel Clive Candy is ambushed in a war game because he plays by the rules, but his captors think differently. They've witnessed the Nazis and no longer believe in the rules. Only might is right. And yet, that is precisely when we should play by the rules. It was C. S. Lewis who said: 'Integrity is doing the right thing, even when no one is watching.'

In public life, someone is always watching. A week in politics is said to be a long time, and as a consequence, those in the Westminster bubble have short memories. But the electorate remembers. Those who want to lead and represent their country will have to make many compromises. But what they must not do is compromise on how they want to lead. It's the same with responsibility.

American philosopher and educator Richard Rorty said: 'National pride is to countries what self-respect is to individuals, a necessary condition for self-improvement.'

Few British people admit to loving their country. They just don't always tell everyone about it. Kipling recognised this:

> Deeper than speech our love, stronger than life our tether,
> But we do not fall on the neck nor kiss when we come together.[3]

This is yet another reason to admire British history and culture. Our style is subtle and understated.

The case of Brigadier Tom Brodie of the Gloucestershire Regiment is an example. During the Battle of the Imjin River at the height of the Korean War in 1951, his men were outnumbered eight to one, surrounded on every side by waves of Chinese communist infantry attackers. But when the British brigadier reported the position to his American superior in the United Nations joint command, he did so with classic British understatement. 'Things are a bit sticky, sir,' he told Robert Soule, the American general, intending to convey that they were in difficulty. The general interpreted it to mean they were finding it rough but were OK. In reality, they held off 30,000 Chinese troops, killing 10,000 of them with Bren gunfire alone, with two soldiers being awarded Victoria Crosses for bravery.

Consider how profoundly yet subtly the theme of love has been explored in English literature by the likes of Blake, Burns, Clare, Coleridge, Donne, Heaney, Keats, Kipling, C. S. Lewis, Marvell, Pudney, Scott, Shakespeare, Shelley, Thomas and Wordsworth.

It's not very British to talk about love, but in the words of Wet Wet Wet, it really is all around. It's there in every military formation, in every workplace, in every school, in every hospital, in every community, in every pub, in every greasy spoon and in every football crowd. It's present anywhere you find hard work. As Kahlil Gibran said: 'Work is love made visible.'[4]

This is something that becomes immediately clear when you travel across the country. People deeply cherish their communities and their homes, but it takes a lot of work to maintain them.

Our traditions are often a cascade from national events. They may start with the service at the Cenotaph or a procession to Westminster Abbey or a proclamation at St James's Palace. But they end in our town squares, the pulpit of every church and beacons being lit on the nearest hill. Traditions aren't something we simply watch on television or admire from afar. They are events we participate in and shape.

All that is understood retrospectively is love. No one ever understands historical hatred for one simple reason. Hate is unsustainable. Only love lasts for ever. Its work is all around us, in our buildings, in our care and respect for history and our work. It is felt both personally and collectively and it is an indelible marker of who we are currently and what we can become.

In politics, though, we're in a new age of hate. It's something that narrows its appeal. Movements built on hate can never succeed. You can be against whatever you want. At some point, though, you will need to say what you are for. And if you don't love your country and its character, you won't get far in trying to influence it.

Some elements of the left hate. Some elements of the right do too. It's difficult to take seriously because it is an all-too-common, habitual hate, casually arrived at. It stains them. They 'hate' lots of things. They have run out of superlatives to express just how angry they are. It is the mark of the childish, the petulant, the ill-disciplined and the downright lazy. It should have no role in public life. Make a contribution, stand for office. Do something positive. Remember you're a representative of all the people, not just those that voted for you.

Getting something done requires everyone and divisive politicians don't help that. When we work together, we can do anything. But some people don't want that. They'd rather luxuriate in the impossibility of accord – what Freud called the narcissism of small differences. The price of such political purity is irrelevance.

Our traditions and way of life are contradictory and sometimes even cut across the rules, especially health and safety ones, but they are not irreconcilable. For instance, in the town of Lewes in Sussex, they burn hate figures on Bonfire Night to celebrate our love of democracy and freedom.

We love the monarchy, but we slam a door in the face of the sovereign's representative when Parliament opens. The Speaker of the House must be willing to serve but must be dragged reluctantly by his colleagues to the chair. We are strongly attached to the church most of us don't go to on Sunday.

The contradictions will always be highlighted by know-it-all, over-educated underachievers. If only their university had given them a telescope as well as a microscope. No one can see the big picture when they're zoomed in so closely. They revile what can't be measured – qualities like faith and hope.

The problem is that most things work because people believe they will. Capitalism is like that. People do not invest because they know they will get a better return. They believe they will. Neither do people get educated if they feel it will make them poorer.

Ignore the revisionists. All around the world, Britain and British history is admired. If there's one thing that identifies the revisionists, it's their hatred. They hate their country. They hate its history. Worse, they hate the one thing that British people are so often most persuaded by – humour. That, in itself, shows how little they understand Britain.

Many things work without knowing why. You can take them apart logically, but it can be harder to fit them together again. It requires more than an engineer's mindset. Besides, the best engineering walks hand in hand with art.

Inside Westminster, it's easy to forget about the outside world. Parliament may be the biggest home advantage anyone will ever have. But most of the life, love and leadership goes on outside in the real world.

The culture of Westminster is self-centred and centripetal. It's different outside. Our way of life and traditions are powered by exactly the opposite forces. These push responsibilities outwards, down to each of us. This respect for our individual freedoms and rights is what permits personal responsibility. This is the essence of our society and community. If you want people to take responsibility, then freedom and democracy is what it takes.

Strangely, days of pageantry begin in an ordinary way. In the still hours before day begins, Parliament Square is filled not by people, but by the dawn chirrups of sparrows. One of the strangest aspects of central London is how quiet some parts are for those up at dawn. At this time, when you walk through the surrounding streets you can hear the hiss of Westminster's 270 gas lamps. The palace and surrounding streets are otherwise silent because the roads have been blocked off. Only the newly erected security barriers stand like a modern portcullis, foretelling the pageantry and procession that will take place later.

For my last State Opening of Parliament, I walked across New Palace Yard completely alone save for an urban fox quietly padding a few feet ahead of me. Its message was clear. You might work here, but this is my home.

Deep beneath the cobbles, in the cellars and passages of Parliament is a subterranean hive of activity. There walks the Yeomen of the Guard, searching for any sign of murder or treason. This is Britain's oldest military unit, established in 1485. These men, sworn to protect the sovereign, have performed this ritual every night before the State Opening of Parliament for centuries. This commemorates the failed Gunpowder Plot of 1605, when English Catholics sought to take out the Protestant King James I and VI and his Parliament.

Tradition isn't just the theatrical or symbolic repetition of the events of the past. Its outward form can seem not just ritualistic but absurd and anachronistic. The ceremonial searching is supervised by the Lord Great Chamberlain, a Great Officer of State whose role dates from at least 1130. It is history piled on history.

But more than that, tradition and ceremony is our way of processing, understanding and commemorating the past. It does not emerge organically or spontaneously but through our own choice and agency. We commemorate that which is important to us at every level.

Recounting this to visitors to Westminster Hall, where the plotters were hung, drawn and quartered, was always slightly embarrassing for me. A previous Mordaunt, Henry the 4th Baron, was imprisoned in the Tower of London for his association with the plotters and was suspiciously absent from Parliament on 5 November. It is also rumoured that some of the conspirators sought shelter in the Mordaunt family church as they fled London. As a child, I asked my father if our family had been in any way responsible. He replied that if a Mordaunt had been involved, they would have 'forgotten the bloody matches'.

Reassuring stuff. No wonder I had to focus.

At the State Opening in 2023, unlike my ancestor, I made sure I was highly visible as the King's Lord President. It was my duty to greet the King and Queen and process with them through the House of Lords.

Prior to their arrival, a member of the government benches, usually the Vice-Chamberlain of the Household, who is both a whip and officially a member of the Royal Household, is taken hostage by the palace to ensure the safe return of the monarch. This insurance policy stems from the contentious relationship that Charles I had with Parliament. This sounds like an ordeal for those to be kidnapped, but in recent times they have made the best of it. They are taken to Buckingham Palace and given a drink or two. One year, the kidnappees threw themselves into the role with such enthusiasm that they exhausted the palace drinks cabinet.

The State Opening is unusual in many ways. It is one of the few times when the three separate and distinct branches of parliamentary power come together – the Commons, the Lords and the King. The building itself is a metaphor for that triumvirate – there is a clear line of sight between the Speaker's chair in the Commons and the sovereign's throne in the Lords. The Commons is elected, the people are paramount, but all the power and authority that the members exercise stems from their monarch. The State Opening ceremony is a regular reminder of the balance between these three elements of Parliament.

The State Opening marks the start of the parliamentary year or session – which can be longer than a calendar year. The King processes to Parliament escorted by the Household Cavalry. He is housed and robed in the sovereign's apartments and then, wearing the Imperial State Crown, walks through the Royal Gallery to his throne in the Lords. The House of Commons is then summoned to hear his speech. The Gracious Speech sets out the government's agenda for the coming session, outlining proposed policies and legislation. It is written for the King by the government of the day.

The task of getting the House of Commons up to the Lords falls to the House of Lords official known as the Gentleman (or Lady) Usher of the Black Rod. Tradition dictates that the Commons slams its door in Black Rod's face as they approach, a gesture meant to remind their lordships that they have no business in the elected House, that it is not at the King's beck and call. This practice dates back to the Civil War.

After three knocks, Black Rod is permitted to enter and deliver the request to attend the King in the Lords. In more recent times, the humiliation did not end there. Dennis Skinner, the Member for Bolsover, took it upon himself to add a further layer of Commons trash talk to the proceedings. Eventually, the Prime Minister and Leader of the Opposition lead the Commons out of their Chamber, through Central Lobby, to the entrance of the House of Lords. Having been commanded to attend, Members of the Commons are not permitted into the Lords' Chamber past what is known as the 'bar', which faces the throne. The result of this is that only about twenty MPs can actually get into the Upper Chamber to listen to and watch the speech. The rest are left to loiter in the trail of the procession until the King has finished.

As Lord President, attending the King, I was permitted into the House of Lords Chamber to experience this process from the Lords' end. Again, the silence is curious. There are several minutes of it while Black Rod fetches the Commons. There is a palpable tension as each of their lordships holds their composure, wary of who might break discipline by engaging in idle chatter – or, worse, doze off and start snoring.

When the King departs, a new parliamentary session starts. The first business in the Commons is to respond to the speech by giving the Loyal Address. There is a proposer, a seconder, then the principal people in the Commons – the Prime Minister, the Leader of the Opposition and other party leaders. The speech is then debated over a number of days and voted on in the Commons and occasionally the Lords.

Why do we still do it all? The State Opening is when men search for gunpowder they know isn't there, when a King delivers a speech that isn't his own, whose audience is the MPs who wrote it. Most of their colleagues, having been summoned, are barred. And yet, it is a piece of theatre with a serious purpose. We step back to honour the process. This is because it is the process that is important. The representatives change, but it doesn't. It tells us that democracy is bigger than any one individual. It's a crucial lesson because when the individual outweighs the democracy, it leads to dictatorship. We serve as representatives in a collective process – none of this belongs to any one of us.

Just outside the Commons Chamber is one of the few places you can see a tradition being actively discouraged in the Houses of Parliament. Historically, those about to make speeches had a tradition of rubbing the feet of the statues of former Prime Ministers David Lloyd George, Clement Attlee and Winston Churchill. But it seems these are now seriously under threat from wear and tear due to the unwanted handling. New MPs are no longer told about the tradition of touching their toes. The four statues in the Members' Lobby of the Commons, outside the Commons Chamber, are among the most high-profile and valuable works of art in Parliament. However, there are now cracks and small holes on the surface of the Churchill statue and substantial loss of surface texture on other statues. Regular rewaxing and recolouring were undertaken to protect their feet and casts had been taken in case they needed to be completely replaced in future. The statue of Baroness Thatcher was unveiled by the former Prime Minister herself in 2007.[5]

Another tradition gone by the wayside is the collapsible top hat MPs used to frisbee to each other to make a 'point of order' during a division – or as my team used to say, 'do' a Point Of Order. You can still do a 'POO' in the Chamber during a division, but you don't need to wear the top hat. Similarly, the doorkeeper's chair still has snuff boxes loaded with the filthy stuff in case anyone calls for snuff in a debate, because smoking in the Chamber was banned in 1694.

In Parliament, the authority of the monarch is ever-present. In both houses, it resides in the Speakers. In this respect, all parliamentarians, elected or otherwise, are using the authority of the King. The power of a constitutional monarch is in this subtle delegated power and privilege. Perhaps this is the symbol of a modern constitutional democracy, in that all elected officials operate with the authority of the royal mandate. Though this is not to say that the power of the monarch only passes through the hands of the executive. Its power is vested in many other representatives.

The Royal Family has other ways to connect to the public. The spectacle of royal procedure, tradition and pageant remains popular. It has even become a major tourist draw. Although not directly involving a royal presence, the Changing of the Guard draws crowds.

There are many times in many locations to see a Changing of the Guard, but the most famous is at Buckingham Palace. It's a ceremonial event that has been performed since 1660. It typically takes place on Mondays, Wednesdays, Fridays and Sundays. The ceremony starts around 11.00 a.m., lasts approximately forty-five minutes and takes place at Buckingham Palace forecourt. It illustrates the seamless transition of responsibilities from one group of guards to another. This tradition is not only a spectacle for tourists but also a significant ritual that underscores the continuity and stability of institutions.

The ceremony begins with the New Guard forming up at Wellington Barracks and marching to Buckingham Palace, accompanied by a regimental band. Upon arrival, the New Guard is inspected and then takes over the responsibilities of the Old Guard. The handover is marked by the symbolic exchange of the palace keys, representing the transfer of security duties. The Old Guard then marches back to their barracks, completing the ritual.

The Changing of the Guard serves as a reminder of the role of the military in safeguarding the nation and its institutions. The precision and discipline displayed during the ceremony are a source of national pride and a symbol of the professionalism of the British armed forces.

The event is not limited to Buckingham Palace. Similar ceremonies are performed at other royal residences, including Windsor Castle and the Tower of London. Each location has its own unique elements, but the core principles of precision, discipline and tradition remain the same.

In addition to its ceremonial significance, the Changing of the Guard also has practical implications. It ensures that the security of the royal residences is maintained at all times, with fresh guards taking over the duties from those who have completed their shifts. This continuous cycle of vigilance is crucial for the protection of the monarchy and the preservation of national security.

The traditions have evolved over the years to include female guards and the use of social media to engage with a global audience. These adaptations ensure that the tradition remains relevant and accessible to new generations.

In a similar way, the Trooping of the Colour, also known as the King's Birthday Parade, is a ceremonial event celebrating the official birthday of the King. The event is held annually on a Saturday in June, regardless of the sovereign's actual birth date. Its origins date back to the early eighteenth century. It was initially a military exercise, designed to ensure that soldiers could recognise their regiment's colours or flags, crucial in the chaos of battle. Over time, this practical drill evolved into a ceremonial event, becoming a key part of the royal calendar.

This tradition began with King George II in 1748, who decided to combine the annual summer military march with his birthday celebration. His actual birthday was in November, a month not well suited for outdoor events. The event takes place on Horse Guards Parade in London, a historic parade ground near Buckingham Palace. It involves over 1,400 parading soldiers, 200 horses and 400 musicians, all coming together in a spectacular display of military precision, horsemanship and pageantry. The parade is attended by members of the Royal Family, who travel in carriages from Buckingham Palace along

The Mall to Horse Guards Parade. The King takes the salute and inspects the troops.

One of the most striking aspects of the Trooping of the Colour is the display of the regimental colours. Each year, a different regiment's colours are trooped before the monarch. The colours are a symbol of the regiment's spirit and service and their presentation is a moment of pride. The ceremony also includes a march-past by the Foot Guards, the Household Cavalry and the King's Troop, Royal Horse Artillery.

The Trooping of the Colour is not just a military parade; it is a vibrant celebration of British history and tradition. The event is marked by the precision and discipline of the troops, the splendour of the uniforms and the stirring music of the military bands. The soldiers wear the iconic red tunics and bearskin hats of the Foot Guards, a sight that is instantly recognisable and synonymous with British ceremonial occasions.

In addition to its ceremonial importance, the Trooping of the Colour is a public spectacle enjoyed by thousands of spectators who line The Mall and watch the proceedings. It is also broadcast live on television, reaching millions of viewers around the world. The event fosters a sense of national pride and unity, as people come together to celebrate the monarchy and the armed forces.

Perhaps the most popular participative events involving royal tradition are the Buckingham Palace parties. These are some of the most delightful British summer traditions, steeped in history and pageantry. They are held annually in the gardens of Buckingham Palace and serve as an opportunity for the monarchy to recognise and reward individuals for their public service and contributions to society. The elegance of these garden parties makes them a highlight of the social calendar, attracting guests from every background.

The tradition of garden parties dates to the reign of Queen Victoria in the 1860s. Initially, these events were known as 'breakfasts' and were held in the afternoon. Perhaps this was the first example of an 'all-day' breakfast. Over time, they evolved into the more elaborate gatherings we see today, complete with tea, sandwiches and cakes. The parties are typically held in the summer months, with three taking place at Buckingham Palace and one at the Palace of Holyroodhouse in Edinburgh.

Each garden party at Buckingham Palace hosts around 8,000 guests. Invitations are highly coveted and are extended to guests from all over the United Kingdom and the Commonwealth. Guests are also nominated by various organisations, including government departments, charities and other public bodies. The selection process ensures a diverse mix of attendees, ranging from community volunteers and military personnel to public servants and representatives of various charities.

The setting for garden parties is the 39-acre garden of Buckingham Palace, which is the largest private garden in London. The garden provides flower beds, a lake and the famous herbaceous border. The Royal Collection Trust meticulously plans the menu, ensuring that it reflects the best of British cuisine.

One of the highlights of the garden parties is the opportunity for guests to meet members of the Royal Family. This personal interaction with the monarchy is a memorable experience for many attendees. The royals have a strong interest in the guests' stories and contributions, making the event even more special.

The dress code is formal. Men typically wear morning dress or lounge suits, while women opt for day dresses with hats or fascinators. The emphasis on formal attire adds to the sense of occasion and tradition. Military personnel are often seen in their dress uniforms, adding to the pageantry of the event.

In addition to the social and ceremonial aspects, Buckingham Palace garden parties also serve a charitable purpose. Many of the guests are involved in charitable work and the events provide an opportunity to highlight and celebrate their contributions.

If all of the above wasn't enough, there are also royal jubilees. These commemorate important milestones in the reign of the monarch. They are marked by a variety of events and activities that bring together people to honour the achievements and longevity of the reigning monarch. The most recent was the Platinum Jubilee celebration in 2022, which marked seventy years of Queen Elizabeth II's reign. She was the first to ever reach this milestone. The celebrations were extensive, spanning several days and including a wide range of activities and events. It was not only a celebration of the Queen's long reign but also a reflection of the changes and developments that had taken place in the UK and the Commonwealth during her time on the throne.

One major event was the Platinum Party at the palace, a star-studded concert held at Buckingham Palace. This event featured performances by some of the biggest names in music and entertainment and it was attended by members of the Royal Family, as well as thousands of invited guests. The concert was also broadcast live, allowing millions of people around the world to join in.

Street parties and community events were also a key part of the Jubilee celebrations. Across the UK, communities came together to host their own parties and events, creating a festive atmosphere throughout the country. These local celebrations were an opportunity for people to connect with their communities and celebrate in their own unique way.

In addition to the public celebrations, there were also a number of official events. These included a Service of Thanksgiving at St Paul's Cathedral, which was attended by the Queen and other members of the Royal Family, as well as representatives from various sectors of society. The service was a moment of reflection and gratitude for the Queen's long and dedicated service.

Museums and galleries across the country hosted special exhibitions, showcasing artefacts and memorabilia from the Queen's reign. These exhibitions provided an opportunity for people to learn more about the history and significance of the monarchy.

The traditions and events surrounding the monarch and Royal Family are central to British life. They also provide continuity in the ever-changing tide of international and domestic politics. In February of 2025, a personal invitation from HM the King helped bridge the gap between an inbound US President and a Labour government with very different political views. The role of the monarch is central to our representative systems, our judiciary, our military and clergy. They are part of the very fabric of our identity. On top of this, they provide the prototype and template for many customs in organisations with or without patronage. The role of the sovereign and family confer a dignity and sense of recognition for any event. The convening power is such that it creates a moment or sense of occasion. Attached to this are some of the most important memories we hold. Take a look at the calendar of local customs later in the book. You will see that the monarchy is involved in every season. It is in our proclamations, our processions, our battle commemorations, charter fetes and games. Politics is absent.

CHAPTER SIX

THE STATE OF US

What are some of the traditions that would be recognisable to our grandparents – even taken for granted in British life? How do these traditions carry into our commercial and legal systems? How are traditions used for environmental assessments? Why is having fun and getting drunk so revered, even by university benefactors, dating back to antiquity?

Frank Gibbons: Here, let's have a look at you.
Ethel Gibbons: What for?
Frank Gibbons: Just to see what's happened to your face. You know, I don't seem to have had time for a really good look at it since I got back.
Ethel Gibbons: Oh, stop it. Leave go.
Frank Gibbons: Here, hold still a minute.
Ethel Gibbons: Now see here, Frank Gibbons.
Frank Gibbons: It's not such a bad face as faces go, I will say.
Ethel Gibbons: Oh, thanks very much I'm sure.
Frank Gibbons: Of course, it's not quite as young
.as it was when I married it.
Ethel Gibbons: Leave hold of me.
Ethel Gibbons: But taken by and large, I wouldn't change it.
NOËL COWARD, *THIS HAPPY BREED*

This chapter is by far the dullest in the book and you would be well advised not to read it. This is where the detail of the British constitution is laid out so you can see how it fits together from the executive and legislative to the judicial and monarchic. Yes, it's not particularly thrilling, but there is, however, a purpose, which will become clear.

Everyone says our constitution is not written down, but shelves of libraries are groaning under the weight of UK case law, so that's not entirely true. Besides, writing things down doesn't necessarily make them more meaningful. The UK tax code alone runs to 10 million words and 21,000 pages. This is ten times the length of the complete works of Shakespeare (880,000 words) and the Bible (800,000 words) combined. Magna Carta, for instance, is barely 5,000 words. The US Declaration of Independence is shorter still at 1,320 words. Quantity and quality are not the same.

Many of our important legal and constitutional principles were not created by fiat but by form. Custom and practice are the parents of a lot of it. In planning permission, for instance, there is the 'ten-year rule'. This states that where a property is occupied for ten consecutive years, it is considered lawful under planning rules. Or put another way, you establish rights over time. In planning, the period starts when the development is substantially completed. This means that patterns of behaviour can form the basis of a law. It is the same in employment law, where custom and practice in a workplace can be adjudicated as to what is 'normal'. In the law governing rights of way, tradition states that these persist despite demonstrable evidence that the paths have not been used for 175 years. Patterns of precedence can establish legal principles. Where the law remains but is no longer relevant, it doesn't need to be reformed, it just becomes defunct through lack of usage. In this respect then, usage or tradition directly dictates legality.

There are many examples of this. The Salmon Act 1986 says that if you are caught handling salmon in 'suspicious circumstances', you can be questioned by police, even though the definition of suspicious is unclear. Watch yourself on the way back from Waitrose. Under the Forbidding Bearing of Armour Act 1313, Members of Parliament are forbidden to wear their suit of armour inside Parliament. Technically, it is also illegal to stay at a burial site for an extended period after a funeral. In some areas, like in London under Section 60 of the Metropolitan Police Act of 1939, it is an offence to shake a carpet or rug in the street. Under Section 7 of the Metropolitan Streets Act 1867, it's illegal to walk your cows down the street in daylight. After dark is perfectly OK. Did you also realise that it's illegal to be drunk in charge of a cow? It's also illegal under the Metropolitan Police District Act 1839 (Section 54) to carry a plank of wood down the street unless you are loading it into a vehicle. The same section deals with the offence of flying your kite in a public place. Remember! No planks, kites or cows (in the daytime at least).

Did you play 'Knockdown Ginger' as a kid? Maybe you knew it better as 'ding dong ditch' or 'nicky nicky nine doors'? Either way, this game is illegal. The Metropolitan Police Act 1839 states that it's against the law to knock on a person's front door and then run off immediately after. Even the poor London cabby must, under the 1939 Public Health Act, ask if their passengers have plague or smallpox. Under the Treason and Felony Act of 1848, it was thought that placing a British stamp upside down on an envelope was an act of treason, although this is debated by experts. You can't gamble in a public library under the Library Offences Act of 1898. The Scots are not absolved from the rules either. It is illegal for a child under ten in Scotland to see a naked mannequin in a shop. Perhaps best of all, under Section 12 of the Licensing Act 1872, it remains illegal to be found drunk inside a pub.

All of these laws were created by statute because they seemed relevant at the time. And this is the problem. Sometimes our statute laws can result from a political imperative, fashion or fad. The Dangerous Dogs Act 1991 is a prime example of a law rushed through in response to public outcry. The law was enacted quickly after a series of dog attacks, several involving children, sparked outrage. The Act prohibits certain breeds, including Pit Bull Terriers, Japanese Tosas, Dogo Argentinos and Fila Brasileiros, and also makes it an offence for owners to allow their dogs to be dangerously out of control.

The Act has been widely criticised as an ineffective and poorly thought-out piece of legislation. Critics argue that it focuses on breed rather than individual dog behaviour, fails to address the root causes of dog aggression and has not demonstrably reduced dog bites. The Act has also been criticised for potentially harming animal welfare by punishing dogs for their appearance rather than their behaviour.

It's not just simple statute that reflects the time of its creation. Constitutions can do as well. The US Declaration of Independence reflects its age. It was significantly influenced by Enlightenment philosophers, particularly John Locke and Montesquieu, whose ideas on natural rights, social contracts and the separation of powers resonated deeply with the document's authors, like Thomas Jefferson. It is rational, organised and logical. Or that's the idea. It is a rigid sound construction that has had subsequent alterations (amendments).

But in America, there was no precedent, so the statute had to take the strain. British laws and conventions, meanwhile, are there but just not all in one place. It is more correct to say that we don't have a codified constitution. Others have described it as a political constitution instead of a legal one. Britain's rulebook evolved over centuries through common law and established conventions. These were established by our traditions.

This gives the British constitution strength but also a flexible quality. It has been designed for the wind tunnel of history, where benign organic neglect is only occasionally overtaken by the imperative of crisis.

In many instances, the problems have emerged from where it has been changed for political purposes. The establishment of a Supreme Court, for example – an American idea – has led to its evolution over time into a constitutional court. Mixing the law and politics is dangerous – ask any American. It's not something that comes naturally to the British. Our system, by custom and practice, has always been independent of politics.

In Anglo-Saxon times, away from London's courts, the King's justice was administered in the counties by the Reeve, who was a local official in England who served as the King's representative. The role was responsible for administering royal justice, collecting revenues and organising peasant labour. The term 'Shire Reeve' corrupted into 'sheriff' as the English language changed.

As Lord President of the Council, I was involved in making High Sheriffs, which was done with a bodkin (a sort of ornamental hairpin shaped like a stiletto) pricking their name on a vellum scroll. This practice dates from the reign of Henry VII (1485–1509), taking place in the middle of March each year. Despite all the new technology, the King still uses a hands-on method to appoint a High Sheriff, which is the oldest secular office in Britain.

The pricking ceremony is an early form of document security. A mark with a pen on the vellum could be erased with a knife, but a hole in the vellum (made from calfskin) could not be removed or repaired invisibly. No official could disguise a hole pierced against the appointee's name.

These officials once held great power, presiding over the law courts, organising military forces and even raising a posse when required. A sheriff in the UK can no longer legally form a posse, as the power of 'posse comitatus' (literally 'power of the county', to summon citizens to assist in law enforcement), was repealed by the Criminal Law Act of 1967. In the US, though, a sheriff can still form a posse in some jurisdictions. Most modern posses are more ceremonial in nature and may focus on volunteer services rather than active policing. Today, the office of High Sheriff is purely a ceremonial role.

Even today, the role of the sheriff in the US is similar to the ancient role in England and is influenced by the English heritage of the

American colonies. A modern-day sheriff's responsibilities include law enforcement, liaising between the people, responding to complaints and caring for prisoners while transporting them to and from court.

The problem with a constitution is that it involves behaviour, the law, politics and economics, and quite frequently, what makes sense politically doesn't always make sense legally or economically. Politics is about weather and waves, but justice is about climate and tide. It's much more long term. As Sir Humphrey Appleby put it: 'Diplomacy is about surviving until the next century. Politics is about surviving until Friday afternoon.'

SIR HUMPHREY ON POLITICS

https://www.youtube.com/watch?v=7hsNfNMoSvE

If change comes to justice, it's better made evolutionarily, not revolutionarily.

The Supreme Court was used politically during Brexit, something it was never intended for. Who would have thought the constitution could be subjective? People tend to focus on what's important to them or aligns better with their desired outcome, but being certain about what is or is not constitutional is not an exact science.

Technically, the UK is a hereditary constitutional monarchy where the Crown has two functions. Firstly, what Walter Bagehot called the preservation of the 'reverence of the population', primarily via ceremonial duties. The Crown is fundamental to the law and the functions of government. It can be seen as representing the state or the sovereign. The sovereign is both the head of state and the head of a nation. In both roles, the Royal Household states that the monarch will provide 'a sense of continuity, a focus for loyalty and an assurance of political independence and neutrality' for key institutions, including the armed forces, the judiciary, the civil service and the Church of England.

Secondly, there are what Bagehot termed the 'efficient', which involve clear works and rules. As well as consenting to the appointment of Privy Councillors, Lord-Lieutenants and sheriffs, the monarch will appoint ambassadors and high commissioners to serve overseas in the UK's diplomatic service. Ambassadors from other countries will present the monarch with letters of credence from their heads of state, providing assurance that they speak with the authority of their nations. High commissioners from Commonwealth realms use letters of introduction, which are exchanged between heads of government and do not involve the sovereign, though they may still meet with the monarch. All foreign diplomats are accredited to the Court of St James's.

The evolutionary nature can be seen in our icons and symbols. For instance, the UK has a Royal Coat of Arms, also referred to as the Royal Arms, used by the government of the UK and by other Crown institutions, including courts in the UK and in parts of the Commonwealth. Different versions of the Royal Arms are used by members of the Royal Family. The monarch's official flag, the Royal Standard, is the Coat of Arms in flag form.

There are two versions of the Coat of Arms. In Scotland, it includes elements derived from the Scottish Coat of Arms, with the other elements derived from the English Coat of Arms. The shields of both versions quarter the arms of the others, which united to form the Kingdom of Great Britain in 1707. The Kingdom of Ireland, which united with Great Britain to form the United Kingdom in 1801, formed the Irish Quarter. This was unaltered following the division into Northern Ireland and the Irish Free State in 1922.

The arms do not include the United Kingdom's fourth constituent nation, Wales. It is instead represented heraldically by two royal badges, which use the Welsh dragon and the Coat of Arms of Llywelyn ab Iorwerth.

At the centre of the Arms is something older and stranger, written in ancient French. Some dispute this story, but that should not stand in the way of it being told. Apparently, at a court function in 1348, Edward III was dancing with Joan of Kent, his first cousin and future daughter-in-law, at a ball held in Calais to celebrate after the Battle of Crécy. Her garter slipped down to her ankle, causing those around her to laugh at her humiliation. Edward placed the garter around his own leg, saying: *Honi soit qui mal y pense. Tel qui s'en rit aujourd'hui, s'honorera de la porter.* ('Shame on anyone who thinks evil of it. Whoever is laughing at this today will later be proud to wear it.') This speaks to chivalry, manners and, perhaps even then, the British sense of humour. Only in Britain could the country's historic motto – even the highest accolade – come about as the result of an underwear malfunction.

You can't 'speak evil of it', in any case. Republican activity is considered a felony under the Treason Felony Act of 1848. In 2003, however, the House of Lords ruled that no prosecution was ever likely because the Human Rights Act 1998 guarantees freedom of speech. By the way, the Crown Proceedings Act 1947 ensures the monarch's personal immunity from legal proceedings in their private capacity. While the Act does not explicitly exempt all members of the Royal Family from being arrested in all circumstances, it does protect them from arrest in certain locations or in the presence of the sovereign.

In a similar way, Crown immunity also means that certain public bodies are immune from specific laws, including health and safety legislation. However, if it is deemed that an organisation needs a rap on the knuckles, Crown censures have been developed for these matters.

The current Royal Arms were established by a proclamation made by Queen Victoria in 1837. In the twentieth century, a version of the arms to be used in Scotland was created. There have been slight changes over time, reflecting the personal preferences of the reigning monarch.

The government uses a simplified version of the Royal Arms known as the 'lesser arms'. The Trade Marks Act of 1994 governs what the Royal Arms can be used for.

The motto features the lion and the unicorn as heraldic supporters in the full Royal Coat of Arms of the United Kingdom. The lion represents England and is associated with the Plantagenet dynasty and the reign of King Richard the Lionheart. The unicorn is the national animal of Scotland. If you visit the Palace of Holyroodhouse in Edinburgh, you will see it on gate posts, carved into walls, on plaster ceilings and more. So, the Coat of Arms features two beasts, one real and one mythological, and only an idiot would comment further on the symbolism.

The Royal Household provides support to the sovereign and members of the Royal Family. It consists of a Private Secretary's Office, the Privy Purse and Treasurer's Office, the Master of the Households Department (which manages all official engagements across royal residences) and the Lord Chamberlain's Office (which organises ceremonial activity and public events, including the State Opening of Parliament). In addition, the Royal Collection Trust takes care of art and artefacts.

Do remember, of course (as if you could forget), that the Lord Chamberlain and the Lord Great Chamberlain are two completely different people. The Lord Chamberlain is a non-executive overseeing the day-to-day operations and ceremonial duties of the Royal Household, while the Lord Great Chamberlain is one of the Great Officers of State, primarily responsible for ceremonial duties when the sovereign is present in Parliament, including the State Opening.

Some in the government, whips and officers in the House of Commons and the House of Lords are members of the Royal Household. In Scotland, the Royal Household is based on the ancient Scottish court. There is the Court of the Lord Lyon, which deals with heraldic and ceremonial issues. The ministers of the Church of Scotland make up the ecclesiastical court. The Royal Company of Archers oversees the household's medical and defensive functions. Finally, there are some hereditary positions, which are purely honorific.

In 1936, there was no permanent statutory provision for the abdication of a monarch. King Edward VIII signed an instrument of abdication, voluntarily terminating his status as head of state. At the coronation, the new monarch takes an oath set out in the Coronation Oath Act of 1688. The oath requires them to rule according to the laws of Parliament, ensure that law, justice and mercy are upheld through their judgements and maintain 'the Protestant reformed religion established by law'. A coronation service itself is not a legal requirement. It is simply a longstanding tradition, but one that is expected by the public. It is based on the Liber Regalis, the royal manuscript, written around 1382. Royal regalia including the Crown Jewels are used, along with the Scottish regalia, which includes the Stone of Scone, or the Stone of Destiny, transferred to Westminster Abbey for the occasion. Events are captured in the Coronation Roll, which in 2023 was produced in a digital format for the first time.

The Regency Act 1937 made general provision for the royal functions to be performed by someone on behalf of the sovereign should certain circumstances require it, for example, where the monarch was infirm of mind or body. Previously, any regency had required a specific Act of Parliament, like the Care of the King During His Illness, etc. Act of 1811, which had allowed the Prince of Wales to take on the duties of George III. However, this only applies to the sovereign's duties within the UK. The act also permits the sovereign to delegate some duties to their Councillors of State.

Some public servants, including those who serve the Crown, take an oath upon assuming office. The Commissioner of the Metropolitan Police is appointed by royal warrant. The inspectors of the constabulary and fire and rescue services are also appointed by the sovereign. This appointment process ensures their independence, as they are neither part of the civil service nor police officers themselves.

The monarch is also head of the UK's armed forces and holds the specific title of Lord High Admiral of the Royal Navy. On enlisting, members of all services are required to take an oath of allegiance to the monarch, with the exception of naval officers. The King's Regulations, which serve as a rulebook for the armed forces, require the sovereign's consent for any changes. Members of the regular forces are not permitted to take part in the activities of any political party or movement.

There is a convention of confidentiality around the sovereign's communications with ministers and the devolved administrations. Every subject has the constitutional right to petition the monarch and UK citizens can send these petitions to the sovereign free of charge.

The Chancellor of the Duchy of Lancaster is a member of the Cabinet and often the de facto Deputy Prime Minister. This role heads the Cabinet Office and manages a source of income for the sovereign that is independent of government funding and the public purse. The Duchy of Cornwall is a private estate belonging to the Duke of Cornwall, a title held by the heir to the throne. Its revenue is used to fund the activities of the duke and his immediate family.

Several royal palaces, including Buckingham Palace, St James's Palace, Windsor Castle and parts of Kensington Palace, are held in trust for the nation by the sovereign. Hillsborough Castle, a historic palace, is available for use by ministers of the Northern Ireland Office. The Palace of Holyroodhouse in Edinburgh is the official residence of the monarch in Scotland. Tradition dictates that the monarch spends part of July in residence. Balmoral and Sandringham are private estates, but they can host official events. Privy Council meetings have also been held elsewhere, such as Dumfries House in Scotland.

Interestingly, Dumfries House has an unrivalled collection of furniture that was saved for the nation by Prince Charles in 2007 when he took out a loan to purchase the 2,000-acre estate. It is now the second-largest employer in the area. The house was lovingly restored and the gardens were planted with specimen trees. The estate is open to the local community, who can walk their dogs and admire its beauty every day. That might have been enough for others but not for the (then) Prince of Wales. The estate is also home to workrooms and showrooms for craftsmen and artisans. From woodwork to textiles, it supports young people as they start their creative careers. It also houses an education centre, which every local schoolchild is sure to have visited. Its purpose is to inspire a passion for science and technology. All of this is complemented by an Ayurvedic meditation centre, a hotel and a vast vegetable garden that grows every type of produce you can imagine. Visit it and you cannot help but be moved by the care, thought and passion that created new life for this ancient estate.

You can see that it's difficult to separate the Royal Family from the fabric of the state. It's an ambiguous relationship, blurred by history and time. It's ripe to be exploited by those who like to pick at threads of our national tapestry. You hear echoes of this in Parliament from time to time. For instance, the House of Commons elects a Speaker, but they are subject to royal approval. Deputy Speakers are elected under common standing orders and have authority under the Deputy Speakers Act 1855. The Speaker is also a Privy Councillor. The monarch hasn't rejected a Speaker since 1679 and the last King to refuse to grant royal assent to bills, except under government direction, was William III (1689–1702); he vetoed the Qualifications Bill in 1696.

The Parliamentary and Health Service Ombudsman is appointed by the King under the Parliamentary Commissioner Act of 1967. Their role is to investigate complaints referred to them by Members of Parliament or members of the public who allege an injustice has occurred.

Parliamentary scrutiny is exercised in the Chamber but also by select committees, the chairs of which are elected by MPs. The Backbench Business Committee is a fairly recent addition to the House of Commons, established in 2010, and gives ordinary members some control over time on the floor of the House. Petitions can be presented and must be answered by the relevant government department.

The House of Lords is made up of the Lords Spiritual and the Lords Temporal. The former consists of the Archbishops of Canterbury and York, the Bishops of London, Durham and Winchester and twenty-one other diocesan bishops of the Church of England, according to seniority. Unlike other peers, they are considered Lords of Parliament, as defined in the House of Lords Precedence Act of 1539.

Lords Temporal are largely life peers appointed by ministers, political parties or through the honours system. At the time of writing, ninety hereditary peers are still permitted to sit and vote in the House of Lords, chosen from the peerage by their fellow hereditaries, as well as the Earl Marshal and the Lord Great Chamberlain, two key roles in the Royal Household. The House of Lords (Hereditary Peers) Bill seeks to exclude all remaining hereditary peers from the House of Lords, including these two great offices of state.

Life peers are ceremonially introduced into the House of Lords, as are all Lords Spiritual. Hereditary peers receive no such ceremony on taking their seat in the Lords. Meanwhile, only the sovereign and their children are permitted to sit beside the Cloth of State, which hangs behind the throne in the House of Lords. Male primogeniture has already ended for the monarch but not for titles and lands for other hereditary lines.

Full members of both the House of Commons and the House of Lords are required to take an oath, swearing allegiance to the sovereign. In the House of Commons, there is no legal obligation to take the oath, but it is customary. According to a 1924 Speaker's ruling, MPs who refuse to swear allegiance will not receive a salary, nor will they be allowed to vote or participate in debates in the Chamber. In contrast, taking the oath remains mandatory for members of the House of Lords.

The House of Lords is also not supposed to filibuster and must consider government business within a reasonable timeframe. Nor is it the done thing to object to secondary legislation, although it has the right to do so. The Parliament Acts of 1911 and 1949 govern the relationship between both houses and limit the length of time the Lords can hold up legislation against the will of the Commons. When bills have been agreed by the two houses, they are sent for royal assent.

With regard to international treaties, the UK operates a dual system. This means those obligations are binding in international law but do not form an integral part of UK domestic law.

The government can raise taxes, borrow money or spend money. But it must have the authority of Parliament and particularly of the House of Commons to do so. The Social Security Administration Act of 1992 mandates that the National Insurance Fund be maintained under the management of His Majesty's Revenue and Customs. Statutory powers given to the Treasury can only be exercised by its Lords Commissioners. This includes the Prime Minister and the Chancellor of the Exchequer, as well as junior Lords of the Treasury. They are appointed by the sovereign via letters patent under the Great Seal.

The Bank of England serves as the central bank for the whole of the United Kingdom and is accountable to the Treasury Committee of the House of Commons. Its directors are also appointed by the monarch. The Comptroller General of the Receipt and Issue of His Majesty's Exchequer and Auditor General of Public Accounts is also appointed by letters patent and heads up the National Audit Office. There is a similar post in Northern Ireland, and Scotland and Wales have their own auditors.

The monarch and Parliament can communicate with each other by messages under the Royal Sign Manual. These are generally acknowledged by addresses in both Houses of Parliament and are presented by representatives. There are different forms of communication, including those made at the sovereign's pleasure, the sovereign's recommendation or the sovereign's consent.

Governments are formed and they also collapse. A government's ability to command the confidence of the elected House of Commons is central to its authority to govern. This can be tested by motions of confidence or no confidence. If the government were to lose a key vote on its programme over its Budget, that would signify it is in real trouble and has lost the authority to govern. There are conventions surrounding the transfer of power and how a prospective government can access enough information to formulate its programme.

Most honours are awarded on the advice of the Prime Minister, who will have their own list managed by the Cabinet Office. There will be an overseas and international list managed by the Foreign Office and the diplomatic service. There is also the military list managed by the Ministry of Defence for members of the armed forces. There are also certain honours, known as the monarch's personal honours, that don't require ministerial advice. These include the Orders of the Garter and the Thistle, the Order of Merit and the Royal Victorian Order.

Since 1968, the Prime Minister also holds the office of Minister for the Civil Service. They are responsible for national security, overseeing the Secret Intelligence Service (MI6), the Security Service (MI5) and Government Communications Headquarters (GCHQ). The Intelligence and Security Committee of Parliament, a committee established under statute rather than a select committee, scrutinises their work. The Prime Minister also appoints the Investigatory Powers Commissioner and the Judicial Commissioners, who oversee the use of covert investigatory powers by public authorities.

Government itself should consist of not more than ninety-five holders of office, with limits placed on salaries and pensions (and not all ministers are entitled to receive them). The law officers of the Crown are the Attorney General for England and Wales, who is also the Advocate General for Northern Ireland, the Solicitor General for England and Wales and the Advocate General for Scotland. Their core function is to advise the government on legal matters, helping ministers to act lawfully and in accordance with the rule of law in the UK's three jurisdictions. The Attorney General is the chief law officer and principal legal adviser to the Crown.

As well as ministries, there are arms-length bodies, which include non-departmental public bodies, executive agencies and non-ministerial departments. Currently, there are twenty-four ministerial departments, twenty non-ministerial departments, 423 agencies and public bodies, 117 high-profile groups such as the Passport Office and nineteen public corporations, including the BBC.

The conduct of UK foreign policy is based on prerogative powers, which do not have a statutory foundation. It operates alongside certain pieces of legislation, such as the Consular Relations Act of 1963, the Territorial Sea Act of 1987 and the International Organisations Act of 1968. It is usually the Prime Minister who will decide to deploy our armed forces. Such decisions do not require the approval of Parliament. However, in 2011, under the coalition government, a convention was established that Parliament's consent would be sought in all but the most exceptional situations.

Thousands of public appointments are made under delegated powers by ministers of the Crown. For a select few, there are pre-appointment hearings conducted by the House of Commons select committees responsible for the relevant area. Royal Commissions can be established under the royal prerogative by the Cabinet, following the sovereign's initial approval.

The Official Secrets Act of 1989 defines a Crown servant as a minister or a member of a devolved administration, any person employed in the civil service of the Crown and any member of the armed forces, constable or member of the National Crime Agency. The diplomatic service has its own code, which is laid before Parliament.

As with the Prime Minister, the Leader of His Majesty's Opposition has a basis in statute.

Local authorities are statutory bodies created by primary legislation. They can create local laws known as by-laws for any part of their district. Their administrators are not part of the civil service. Elected councils across the country use ceremonial maces, which denote royal authority. The accession proclamation for a new monarch is read by the high sheriffs of each county in England and Wales or by mayors and Lord Mayors. In Scotland, it is read by the sheriffs in the counties and Lord Provosts and provosts in cities and towns. In Northern Ireland, it is read by mayors and Lord Mayors. The local government landscape has been permanently in flux.

The City of London Corporation is the governing body of the Square Mile. Its ancient liberties and customs are well protected in the clauses of the Magna Carta (1215) and remain in force to this day. By tradition, the Lord Mayor of London and the City's Aldermen attend part one of the Accession Council. The Lord Mayor is approved by the monarch and swears an oath of allegiance at the Royal Courts of Justice. The Lord Mayor will present the hilt of the City of London's sword to the monarch, who touches it and then returns it to the Lord Mayor.

The UK has an established church in England and a 'national' church in Scotland. The Church of England has no legal status. It was not created but evolved and dates from an age when the church and the nation were largely indistinguishable from one another. Magna Carta states that the English church 'shall be free and have all her whole rights and liberties inviolable'. The rights and privileges of the Church of England are found in Acts of Parliament, in measures and canons, in the common law of England, from the judgments of ecclesiastical and temporal courts and in customs and in divine law.

The Acts of Supremacy of 1534 and 1558 declared the monarch to be the Supreme Head and Supreme Governor of the Church of England. Their obligations are described in the coronation oath. The Bill of Rights of 1688 barred Roman Catholics from ascending to the throne. This was reinforced in the Act of Settlement 1701 and then extended to Scotland, now part of the Union, with the Scotland Act of 1706.

The appointment of bishops is governed under the Appointment of Bishops Act of 1533. There is an additional process for the Archbishop of Canterbury, with the final approval coming from the Privy Council.

The Crown also appoints twenty-eight of the forty-four cathedral deans, and military chaplains are commissioned officers under the King's Regulations. Under the Prisons Act of 1952, every prison establishment in England and Wales must have a chaplain who is a clergyman of the Church of England. When a bishopric becomes vacant, the Crown has the right to exercise its patronage. Bishops, priests and deacons of the Church of England are required to swear an oath of allegiance under the Clerical Subscription Act of 1865.

The church is governed by the General Synod, made up of bishops, clergy and laity. Any measures it wishes to introduce require parliamentary oversight. By convention, the government doesn't legislate for the Church of England without its consent. Royal peculiars are Church of England parishes or churches that are exempt from the jurisdiction of the diocese and instead fall under the authority of the Crown. Both Westminster Abbey and St George's Chapel, Windsor, are notable examples. They are governed by reference to their own ancient statutes and rules. The Archbishop of Canterbury also holds ecclesiastical powers under the Ecclesiastical Licences Act of 1533, which could include special marriage licences. The Church of Scotland is governed by the General Assembly, which functions as a legislature, a court and an executive body. Although it is the 'national' church, it is not established and is not governed by the monarch, who is considered simply an ordinary member when he or she is in Scotland. The King has one special privilege: he can appoint a Lord High Commissioner to represent him at the annual meeting of the General Assembly of the Church of Scotland in Edinburgh, but this representative is only an observer and has no rights in the assembly.

The United Kingdom has three separate legal jurisdictions: England and Wales, Scotland and Northern Ireland. The independence of the legal system is an important principle.

The Constitutional Reform Act of 2005 established the Supreme Court of the United Kingdom as the final Court of Appeal for all civil cases in the UK, as well as criminal cases in England, Wales and Northern Ireland. The process for appointing Supreme Court judges includes approval from both Houses of Parliament, with the Lord Chancellor required to consult the First Ministers of Scotland and Wales as well as the Northern Ireland Judicial Appointments Commission.

The motivation for its establishment was to separate of the judicial functions of the House of Lords (its Appellant Committee, which the court would replace) from its legislative functions. It ended the judicial functions of the House of Lords, other than the trial of impeachments, where Parliament can arrest and depose ministers. Before it was created, some sounded a word of caution. They feared the new court could become more powerful than the House of Lords structures it would replace.

The UK Supreme Court has come under criticism for evolving into an 'activist' court. It has been accused of creating policy, as opposed to being a mere legal interpreter. The charge is that it is no longer a check and balance but a political operator.

One such charge was made during Brexit: the challenge to the Prime Minister's decision to prorogue Parliament. As it happened, a way through the parliamentary stalemate was found in the form of a general election. Again, constitutional flexibility saved the day. However, there remain concerns over the legitimate role of the court and how much judge-made law is acceptable. This has been of particular concern with regards to successive legislation to strengthen UK border protection against illegal and irregular immigration. The court will continue to evolve and will be a topic of political debate as well as legal. One potential change, suggested by Policy Exchange, is to have a greater pool of Supreme Court judges on rotation, so that they do not attain the celebrity status and political nature of their US counterparts.

The Judicial Committee of the Privy Council is a statutory body that deals with appeals to the King in Council. It hears appeals from the Crown dependencies, British overseas territories, Commonwealth realms, Commonwealth republics and, by proxy, on behalf of the Sultan of Brunei from the Court of Appeal of Brunei. It will also hear appeals from the Court of Chivalry on heraldic disputes, the prize courts related to the seizure of ships, the Court of Admiralty of the Cinque Ports, dealing with piracy and collisions at sea, and certain ecclesiastical courts.

Tribunals are independent judicial bodies set up by the UK's legislature to rule on disputes between individuals, organisations and state agencies.

In Wales, there is the Court of Appeal, the High Court of Justice and the Crown Court. In addition, there are the county courts, the family courts and the magistrates' courts, along with specialist courts such as the coroner's court.

In Scotland, the Court of Session is the highest civil court, while the High Court of Justiciary is the highest criminal court. Other courts include sheriff courts, which handle both civil and criminal cases at the local level, Justice of the Peace courts, the Scottish Land Court, for disputes between landlords and tenants in agriculture and crofting, and the Court of the Lord Lyon, which holds authority over heraldic disputes.

In Northern Ireland, there is the High Court of Justice, the Court of Appeal and the crown courts.

Although UK courts are under no obligation to implement judgments made against the UK by the European Court of Human Rights, the House of Lords has ruled that domestic courts should take into account clear and constant jurisprudence from this court.

The International Criminal Court is a treaty-based court dealing with the most serious offences and crimes against humanity. It was incorporated into law in England, Wales and Northern Ireland through the International Criminal Court Act 2001 and in Scotland by the International Criminal Court (Scotland) Act in the same year. The International Court of Justice is part of the United Nations and adjudicates on general disputes between nations and on international legal issues.

Magna Carta is the basis of trial by jury. Habeas corpus, initially a prerogative writ, is now governed by a combination of statute law, case law and court rules. The UK has enacted various pieces of domestic human rights and equality legislation and the European Convention on Human Rights was incorporated into UK law through the Human Rights Act of 1998.

The prerogative of mercy is granted by the monarch under the advisement of ministers. It can only be exercised in relation to criminal proceedings.

Use of the Wednesbury principle can stem from a Court of Appeal judgment and concerns the ability to intervene in the decision of a local authority or public body.

The sub judice rule is a convention of the House of Commons. No matter that is awaiting adjudication by a court of law should be brought to the floor of the House. However, the Speaker has the authority to waive this rule if deemed necessary.

So much for Britain, but it doesn't stop there. The Commonwealth is a voluntary association of fifty-six countries that recognises the UK sovereign as its head. It is bound by shared values and the goals of democracy and development. As a non-constitutional entity, the Commonwealth allows the British monarch to sometimes act or speak without the advice or direction of UK ministers. For example, in the monarch's Commonwealth Day message or Christmas speech, which is broadcast to all Commonwealth nations, the monarch speaks independently. However, when addressing the Commonwealth in this capacity, the speech is coordinated and agreed upon in advance by all member governments.

Fourteen overseas territories form part of the UK realm but are not part of the UK itself. Governors are appointed by the monarch on the advice of the Foreign Secretary. Each territory will have its own codified constitution, although the UK Parliament retains unlimited power to legislate on their behalf. In nine of these territories, there is an elected legislature which passes bills, just like the UK Parliament, before submitting them to the monarch or the governor for royal assent.

The crown dependences include the Bailiwick of Jersey, the Bailiwick of Guernsey and the Isle of Man. These too are part of the UK realm. The monarch is the head of state and is represented by a lieutenant governor. In the Channel Islands, the King is styled as the Duke of Normandy and in the Isle of Man, he is referred to as the Lord of Mann.

So, what are the elements that make up this highly reasonable and flexible rule book?

Primary legislation issued as an Act of Parliament is the highest form of law and takes precedence over other forms. The statute book also includes laws enacted by parliaments from separate countries of the British Isles prior to the Union of the United Kingdom being formed. This includes the Parliament of England from 1267 to 1706, the Parliament of Scotland from 1424 to 1707, the Parliament of Great Britain from 1707 to 1800 and the Parliament of Ireland from 1495 to 1800. Between 1921 and 1999, there were also sources of Northern Ireland legislation. Primary legislation also includes legislative instruments made by the Privy Council under the royal prerogative. The royal prerogative is the residual power vested in the sovereign, which is only exercised on the advice of their ministers. This is usually done in writing.

Secondary legislation is that made under the authority contained in primary legislation. The statute book also originated from EU laws, which were assimilated into UK law following the UK's withdrawal from the European Union. There are also codes of guidance, conduct and practice issued by the government and also regulators and public bodies.

The Crown Office resides in the House of Lords and carries out certain functions, such as the issue of letters patent under the Great Seal or for parliamentary elections and senior judicial and ecclesiastical appointments.

The *London Gazette*, the *Belfast Gazette* and the *Edinburgh Gazette* are official journals of record and include notices of the state and Parliament, including proclamations.

There are also what are known as constitutional conventions. These are customs and practices which aren't recognised by the courts but are really an ethical code. An example of this would be the King appointing a Prime Minister. Parliament also has such practices and customs.

There are also light-touch guides. For example, the Cabinet Manual will tell ministers the main laws, rules and conventions affecting the government's conduct and operation. Then there are more heavy-going rule books such as *Erskine May*, which acts as a guide to parliamentary practice spanning over 1,000 pages. MPs swear on it on entering Parliament. Secretaries of State become Privy Councillors (all Cabinet ministers must be, as the Cabinet is technically a committee of the Privy Council) and are sworn in by the sovereign at a Privy Council meeting. Audiences are a set number of times a year. For the Prime Minister, it's weekly; for the First Minister of Scotland it's around twice a year. Key positions will spend time with the sovereign or have official residences. There will be other ceremonies for other posts, such as the Paymaster General.

In addition to citizenship resulting from being born in the UK or a qualifying territory, there are various forms of British citizenship, provided at least one parent is a British citizen. Those who qualify are also Commonwealth citizens. Other forms include British overseas territories citizenship, British overseas citizenship, a British national, a British subject and a British protected person.

For someone to be naturalised as a British citizen, they have to go through the relevant citizenship oath and pledge in a citizenship ceremony. British citizenship can also be renounced if the Secretary of State deems it in the public interest. There isn't a list of rights and responsibilities of British citizens, but there is generally considered to be a shared common bond. This was outlined in the 2008 report by

Lord Goldsmith as the right of abode and free movement; the right of protection and duty of allegiance; civic rights such as being able to vote, undertake jury service or hold public office; and social and economic rights, including the duty to pay taxes and the ability to access benefits and services.

The national anthem of the United Kingdom derives from custom rather than any statute. Scotland and Wales have their own unofficial anthems: 'Flower of Scotland' and 'Land of My Fathers' (*Hen Wlad Fy Nhadau*) respectively. There is no agreed unofficial anthem in England or Northern Ireland. This has sparked some debate and resulted in some politicians campaigning for England to have its own anthem.

The flying of flags, including the Union flag, is not governed by law but is guided by recommendations from the Department of Culture, Media and Sport. However, in Northern Ireland, specific legislation governs flag usage through the 2000 Flags Regulations and its subsequent amendments.

The Great Seal of the Realm is the principal seal of the Crown and is used to show the monarch's consent to state documents. The practice of using this seal began in the reign of Edward the Confessor in the eleventh century, to avoid the monarch having to sign every official document. The seal is unique, with only one matrix existing at any one time, making it difficult to forge an official document. There is a system of colour coding for seals. Red sealing wax is used for most letters patent. Dark green seals are affixed to letters patent that elevate individuals to the peerage. Blue seals are used for documents that relate to members of the Royal Family.

So, what does all this mean? And what is the point of this weight of history? It means that our constitutional system appears to be unchanging, even unchangeable. It is though, in reality, slowly evolving all the time. Is its pace of change equal to the pace of change in the executive or the wider world? No. Nor should it be. The correct functions of the constitution, the Royal Family, the courts and the authorities are to enable consistency, confidence and continuity. They are the bones of the body. They provide something against which the muscles and sinews of the state can act.

Some may want to attack this as bureaucracy. This is like accusing the bones of the body of not thinking. That's not their job.

This is an important point in Britain. The state does not stand in the way. The legal maxim is that 'everything which is not forbidden is allowed'. This essentially means that any action is permitted unless there's a specific law prohibiting it. This principle, also known as 'general power of competence', grants individuals a broad scope of action unless a specific rule restricts it.

The opposite principle is that 'everything which is not allowed is forbidden'. This has begun to creep in to the approach taken by departments and public bodies. Permission to carry on is not their default setting. Agency is removed. This is not historically our approach.

In Britain, you should be free to do whatever you want unless there is a law against it. In other countries, there is an assumption that government must first permit something for it to be allowed. We should never allow that to come here.

Our system may require methodical, clear planning, notice and scrutiny, but it will not stand in the way of free action unless there is a law against it. In this way, the system provides continuity, confidence and consistency, which allows for change.

As we are seeing unfold in other parts of the world, this continuity is vital. It takes time to build up trust. It underpins everything. It takes decades to achieve, but it can be lost in days and when it is, the potential for all coordinated and assimilated change is lost. In other words, if you really want lasting change, then the price is meticulous planning and considered action. Sure, you can have a revolution, but the price of that is a complete loss of confidence, which inhibits change.

As someone once said: 'The rules are made for the obedience of fools and the guidance of wise men.'

Like good health, stability is conspicuous only by its absence. This is a great lesson about the British constitution. It is designed to withstand, but not resist, change. If the argument is that it cannot change fast enough, then consider the alternative that it changes so fast that people lose confidence. It is a lesson that the Conservative Party, indeed any party, must learn, because if anything, stability allows accelerated change. It doesn't stand in the way of it.

Our traditions and customs are not there just for amusement or entertainment. They're a vital part of effectiveness, allowing values, culture and history to be shared. Wherever culture is ignored or bypassed, there tends to be lower morale, lower cohesion and lower levels of satisfaction. These complicated rules and processes are held together not by some giant manuscript but by habit, ceremony and the rhythms of these great institutions.

CHAPTER SEVEN

DEFENCE OF THE REALM

———————————————◦❯❯—✦—❮❮◦———————————————

Some of the military traditions detailed in this chapter date back hundreds of years. They come from every branch of the services and from many different units. Why does the military place such a strong emphasis on discipline and conformity yet allow a tradition of idiosyncrasy? How do traditions help shape the ethos and identity of military units? What effect do they have on efficiency?

———————————————◦❯❯—✦—❮❮◦———————————————

I've seen something today that I wouldn't believe could happen in this country. I've seen thousands of people – British people, mark you – carrying on like maniacs, shouting and cheering with relief for no other reason but that they've been thoroughly frightened. And it made me sick and that's a fact. And I only hope to goodness we've got guts enough to learn one lesson from this and we shall never find ourselves in a position again where we have to appease anybody.
FRANK GIBBONS IN NOËL COWARD'S *THIS HAPPY BREED*

When it comes to the spending required for the defence of the nation and our military traditions, there are quite a few myths. For a start, economists will explain the dilemma of 'guns or butter?' This is the principle that you can spend money either on our defence or on our communities. It's like saying I won't fix my front door, I'll buy a new TV instead. Result? You're probably going to lose the telly you bought and much more besides. They believe that spending is binary. It's an argument as old as it is wrong.

Investment in our military is returned many times more than official estimates. It is spent on training, social welfare, research, technology and education. This last factor is particularly important, because to learn our military traditions is also to learn our history.

Britain has not been on the losing side of a war in 200 years. This is not a matter of luck or just sheer accident. There are reasons and you will find them in our history and traditions. Like excellence in general, winning is a habit.

Chief among these reasons is that Britain stayed engaged internationally. It developed systems of trade that allowed mutual benefit to flow back and forth. The British Empire was founded on trade, not plunder. Trade brings mutual understanding, communication and interdependence. It also brings legal systems for dialogue, resolving disputes and setting mutually agreed rules. Plunder is unsustainable and morally wrong. Wars break out when systems of trade break down. Nations just take what they want.

The Japanese oil embargo imposed by the US in 1941 was a response to Japan's expansionist policies in Asia. This effectively cut off Japan's access to crucial oil supplies and trade and was a major factor contributing to the attack on Pearl Harbor. History has important lessons.

Britain was the first major global power to abolish the slave trade. On 25 March 1807, the British Parliament passed the Slave Trade Act, making the slave trade illegal throughout the British Empire. While this act did not end slavery itself, it prohibited the trade of enslaved people. Britain abolished the slave trade due to a combination of moral, economic and political factors. The abolitionist movement was driven by moral and religious arguments and gained significant public support.

In practice, though, the trade in slaves was ended by the power and professionalism of the Royal Navy.

The Navy's West Africa Squadron was the main force in the fight against the slave trade, operating between 1808 and 1860. The squadron was based at Freetown in Sierra Leone and played a significant role in capturing slave ships and liberating the enslaved. Between 1808 and 1860, it captured around 1,600 slave ships and freed approximately 150,000 Africans.[1]

Incidentally, the US Congress made it illegal to import enslaved people from abroad on 1 January 1808. The act banning the slave trade was effective from the start of that year. Slavery, however, was only officially abolished within the US with the ratification of the Thirteenth Amendment to the Constitution on 6 December 1865. As in Britain, it was only ended by military means, by the Army of the Union defeating the Confederate Army in the American Civil War. Again, the lesson is clear: policy is nothing without the power to police it.

There is little point in having grand moral convictions unless you realise muscle is needed to carry them out. In any case, militaries fight better for a moral cause than they do an immoral one. Our military is representatively drawn from our own populations. If a war is unpopular with civilians, it will be unpopular with soldiers. This proved the case in Vietnam.

There are two important points here. In an uncertain world, you can say and think what you like, but if you can't implement or defend your principles with force, then nothing else matters. Close behind that is the moral ethos. If you do what you know to be right, just, good and true, then you become a reliable partner.

Commercial contracts may be written in ink, but military alliances are written in blood. If you are an unreliable player militarily, then you are unreliable commercially and culturally, too. All success is built on trust and reliability. These are the table stakes of an effective, commercially successful, nation state.

If you focus on defence, national resilience follows in its wake. This includes ownership of sovereign steel production, lower-cost energy and supply chain integrity.

The commercial factor applies within countries as well. For decades, the military has been a social escalator that takes people from the lower ranks to the higher ones. It fosters discipline, skills and camaraderie. It's a source of local as well as national pride. To join the military is still seen as joining something admired and popular.

In January 2024, the Army received the highest number of applications (over 10,000) for regular service. The reserve service has been transformed in both quality and quantity.

Of course, there are downsides and employment drawbacks. You don't join the military for money. It's not always an economic argument. It's one that must begin in our schools. When you believe strongly in something and its traditions, there are some things that are just more important.

You don't even have to believe in King and Country either. You can still serve in the military if you're a republican. After all, you are signing up to potentially lay down your life to protect the rights of those who may deeply disagree with you. Like so many aspects of the British way of life, it's contradictory. We will fight to the death for another person's right to say they disagree with us. The military has always welcomed those with strong beliefs.

The chief return on our military expenditure is really in what *doesn't* happen. We don't get invaded. We don't get pushed around by bullies. Our goods don't get intercepted as they travel between ports. No one thanks the military for what doesn't happen. We just take it for granted.

History is full of events which were unexpected. The military is our insurance against the unforeseen and the unimaginable. The events that currently surround us provide a live update on why history has not come to an end. Deterrence still matters.

Alliances are being formed and reformed. NATO is boosted by its most recent members, Finland and Sweden. Finland joined as the thirty-first member in April 2023 and Sweden followed in March 2024, becoming the thirty-second member. The US is quite right to question why it should provide a disproportionate amount of the organisation's military forces. This too was a tradition and an understanding in the nuclear age. America's protection of Europe was based on the fact that its nuclear weapons were held outside the US, which made a first strike on European soil far more likely.

More recently we have established new partnerships: a new Atlantic Charter, AUKUS, the Global Combat Air Programme with Italy and Japan. We are also exporting more. Our resolve and commitment to NATO has led the way in getting others to step up. Britain remains one of the only nations to operate both fifth-generation carriers and fifth-generation combat aircraft. It is only Britain and the US that operate the RC-135W Rivet Joint, a specialised electronic surveillance aircraft. This is a modified Boeing RC-135 with an extensive sensor suite for collecting and analysing intelligence, particularly signals intelligence and electronic intelligence. This has proved vital in Ukraine.

We are lucky in this country to have such an embedded military ethos, tradition and culture. It's important that we don't lose sight of that – we need to keep it strong and see its value. I was brought up around military people. My father was a member of the Parachute Regiment, while I have served in the Royal Naval Reserve (motto: *Si vis pacem, para bellum* or 'If you wish for peace, prepare for war'). We've turned a corner in recent times; our military has reached its lowest ebb of funding and now there is a consensus that it needs massive and rapid reinvestment and growth. This is music to the ears of those of us who have long campaigned for stronger armed forces. We have moved on from the why and the what to the how and the when.

We know the government is short of cash – that's why we will need to fund military expansion using the power of the private sector. Fortunately, there are many forward-thinking organisations that are ready for this moment. Again, our history helps us because we've been here before. We only need the military when we need them. Otherwise, we don't care. Kipling wrote about the relationship between the soldier and the civilian in this poem, written in 1890:

TOMMY

https://www.kiplingsociety.co.uk/poem/poems_tommy.htm

Incidentally, Kipling didn't coin the name Tommy. The Duke of Wellington was once asked to name a typical British soldier and he replied: 'Tommy Atkins'. It is from this that we derived the term 'Tommies'. The real Tommy Atkins died of his wounds, which consisted of a sabre cut to the head and a bullet through his lungs. His last words were to Wellington, as his general looked at him with pity and concern. 'It's all right, sir,' he said, 'it's all in a day's work.'

Some might say, well what if there isn't another war? Why do we need all this reinvestment? The answer is because investment in our defence industries is an each-way bet. Not only does it prevent wars but it also advances technology, stimulates research, generates engineers and is an escalator for talent.

The best example of this is the military expenditure in Silicon Valley in the US during the Cold War. This spawned an enormous expansion in computer technology, which led to some of the most powerful companies in the world. This is the prize open to us as the largest technology investment zone outside of Silicon Valley.

We should remind ourselves that California became the capital of the US military-industrial complex. Military spending drove the state's economic growth, bringing in new industries and with them housing developments, highways, offices, shopping centres and all of the other features that transformed the Californian landscape in the late 1950s. All of these developments were largely paid for by government dollars via the salaries of a large military workforce and revenues from military hardware and software from California tech businesses. In peacetime, the return on military investment is measurable. In wartime, the return is priceless in protecting everything we hold dear.

The state of California, even today, remains among the top recipients of defence contracting. For the 2019/20 fiscal year, according to the Office of Local Defense Community Cooperation report, California ranked third in total defence spending at $61 billion, behind Virginia ($64 billion) and Texas ($83 billion).[2] The leading business was the Northrop Grumman Corporation. Among its numerous defence products, the company makes the B21 Raider, the successor to the B2 Stealth Bomber, a variety of drones and the latest directed-energy weapons, including high-powered lasers.

The relationship between defence and business in the UK is a shadow of its former self, but the potential remains huge. It is one of the most exciting opportunities for investors – a long-term, stable, predictable environment with ready access to some of the most ingenious minds at the heart of a global trading network.

We can learn much from our traditions about how the future might turn out. The lessons are still there from history. If we look for instance at Nelson's navy, we can learn that it was the most technically advanced of its day. It was skilled, well-disciplined and trained. It was also supported by an enormous technology industry in the materials of the time – this included navigational science, meteorology, communications, metallurgy, cartography, propulsion technologies, logistics, ballistics, targeting technologies, differential calculus and trajectory analysis – even nutrition and specialist officer training.

This investment in technology is what we need again. The spin-off benefits would be felt in so many areas: commerce, finance, professional services, manufacturing and logistics.

If anyone wants to see the naval tradition writ large, pay a visit to the Trafalgar Night dinner (around 21 October) in the Painted Hall in the Old Royal Naval College at Greenwich. Designed by Christopher Wren, it is another UNESCO Heritage Site. It was completed between 1707 and 1726 by Sir James Thornhill and is one of the country's many wonders.

By far the best way of attending this event is by Thames Clipper. These are the riverboats that serve many destinations on the River Thames. Greenwich Pier is a short walk away from the college.

On the evening, beef is traditional, every table has a bottle of port, which is sometimes augmented by a bottle of rum, and consequently, the singing is hearty. The traditional songs are, of course, 'Rule Britannia' and 'Hearts of Oak'. I once witnessed a senior military officer quite literally sing himself off his chair and end up under the table laughing his head off. This, too, is part of the tradition. Deviation from dinner etiquette is frowned upon and may result in fines. One of the trickier traditions to adhere to is not popping to the loo until the command 'ease springs' is given at the end of the meal. This may have been designed to ensure diners didn't go large in the bar beforehand (although, more sensibly, it might be simply to make sure everyone is present when the Loyal Toast is called at the end of the meal).

Fortunately, the Royal Navy has the convention of sitting down during the Loyal Toast. This is because of a tradition dating back to King William IV, who, as a naval officer, often hit his head on deck beams when standing up to toast the monarch on board ships. He authorised all naval personnel to remain seated during the toast to avoid such discomfort.

The autumn brings battle commemorations. A large number of the notable actions the Royal Navy honours take place towards the end of the year. All armed forces personnel are particularly attuned to weather conditions. They will reflect on what their forebears must have felt going into action against an uncertain climate.

The twilight of the year is a time for reflection for a native of these isles. It means you are connected to something much bigger and beyond your control. You feel the change in season, just as Nelson's men would have done off Cadiz.

At such dinners, we talk about Nelson, about his men and about the ships in which they served, about triumph in battle and about what that meant – the founding of modern Britain. The Royal Navy was a guardian of free trade and an enabler of maritime exploration. It helped make Britain the workshop of the world. We needed the high seas to deliver our products and receive payments.

But there is something else about Nelson's victory which is peculiarly British. It was achieved collectively and personally, against the odds and in the face of many failures. Failure is a theme we dwell on. Not just ordinary but epic failure. We like plucky Brits. We cheer the underdog.

And this is what makes Nelson special. When he was a young man, he suffered several setbacks in his career – for instance, having discovered himself to be prone to sea sickness. No one talks about Nelson's throwing up over the side of the boat. Nor his scurvy or dysentery. No one talks about him being left on the beach between the wars when he was a young officer. No one talks about the time he spent as a boy living in Norfolk. No one talks about the pain that he suffered from multiple injuries or his disabilities. No one talks about his debts, his failed marriage or the fact that he was unsuccessful in getting into Parliament three times. No one, while passing the port, talks about the Dutch Navy's victory at Chatham when our fleet was burned by fast-moving catamarans. We do not celebrate failure and we do not celebrate defeat.

And yet, victory and Nelson are both the direct provenance of defeat and failure. How do we know this? Because some of our greatest countrymen who achieved our greatest triumphs have suffered defeat after defeat. It was Churchill himself who said that failure is not final. It is the ability to carry on that matters. Determination wins. So many of us will have had our successes, but if we're honest with each other, we learn the most from our failures. We have to treat failure in the same way that we treat victory and success because it's easy to cope with success.

What really matters is what you do when you're defeated. When you feel you cannot go on. When you have exhausted all that you have to give. When you have tried everything you can think of. It is such moments that our armed forces train for.

This is the test of the philosophy of a person and a nation. Not how well it fights in success. It's how well it rallies and fights in defeat, and there are many times in history when the causes look lost. It is a test for governments too. It comes down to will.

A short while ago, Ukraine was written off by most of the foreign offices of the Western world. Ukraine had other ideas. Europe by herself has all it needs to support Ukraine against Russian aggression. To date, she has not committed to using it.

This is a lesson that can be seen throughout history. From Henry V at Agincourt through to Winston Churchill after the fall of France. Just because the odds are stacked against you, it doesn't mean to say that defeat is a foregone conclusion.

This is why Nelson is such an important figure to the moral component of fighting. Anybody who knew Nelson would say that he considered himself to be a failure. He was a hypochondriac. He felt he was about to die. His vulnerability inspired loyalty. His emotional state was an essential part of his leadership.

So was love. He looked after those in his charge. Nelson bought blankets for his men from his own salary. On discovering that his signaller, John Pascoe, had missed the mail ship, he ordered a signal to be sent so that it would return to pick up the letter Pascoe had written to his family.

Nelson understood how people felt. He knew what people needed to feel. Perhaps because he had faced death so much, he knew what was vital in life.

One of the lesser-known tales about him concerns Emma Hamilton. Her husband needed to raise money and had decided to sell some art, including the Romney portrait of Emma as Circe. Did Nelson purchase it as a gift for her, as a romantic gesture of his affection and evidence of his means? No. He bought it but then attached a condition that Sir William Hamilton would tell Emma that he (Hamilton) couldn't bear to part with the painting. Nelson secretly bought the picture to prevent Emma's distress at losing an image of her painted at her most beautiful.

Nelson was not born into aristocracy or endless opportunity. Often, when people who don't normally get one are given a chance – that's when the sparks start to fly. Trafalgar Night doesn't just celebrate a ship called *Victory* and a historic sea battle. It asks us to consider the present and the future we hope for.

Trafalgar is not past, it's prologue. All the fighting spirit that Nelson and his men displayed is still alive and well. Not just in the rank and file of our armed forces, but in every Briton. Trafalgar Night is not confined to mess dinners. It is in pubs, clubs and social media accounts across the land. It is celebrated by anyone who can see opportunities in the future and remain unafraid of failure. It's a celebration of those who carry on, who look after those in their care, those who are humble in victory and who open up their hearts to inspiration.

The captured French Admiral, Pierre-Charles Villeneuve, said: 'To any other Nation, the loss of a Nelson would have been irreparable, but in the British Fleet off Cadiz, *every Captain was a Nelson.*'

Trafalgar Night events are held across the UK and around the world. Collingwood, who took over command when Nelson was wounded, is also remembered with a toast at his monument at Tynemouth in the north-east.

HMS *Victory* remains a commissioned ship of the fleet at Portsmouth Historic Dockyard. It is also a national focal point on Trafalgar Night, along with Nelson's tomb in St Paul's Cathedral.

Later in the year, Pickle Night is held on 6 November. This is an evening specifically for non-commissioned officers. This was born of practicality. During the 1970s at HMS Nelson, an onshore base in Portsmouth, the president of the Warrant and Chief Petty Officers' Mess asked to hold a Trafalgar Night event. But how to find a prestigious guest to propose the toast, when everyone would be at the commissioned officers' event? Vice Admiral Sir John Lea suggested they should celebrate the arrival of HMS *Pickle*, the ship that bore Nelson's body back to England with news of the victory and the tradition was born.

By the way, the Royal Navy needs little reminder about the importance of minorities or the potential to be found in unorthodoxy. Nelson was a disabled, one-eyed, hypochondriac adulterer who suffered from chronic seasickness. Perhaps the best DEI lesson of all can be found in our own history books.

HEARTS OF OAK

https://www.youtube.com/watch?v=4NXFCDgyanA

RULE BRITANNIA

https://www.youtube.com/watch?v=akbzRuZmqVM

Trafalgar Night is one example of combat remembered in military traditions. It has to be said that the evening is as popular with the Royal Navy as it is with the Army and the Royal Air Force (who hold similar events, such as the RAF's Battle of Britain dinners in September each year). It celebrates British bravery and sacrifice in combat, so its message is common to all who serve the crown.

Our military is rightly revered because of its ethos and commitment. They are the very best of us. How can we say that? Because combat is the ultimate test of a person. Preparing for it is as much a matter of tradition as it is training. The whole ethos of the military is that teams of people are more difficult to defeat than individuals. Traditions bring people together. So does discipline. These are the cornerstones of extraordinary performance under pressure. Teams are drilled and trained to respond almost by reflex – quickly, precisely and professionally. It's essential for survival. In times of crisis, the routine and the traditions kick in and you carry on.

Thus, the military is the ultimate in teamwork. In basic training, everything is designed to make you work as a team. Everyone is trained and treated the same. From this comes basic unit cohesion. You eat together. You sleep together. You dress together. You rehearse tasks together. It teaches people to follow orders quickly without question. This means you also need to have complete faith and trust in your leaders.

No matter which service you join, the training is similar. All success depends on everyone in the team working together. This is not just about one service. Each service depends on the other to constitute a military fighting force. No individual, no general, no admiral, no air marshal is above the team. Individuals are only venerated when they bring victory to the team.

There is always tension between the military's need for cohesion and the public's need for heroes. It's a delicate balance. Even when awards are made, it's quite common for the recipient to dedicate it to their mates or unit rather than take credit themselves.

The rule is generally that difference and personality are allowed but only at the unit level. Apart from unit morale, this is also because you need to be able to recognise certain specialisms under combat conditions – for instance, musicians, who were signallers on ancient fields of battle.

It's not just the insignia but also where it's worn. For officers, this is on the shoulder, signifying the weight of responsibility. For other ranks, it's on the arm. Historically, enlisted personnel were more likely to roll up their sleeves to work, so their rank is displayed on the upper part of the sleeve.

Most of the British Army uses the rank of private to denote the lowest level. A handful of regiments use other terms – such as 'Kingsman' or, for the Rifles, 'Rifleman' – instead of 'private', a notable one being the Duke of Lancaster's Regiment. This is a custom inherited from the King's Regiment. It was officially sanctioned in 1951 but was also used informally prior to this.

The King's Man is also the term given to the Royal Marines Cadet who is awarded the King's Badge. This is an honour reserved for the very best Royal Marines of their training class. At the passing-out parade at Lympstone, the honour is awarded to the leading recruit. Not every course has someone of that calibre and so in some years, it has not been awarded.

Some of the traditions and customs of the UK armed forces are on display for all to enjoy, whether these be set-piece events that take place year in and year out, or the distinct uniforms worn by branches and units when on parade. However, much is hidden from public view and not understood. These traditions are based on practicality. The colour of a uniform or a method of training is designed to make a soldier, sailor or airman more operationally effective. However, uniforms, traditions and customs are also designed to form bonds and tell a story.

Perhaps the most recent and starkest example of this can be seen in the modernisation of the Ukrainian Army's military uniform. Modern updates have been designed to erase reference to Russian tradition, instead highlighting the traditions of Cossack uniforms. This can be seen in the tailoring, the arrangement of buttons and changes to headgear. The story is clear. Ukrainians are not Russians. Ukrainians have their own culture and identity and they always have. And those who fight for Ukraine's freedom personify those traditions and embody that history.

The Russo-Ukrainian war illustrates an important point. How could a military force so inferior in number and materials hold off the advancing Russian Army? The answer is resolution and cohesion. Culture made a difference, too.

Allan English, in his 2004 analysis of military culture, claimed culture to be the 'bedrock of military effectiveness' and the difference between competing nations being able to use their technology effectively.[3]

The UK's defence doctrine places great importance on the moral aspects of an effective fighting force, viewing it as more important than physical or mental preparedness. It is the parent of courage. The doctrine sets out that

> the warfighting ethos is the characteristic spirit of the cultures of our Armed Forces manifested in our attitudes and aspirations. It provides us with the vital moral, emotional and spiritual capacity to overcome fear and cope with war's visceral and highly ambiguous nature.

In 2023, the UK's doctrine was updated to place even greater emphasis on this moral component, in light of a more complex and confused international landscape and new types of emerging grey zone warfare. The update noted the importance of traditions and customs:

> The deep and distinctive organisational cultures of defence have emerged and evolved over centuries. Comprising complex traditions,

practices, organisational structures, artefacts and unwritten norms, our cultures underpin effective fighting power and our warfighting ethos.[4]

A military can only be as moral as the politicians commanding it. This is why troops can never be committed lightly. Lives are at stake. When politicians are involved in committing forces, it is one of the most solemn and humbling occasions. Principles and policies are fine, but someone has to defend them.

Defence customs and traditions are there to help identify, communicate, train, improve, inspire and prepare but also to create the conditions in the hearts of ordinary men and women to do the unthinkable.

Unless you or a member of your family is a part of the armed forces, it is unlikely that you will be familiar with the different organisations that constitute them. Whereas the Royal Navy and the Royal Air Force pride themselves on similarities, the Army takes pride in its differences. It's a crime if two naval personnel are not in the same rig. For the Army, it's a crime if they are. Let's briefly look at the structures of the armed services.

THE ROYAL NAVY

The Royal Navy is divided into six branches: the Royal Marines, Royal Fleet Auxiliary, Surface Fleet, Fleet Air Arm, Royal Navy Submarine Service and the Maritime Reserve.

The Royal Marines are experts at amphibious warfare and highly specialist tasks, such as security for the nuclear deterrent. A comparatively large number of marines go on to serve in the special forces, in particular the Special Boat Service.

The Royal Fleet Auxiliary is part of the Naval Service, but its members are civilians. While they train at Royal Navy establishments, they do not undertake weapons training and in the course of their regular duties they do not carry firearms. They provide logistical support to the Navy, including supplies, refuelling and maintenance.

The Surface Fleet requires little explanation; it comprises all surface vessels used in maritime operations.

The Submarine Service has several prime roles. These include the operation of the nuclear deterrent, intelligence gathering and covert operations. The submarine fleet is the UK's only stealth medium.

The Fleet Air Arm operates aircraft for reconnaissance, anti-submarine warfare, carrier and littoral strike, and search and rescue.

Finally, there are the Royal Navy and Royal Marines Reserves. Their shape and specialisms are designed to supplement the regular fleet. Their tasks range from counter-terrorism to anti-piracy work.

The shape and specialisms are designed to supplement the regular fleet. Within these branches, there are specialist trades. In engineering, you can specialise in aircraft, communications marine engineering, submarines or weapon systems. In logistics and personnel, you can be an expert in supply chain, catering, physical training or be a chaplain, writer (administrator) or police officer. There are a variety of professions within the health and medical branch, from being a biomedical scientist or environmental health officer to a radiographer or dental professional. And then there are warfare specialisms. These range from meteorology and oceanography to mine warfare to aviation or other specialisms in handling ships or fighting them. There is also, within the Royal Marines, the band service, which is integral to every tradition the Navy remembers.

It's worth looking in detail at one particular area of the Navy to illustrate its uniqueness.

THE ROYAL NAVY SUBMARINE SERVICE

Submariners are a special breed of warrior. They work in the dark depths of the oceans around the clock, in all conditions. The British submariner plays a leading role in the nightmares of all those that mean us harm.
LIEUTENANT COMMANDER HUGO MITCHELL-HEGGS, HEAD OF HUMAN PERFORMANCE IN THE ROYAL NAVY SUBMARINE SERVICE

Although a relatively young service, traditions and customs onboard a submarine have a distinct culture and history. Submariners are still known as 'pirates' because when they first started to be used as warships in 1901, Admiral Sir Arthur Wilson said that they were 'under-handed, unfair and damned un-English' and that 'captured enemy submariners should be hanged as pirates'.

For this reason, the Jolly Roger is still allowed on hunter-killer/ attack submarines. The name of the flag may have originated from the French phrase *joli rouge* meaning 'pretty red', a reference to its original blood-red colour, which in English became 'Jolly Roger'. During the First World War, Lieutenant Commander Max Horton (later Admiral Sir Max Horton, Commander in Chief Western Approaches in World War II) began flying the Jolly Roger after returning from success- ful submarine patrols in his submarine HMS *E9*. Initially, he flew a separate flag for each successful patrol but later switched to a single large flag, onto which symbols were sown to indicate the submarine's achievements. The practice was never approved by the Admiralty, but they were unable to stop it.[5]

The unusual lifestyle was also set by the imperatives of the service. Different lights onboard told you which part of the day it was.

The food is worthy of special note. It tells you what day it is: curry on a Wednesday, fish and chips on Friday, steak on Saturday, roast lunch on Sunday, followed by pizza and a pub quiz in the Senior Rates Mess on Sunday night. This even extends into entertainment. There's horse racing, where every department creates a horse and dresses a jockey for a dice-rolling horse race night (with some gambling/charity dona- tions). Other delicacies include 'the train smash' where occasionally all the leftovers from breakfast get blitzed into a bucket (sausages, bacon, tinned tomatoes, baked beans) and offered at lunch to avoid waste and provide another option. This is supplemented by a 'salad', which is made with Branston pickle, bacon and sausages or the cooked krill that comes from cleaning the seawater filters. There are 'Middle Watch' spuds – potatoes baked on the main engines with cheese, butter and anything else that can be stolen from the wardroom pantry fridge.

Communications are drastically limited. This comes down to family grams, which are a maximum of sixty words in length and can only be sent one way, from family to submariner, once per week. So, if you don't get your family gram, you can understand how concerning it is.

Captain (retired) Paddy Parvin illustrates the difficulties of life in submarines:

> I mean who in their right mind puts a high-power density nuclear reactor in a tin can, brimming with explosives and high-pressure systems, upwards of a hundred and thirty men and women, and then throws it into the Atlantic and expects it not only to survive but to thrive and show the rest of the world how it's done? We do.
>
> Operating in the Royal Navy's Silent Service requires exceptional skill, resilience and discretion, as missions often involve extended periods submerged in isolation and the utmost secrecy. The unforgiving environment of a submarine fosters unmatched camaraderie, banter, a borderline-sick sense of humour and, above all, trust among crew members, while the technical complexity of their work demands a high degree of professionalism and adaptability. Combined with a proud heritage of excellence and innovation in undersea warfare, British submariners embody a distinctive blend of toughness, ingenuity and dedication to duty.

Another peculiarity of the Submarine Service and wider Naval Service is the board game of Uckers. This is very similar to (but definitely isn't) Ludo. Getting eight pieces on Uckers is the equivalent of being seven-balled in pool. Your name gets written on the back of the board to etch your disgrace in eternity.

THE SUBMARINER'S LIFE

https://www.youtube.com/watch?v=teibnMTikuM

The submariner's insignia is the 'dolphin', which is earned by undertaking the arduous submarine qualification. This can take years to get to from joining the service. Submariners need to demonstrate they understand how every system on board works, how to make it safe in the event of an emergency and have broader knowledge of how the submarine operates, as well as emergency procedures etc. It culminates in an oral board that can go on for six hours. Once earned, you are a trusted member of the ship's company (and not a passenger/'oxygen thief').

In the Submarine Service, the Dolphins Ceremony is a significant event. This is where newly qualified submariners receive their warfare insignia, a badge depicting two dolphins and a crowned anchor. This insignia signifies a specialisation earned after completing extensive training, marking a milestone in their career. The ceremony involves the tradition of presenting the 'dolphins' in a glass of rum. Instead of a senior officer pinning them on to the chest, the submariner drinks the tot and catches the badge in their teeth. It is a proud moment for the individual and the submarine crew.

THE ROYAL AIR FORCE

The Royal Air Force (RAF) is divided into squadrons and units. There are currently eighty-six active squadrons and thirty-two operational units. Each squadron has its own crest and motto. Some old and famous squadrons have been resurrected for modern purposes. For example, 617 squadron (motto: *Apres moi le deluge*), which flew the Dambusters raid under Guy Gibson, along with other missions, was revived in 2018 to fly the fifth-generation F35 lightning aircraft. The unit is composed of both RAF and Royal Navy personnel and operates from the Royal Navy's Queen Elizabeth-class aircraft carriers.

THE RAF MARCH PAST

https://www.youtube.com/watch?v=5QaxpOQAWOY

There is no fixed size to an RAF unit; its size is determined by its task. Squadrons are subdivided into smaller organisations known as flights.

Squadrons and units are grouped together and co-located where there is synergy between their outputs: for example, training, policing or operations. These, in turn, are organised into groups and there are currently four.

No. 1 Group is focused on generating the fighting force and getting it into the sky, including the Air Mobility Force, the Combat Air Force and the ISTAR (intelligence surveillance targeting and reconnaissance) Force. It also has aircraft and parachute display teams. No. 2 Group is mainly responsible for the RAF's stations themselves, from which No. 1 Group operate. No. 11 Group provides command and control of air operations worldwide, including air defence of the UK. No. 22 Group provides recruit and specialist training and is also home to the Air Cadets.

Alongside all of this is UK Space Command, which sits inside the RAF in much the same way that the groups do. There are also Expeditionary Air Wings, comprising all staff required to support, make ready and then operate deployed fleets of aircraft.

THE RAF BURNING PIANO

The tradition of the RAF burning pianos reflects the unique culture and camaraderie within the service. This peculiar custom is believed to have originated during the Second World War. The exact origins are somewhat murky, but several popular stories attempt to explain it.

One widely accepted tale suggests that the tradition began as a form of tribute to fallen comrades. During the war, RAF pilots would often gather around a piano in the mess hall to sing and play music, fostering a sense of unity and morale. When a pilot was lost in combat, burning a piano became a symbolic gesture of mourning and respect, representing the loss of a member of their close-knit community.

Regardless of its true origins, the piano-burning tradition has endured and evolved over the years. Today, it is often performed during significant RAF events and ceremonies, serving as a reminder of the service's rich history and the bonds formed among its members.

Although these modern events are more staged and less impulsive, it is nevertheless not uncommon to see the piano in an RAF mess chained to the wall and clearly labelled 'Do Not Burn', suggesting the impulsiveness remains.

RAF PIANO BURNING

https://www.youtube.com/watch?v=2yFRDb29mus

THE ARMY

The British Army is organised into the Household Cavalry and Armoured Corps, infantry, special forces, combat support and Army Air Corps, combat service support and the overseas regiments. The regimental system has been described as the bricks from which the British Army is made. But this system has more than an administrative purpose. These regiments are permanent organisations, each with its own history, traditions and insignia. Although the shape and size of the British Army has changed dramatically over the centuries, many of these traditions still survive and have been adopted by successor units. The stories and the values such customs relate to are reflected in their rituals, insignia and uniforms.

The Household Cavalry and Royal Armoured Corps consists of the Line Cavalry, the Royal Tank Regiment and the Yeomanry. The Household Cavalry is a regiment of the British Army, composed of the two most senior regiments: the Life Guards and the Blues and Royals. The latter is the historic amalgamation of two regiments raised in 1661 – the Royal Horseguards and the 1st Royal Dragoons, which are a heavy cavalry regiment.

HCav (as it is known) is divided into two units: the Household Cavalry Regiment (HCR) and the Household Cavalry Mounted Regiment (HCMR). The HCR is the operational unit, providing armoured reconnaissance capabilities, while the HCMR is primarily involved in ceremonial duties. Each regiment has its own traditions and uniforms. The Household Cavalry Foundation supports serving soldiers, operational casualties, veterans, their dependents and the welfare of its retired horses.

This is Giles Stibbe OBE, director of the Household Calvary Foundation, talking about the history of the ceremonial dress as worn in Ripley's portrait 'The Squadron Leader of The Blues and Royals', which graces the front of this book. You'll find more about Ripley on the dust jacket.

https://www.youtube.com/watch?v=KdeZBIvHC9I&t=28s

You will see the Household Cavalry performing the Changing of the Guard ceremony each day at Horse Guards in Whitehall. The Life Guards were originally made up of only gentleman troopers, but from the 1780s, commoners were allowed to join. The term 'cheesemonger' is the phrase for new members of the Life Guards. It came from those who worked in a trade prior to joining.

The Line Cavalry is made up from the 1st Queen's Dragoon Guards, the Royal Scots Dragoon Guards, the Royal Dragoon Guards and the Light Dragoons, the Queen's Royal Hussars, the King's Royal Hussars and the Royal Lancers. The Yeomanry consist of the Royal Yeomanry, the Royal Wessex Yeomanry, the Queen's Own Yeomanry and the Scottish and North Irish Yeomanry.

The infantry consists of the Foot Guards, line infantry and rifles, airborne infantry in the form of the Parachute Regiment (the Paras) and special operations in the form of the Ranger Regiment.

The Grenadier Guards, the Coldstream Guards, the Scots Guards, the Irish Guards and the Welsh Guards form the Foot Guards. These are the guards you'll see taking part in the Trooping of the Colour.

The Royal Regiment of Scotland, the Princess of Wales's Royal Regiment, the Duke of Lancaster's Regiment, the Royal Regiment of Fusiliers, the Royal Anglican Regiment, the Royal Yorkshire Regiment, the Royal Welsh, the Mercian Regiment, the Royal Irish Regiment, the Royal Gurkha Rifles and the Rifles form the line infantry. The Rifles were known as the M4 Rifles, in reference to the motorway that runs the length of Berkshire and Wiltshire.

The Mercian Regiment's mascot, a Swaledale Ram known as 'Private Derby', is on the official strength of the regiment. As one of very few official mascots, he has his own regimental number and is funded by the Crown. He is even on the ration strength and draws his rations like any other soldier. The Paras, meanwhile, have 'Pegasus', a miniature pony of the Thelwell variety.

Army special forces consist of the Special Air Service and the Special Reconnaissance Regiment.

Combat support in an Army Air Corps consists of the Army Air Corps, the Royal Regiment of Artillery, the Corps of the Royal Engineers (commonly known as the Sappers – the engineering arm of the British Army), the Royal Corps of Signals, Intelligence Corps, the Honourable Artillery Company and the Royal Monmouthshire Royal Engineers.

Combat support consists of ten regiments or units. The Royal Logistic Corps, the Corps of Royal Electrical and Mechanical Engineers, the Adjunct General Corps (which encapsulates education and human resource services, legal services, guards staff and police), the Royal Corps of Army Music, the Royal Army Chaplains' Department, Small Arms School Corps (providing instruction to infantry weapons trainers throughout the Army, in order to maintain proficiency in the use of small arms and support weapons and in range management), Royal Army Physical Training Corps, General Service Corps, the Royal Army Medical Service and the Royal Army Veterinary Corps.

Finally, there are the overseas regiments such as the Royal Gibraltar Regiment, the Royal Bermuda Regiment, the Royal Montserrat Defence Force, which is the home defence unit of the British Overseas Territory of Montserrat, the Cayman Islands Regiment, the Turks and Caicos Regiment and the Falkland Islands Defence Force, a locally maintained volunteer defence unit.

The three services make up the UK's defence capabilities. They work together with the Ministry of Defence (MOD) and civilian support organisations. They also work alongside many other organisations and, in particular, the UK's intelligence services. These include MI6, primarily concerned with foreign intelligence; MI5, which protects the UK against domestic threats; GCHQ, which specialises in signals intelligence and reconnaissance; and Defence Intelligence (DI), providing products to the MOD.

Maggie Smith sang about the various divisions when playing a First World War music hall recruitment singer.

OH WHAT A LOVELY WAR!

https://www.youtube.com/watch?v=ynEWZF1bkLQ

UNIFORMS

Until the English Civil War, the only elements of the British military that wore uniforms were small security units charged with protecting the Royal Family. These were rather like the Yeomen Warders, who now protect the Tower of London. Apart from these, there was only a part-time militia for home defence and occasional expeditions abroad.

In 1645, the Parliamentarian New Model Army adopted russet, a rough homespun fabric, and this tradition persisted in the English Army of the Restoration. Oliver Cromwell recruited men for the New Model Army based on their dedication and prowess, rather than their wealth or name. He famously said: 'I'd rather have a plain, russet-coated Captain that knows what he fights for and loves what he knows.'

In parallel, Scotland created a standing army, which, after the Acts of Union, merged with the English Army in 1707. After the Crimean War, what was known as the British Board of Ordnance was amalgamated into the British Army. This consisted of the Royal Artillery, the Royal

Engineers, Royal Sappers and Miners and other units responsible for logistics.

The Scottish Army's colours were originally grey, but it began to adopt the red of the English Army in the 1680s. This practicality and consistency did not last long. Following the Napoleonic wars, uniforms became more elaborate and distinct. From 1873, a brighter shade of scarlet was adopted into all the uniforms.

Other colours were later introduced. In the nineteenth century, the elite Hungarian Hussars and Polish Lancers, who wore blue coats, inspired the creation of new units in the British Army. Riflemen wore green for reasons of camouflage.

As weapons with greater accuracy and range were developed, camouflage became important. In 1902, the British Army adopted a universal khaki uniform, and in 1938, British Army battle dress, as it was known, became the prototype combat uniform for many armies around the world. This was most famously associated with the Brodie helmet. This is a steel combat helmet designed and patented in London in 1915 by John Leopold Brodie. A modified form of it became the Steel Helmet, Mark I in Britain and the M1917 Helmet in the US. Traditionally, it was nicknamed the battle bowler, Tommy helmet, tin hat and in the US, the doughboy helmet. The German Army called it the *Salatschüssel* (salad bowl).

With military roots dating back to the 1800s, khaki originated when Henry Lumsden, a British Lieutenant, and his subaltern William Hodson pioneered the use of a drab-coloured uniform for field service that came to be known as khaki. He traded in his red felt uniform for something cooler and more comfortable during his and his troops' time in India. Using a plant dye called Mazari, they dyed their cotton pants to help blend in with landscapes. One of the reasons full dress was phased out was that scarlet cloth required expensive cochineal dye.

Full dress is the most traditional ceremonial order worn by the British Army. It usually consists of a coloured, high-necked tunic and elaborate headwear. They are based on pre-1914 uniforms and each regiment and corps has its own pattern.

Modern regiments such as the Army Air Corps still incorporate a nod to the traditional in their uniform. Gloves are either white in the case of the Rifles or black in the case of the Royal Gurkha rifles, the Royal Army Chaplains' Department and the Royal Irish Regiment. The Life Guards all wear white leather gauntlets when on horseback. This includes the Blues and Royals, the Queen's Royal Dragoons, the Royal Scots Guards, the Royal Dragoon Guards and the Royal Lancers.

Although it was withdrawn from general issue at the start of the First World War, full dress is still 'the ultimate statement of tradition and regimental identity in uniform' as described in the Army dress regulations. It is worn regularly by those parts of the Army most involved in ceremonial occasions.

All uniforms in the armed forces celebrate history, specialisms, length of service and their current and former deployments. The variety and complexity of Army uniforms do something beyond practical communications. The variance may partly lie in practical constraints – for example, shortages of a particular fabric – but this does not solely explain either the variety nor the celebration of it.

For an organisation that prides itself on consistency and fighting as a whole, it has a remarkable tolerance for self-expression. Uniforms are a link to where we're from and what we're good at. They honour what went before us. They keep alive the connection between those who served our country and those who currently do. Perhaps it is because the Army has always been the largest element of our armed forces that this becomes of paramount importance.

During the Napoleonic wars, the Royal Navy came close to the size of the Army, at just 30,000 men smaller. By the end of the Second World War, the fleet stood at 861,000 men, compared to almost 3 million in the Army.

Historically, musicians were a vital means of communication on the battlefield and so their uniforms were designed to stand out. They would have laced coats and different colours. This extra bling can still be seen today in the Infantry Regiment Corps of Drums and in the different-coloured helmet plumes worn by the trumpeters in the Household Cavalry. Today, it is only military musicians that wear shoulder wings.

Depending on regiment and rank, you'll see a range of accessories. These include cocked hats, metal helmets with plumes of various colours, black fur busbies with different coloured plumes, caps, bearskins, feathered bonnets, berets and caubeens, pith helmets and hackles.

If that wasn't enough, each regiment has an allotted facing colour or inside lining folded back on itself. These indicate and identify a regiment where full dress isn't worn or if that regiment has never had a design of full dress, as in the case of the Intelligence Corps, the SAS or the Special Reconnaissance Regiment. Neither do they currently have a design for mess dress (formal evening wear).

For the Army, frock coats may be worn by officers of senior rank for formal occasions but not when on parade or in command of troops. In contrast, Navy grey coats are worn by officers on parade. Of course, one type of frock coat would be a wasted opportunity for confusion. Officers of the Household Division, Honourable Artillery Company and King's Troop wear a different style that is single-breasted, with ornate black braiding and loops. Directors of music and bandmasters wear a similar style if they are affiliated with cavalry regiments and others wear plainer double-breasted coats. Further complexity is added with different colours and fabrics.

Different buttons were not enough complexity. Why not space them differently, too? This brings us to another icon of British life – the guards. You can identify the guards easily by counting their tunic buttons. Grenadier Guards have buttons in a single line. Coldstream Guards (the oldest continuously serving regiment in the Army) have buttons in twos. Scots Guards have them in threes. Irish Guards have them in fours and Welsh Guards have them in fives.

The five regiments of foot guards can also be distinguished by the colour and placement of the plume on their bearskins and their collar badges. Specifically, the Grenadier Guards have a white plume on the left, the Coldstream Guards have a red plume on the right, the Irish Guards have a blue plume on the right, the Welsh Guards have a white/green/white plume on the left and the Scots Guards have no plume.

THE FIVE REGIMENTS OF THE ROYAL GUARD – UNIFORMS EXPLAINED

https://www.youtube.com/watch?v=bA43ZYB2Vf0

Number One Dress originated in the late nineteenth century from the undress uniforms for semi-formal or ordinary duty occasions. This is worn on the most formal occasions, by senior officers and aides to the Royal Family. The modern version was issued for the 1937 coronation and was intended to be a more economical version of full-dress uniforms. Units participating in the 1953 coronation wore the uniform too.

Number Two Service Dress is worn for formal duties by all units. Differences can be seen in the colour of badges, the use of coloured cloth backings, lanyards, badges, coloured socks and buttons and whether a leather Sam Browne belt is worn – or in the case of the Queen's Dragoon Guards, one made of pigskin or a sash.

Differences persist with warm weather dress and even combat dress.

If complexity and difference are the watchwords of Army uniforms, then consistency, simplicity and practicality sum up the other two. Indeed, it is not just consistency between branches and units within the service but also between the Royal Navy and others. Royal Navy uniform could be said to be the prototype for navies across the globe, especially those with Commonwealth or British Empire connections.

Navy uniforms were first introduced by the Admiralty in 1748 for officers and in 1857 for ratings. Until 1890, ratings wore blue jackets. In 1997, there was a major programme to standardise all ceremonial uniforms for ratings, the first time in history that this was done.

Modern-day uniforms consist of ceremonial day dress worn by a handful of senior officers. Number one dress is worn on ceremonial occasions. Number two dress or mess dress is worn for formal dinners. Number three dress is worn for general duties by officers. Number four dress is the Navy equivalent of combat uniform. Finally, number five dress consists of job-specific kit, including the multi-terrain or camouflage pattern. There is also a white uniform worn in the tropics. For ceremonial duties, grey coats are still worn.

The executive curl, or Elliot's Eye, is the ring above the gold lace indicating an officer's rank, worn on their sleeves or on rank slides worn on their shoulders. One story is that it is in memory of Captain George Elliot, who, when wounded in the arm in the Crimean War, used the gold on his sleeve as a sling. There are also theories that Elliot's Eye refers to the method of making an eye in a hemp cable and is said to have been introduced into the service by the Honourable William Elliot, a member of the Board of Admiralty in 1800 and 1801. It may perhaps best be explained as the simplest possible form of the various loops, trefoils, Austrian and Hungarian knots that were popular embellishments on service uniforms at the time.

Braiding is used to differentiate between the Royal Navy, the Royal Navy Reserve and the Royal Fleet Auxiliary. The Royal Navy Reserve was formed in 1859 and was distinguished by the width of the braiding, being half what it was for the regulars. The braid formed two waved lines as opposed to the single braid worn by the regulars. In place of the curl, reservists had a six-pointed star. In 1903, this was modified for the Royal Naval Volunteer Reserve, including the curl becoming a square.

Officers in the Women's Royal Naval Service wore sky-blue braiding formed into a diamond-shaped curl. The Royal Fleet Auxiliary also uses a diamond shape in its executive curl. In 2007, the last distinctions in insignia between regular and reserve services were eliminated, with officers of the reserve no longer wearing the letter 'R' in their executive curl.

The history of naval uniforms was born from practicality. Ratings' uniforms consisted of a jumper, square-neck T-shirt, lanyard and collar. Bell bottoms and flared trousers were worn. You can't climb rigging in tight trousers.

Like the Navy, RAF uniforms were consistent. The predominant colours are blue grey, Wedgwood blue and crab fat blue. Number one uniform is service or formal dress, number two uniform is working service dress (number seven in warm weather), number three uniform is operational clothing, numbers four, five, six and eight are various mess dresses, nine, ten and eleven are uniforms for the music service, and twelve, thirteen and fourteen are for physical training or flying.

The RAF was established as an independent standalone service in 1918. The initial pale blue cloth used was available at low cost, given that a large amount had been produced for the imperial Russian cavalry – however, the Bolshevik Revolution had other ideas. Soon the pale blue colour was discontinued; it was deeply unpopular as it was highly impractical. It was replaced with blue grey, which has remained in use to this day.

A key distinction between the RAF and the other services is that all ranks wear a starched collar and tie. Officers were distinguished from airmen through cap badges, patches and the type of fabric used in the uniforms. Airmen were also expected to wear ordinary shoes, with only officers wearing shoes with toe caps. The gloves were different as well, with officers wearing brown leather ones and airmen knitted woollen ones.

One common theme between each of the services is the need to rename something or someone with a nickname. Nicknames reflect our culture. They point to our traditions, habits, lifestyle and ideas. They are a rebellion against officialdom. If senior leadership has named something, the troops will rename it.

This applies to military formations, too. The Royal Berkshire Regiment were known as the Biscuit Boys because of their close proximity to the Huntley and Palmers factory, who were at the time suppliers to the British Army. The Wiltshire Regiment's earliest nickname was the Splashers. This referred to an incident at Carrickfergus during the Seven Years' War when they ran out of ammunition and were forced to melt their buttons, or a 'splash', into musket balls. They were also known as the Moonrakers. According to Wiltshire legend, customs officials had captured some locals pulling kegs of alcohol out of a pond using rakes. Their defence was that they were actually using their tools to retrieve cheese, which looked like the reflection of the moon in the water.

The second battalion of the Wiltshire Regiment, or the 99th Foot, was asked in 1858 to guard Queen Victoria's pavilion in Aldershot. This earned them the nickname 'The Queen's Pets'. The expression 'dressed to the nines' is a reference to the 99th because their uniforms were kept in such an immaculate condition.

The Duke of Edinburgh's Royal Regiment were the Farmers Boys. Their first regiment, with the abbreviation 1 DERR, became known as the 'Wonders'.

Perhaps the single greatest moment in *University Challenge*'s history was in answer to this question:

https://www.youtube.com/watch?v=c5-6F42y3Hk

The answer was not homosexuals, but regiments of the British Army. The full list of renamed Army regiments can be found here:

https://en.wikipedia.org/wiki/List_of_nicknames_of_British_Army_regiments#A

The Royal Navy also has a word for everything:

https://arkroyal.net/index.php?option=com_content&view=article&id=24&Itemid=145

It's worth noting that nicknames aren't always consistent across the different NATO countries. If you are told to stop 'wanking' by someone in the American air force, it means stop whingeing.

THE CHELSEA PENSIONERS

The Chelsea Pensioners are distinguished veterans of the Army who reside at the Royal Hospital Chelsea (RHC) in London. The Pensioners are instantly recognisable around Chelsea by their scarlet tunics and tricorn hats. The hospital was founded in 1681 by virtue of a royal warrant signed by King Charles II. Construction of the RHC commenced in 1682, with the first Chelsea Pensioners moving in in 1692. It was built by Sir Christopher Wren, under the commission of King Charles II, in what was then the site of an old theological college, near the village of Chelsea. These men and women have served the nation with honour and in their retirement have chosen to become part of a unique and historic community that offers not just a place to live but a home, filled with camaraderie, dignity and service.

Any former soldier of the British Army over state pension age who is facing spending their advanced years alone can apply for residence at the Royal Hospital as a Chelsea Pensioner. While provision was primarily for non-commissioned ranks, former commissioned officers can join, although they revert to their last substantive 'other rank'.

The Chelsea Pensioners have some unusual traditions, such as saluting with their left hand when parading before the Reviewing Officer on Founder's Day in front of the statue of King Charles II. This may date back to Queen Victoria, who said when her troops saluted her from her left-hand side, she wanted to see their faces.

The Pensioners have a tradition of the stirring of the Christmas pudding, which has taken place for over eighty years. Held in the Great Hall, this festive occasion begins with the Royal Hospital band and Christmas music. The Pensioners and staff gather to add ingredients – seventy eggs, five kilograms of currants and fourteen pints of Guinness plus rum, brandy and port – to a giant mixing bowl. The chaplain blesses these ingredients before they are mixed and the pudding is later cooked in the Royal Hospital kitchen.

Dating back to 1949, the Returned Services League of Australia have donated a Christmas cake to the Royal Hospital. Initially, this was done as a token of respect and affection for our 'old soldiers' who had served alongside the 'Diggers' in the two world wars and thereafter. More recently, the cake donation is made by the League from different states each year by rotation and now celebrates the enduring friendship between the UK and Australia.

They also have the ceremony of the Christmas cheeses. This is an event dating back over 300 years. Originating from a local cheesemonger's gift to the 'Red Breasts of Chelsea', this ceremony has been upheld with the support of Dairy UK since 1959. It features entertainment, including performances by surprise guests, speeches from the governor and the Dairy UK chairman and a blessing from the chaplain. The highlight is the ceremonial cutting of a large British cheese by a Pensioner, followed by a festive celebration with canapés, bubbly and the singing of 'The Quartermaster's Stores'.

The Royal Hospital's historic buildings, such as the Great Hall and the Long Wards, have been meticulously restored. The Great Hall, with its mural of Charles II on horseback, and Wren's original Figure Court remain central to its identity. Today, the hospital continues to serve as a living monument to the nation's gratitude, providing a home, care and community to the veterans who have served their country.

GUIDED TOUR OF THE ROYAL HOSPITAL CHELSEA

https://www.youtube.com/watch?v=7UBZXvyW-2Q

THE CEREMONY OF THE KEYS

The Ceremony of the Keys at the Tower of London is a daily gate-closing ritual performed by the Yeomen Warders (Beefeaters). It takes place every night at 9.53 p.m., when the Chief Yeoman Warder, dressed in Tudor uniform and carrying a candle lantern, leaves the Byward Tower with the military Escort to the Keys. This is made up of armed members of the Tower of London Guard. The Warder passes his lantern to a soldier and marches with the escort to the outer gate. The sentries on duty salute the keys as they pass.

The Warder first locks the outer gate and then the gates of the Middle and Byward towers. The Warder and the escort march down Water Lane until they reach the Bloody Tower archway, where a sentry challenges the party to identify themselves:

Sentry: Halt! Who comes there?
Chief Warder: The keys.
Sentry: Whose keys?
Chief Warder: King Charles's keys.
Sentry: Pass King Charles's keys. All's well.

The Warder and escort march down to the bottom of Broadwalk Steps, where the main Tower Guard is waiting to meet them. The party halts and the officer gives the command to present arms. The Chief Warder steps forward, doffs his bonnet and proclaims:

Chief Warder: God preserve King Charles.
Guard: Amen!

On the answering 'Amen', the clock of the Waterloo Barracks strikes 10.00 p.m. and the Last Post is sounded, marking the end of the ceremony. The Guard is dismissed.

The Chief Yeoman Warder, carrying the King's keys and a lantern, makes his way along Water Lane, then closes, locks and secures the outer and inner gates of the Tower with the help of the Tower's Watchman. The Chief Warder takes the keys to the King's House for safekeeping overnight.

The Ceremony of the Keys is the oldest military ceremony in the world.

THE CEREMONY OF THE KEYS

https://www.youtube.com/watch?v=UPPl6bFwHOg

The Crown Jewels are kept in the Jewel House in the Tower of London and are guarded by armed security. They are worth an estimated £5 billion. They include St Edward's Crown, which is made of solid gold and decorated with rubies, amethysts and sapphires. This crown was last used for the coronation of King Charles III in 2023. It replaced a medieval crown that was melted down in 1649 after the execution of Charles I. There's Mary of Modena's Crown, which was created in 1685 for the second wife of King James II. This crown originally contained 550 diamonds, but the diamonds were replaced by rock crystals in the 1720s. There's also Queen Mary's Crown, which was used for the coronation of Queen Camilla in 2023. This crown was reset with the original Cullinan diamonds and had four of its eight half-arches removed. And, of course, there's the Imperial State Crown worn by King Charles III for the procession from Westminster Abbey to Buckingham Palace. The Crown Jewels are also used in ceremonies such as the State Opening of Parliament.

THE VERNON BELL

In 1754, some men from the 1st Battalion, 62nd Regiment of Foot were drafted into the Royal Navy to serve as marines. As a consequence, 'Rule Britannia' was played before their own regimental march at the end of band programmes and in the guard house. Every half hour, a non-commissioned officer would strike the ship's time on a bell. This tradition was carried over to the Duke of Edinburgh's Royal Regiment.

HMS Vernon, a naval establishment in Portsmouth, established an affiliation with the regiment at the request of the Duke of Edinburgh. The bell is still struck by the police or guard to indicate the time of day, as is the custom in the Royal Navy.

ROLLING IN

The term 'rolling in' refers to the drum rolls played by a drummer who led the officers into the dining room on guest night. Great efforts were made in 1914 to capture a German side drum so it could be used for this purpose. This tradition was still observed in the Duke of Edinburgh's Royal Regiment after its amalgamation.

WHITE TIE NIGHT

This is the tradition of dining in civilian clothes once a year, initiated by the 66th Regiment. The officers were apparently invited to a ball by a distinguished French lady. Their commanding officer, out of consideration for a defeated enemy, ordered that plain clothes should be worn. However, due to the campaign, many officers only had uniforms. They were ordered to obtain civilian dress and keep it with them at all times. The custom of dining out in civilian dress was observed throughout the regiment's life.

The role of traditional battle honours has also been reinstated. The first battle honours were given to the 18th Regiment of Foot, later the Royal Irish Regiment, for their part in the siege of Namur in 1695. Until 1932, honours were awarded to a specific unit and if it was disbanded, the honour was lost. This was changed so that honours were awarded to the parent regiment of the battalion whose actions led to the award. That way, the honours would still be carried forward if the shape of the Army changed.

GUNFIRE

Gunfire is made of black tea and rum. It was a cocktail in existence during the 1890s and is served by officers and non-commissioned officers to the lower ranks before a morning attack and also as a celebration before the passing-out parade. It was also traditionally served to soldiers before they got up on the morning of Christmas Day if they were deployed at that time. Different regiments carry out the ritual on other days that have significance for them. The Royal Dragoon Guards substitute the rum for whisky on Saint Patrick's Day.

THE MINDEN ROSE TRADITION

This is associated with the Battle of Minden, a famous battle during the Seven Years' War, which took place on 1 August 1759.

An Anglo-German army, under the overall command of Field Marshal Ferdinand of Brunswick, defeated a French army commanded by the Marshal of France, Marquis de Contades. Two years previously, the French had launched a successful invasion of Hanover and attempted to impose an unpopular treaty of peace upon the allied nations of Britain, Hanover and Prussia. After a Prussian victory at Rossbach and under pressure from Frederick the Great and William Pitt, King George II disavowed the treaty. In 1758, the Allies launched a counter-offensive against the French and Saxon forces and drove them back across the Rhine.

The French launched a fresh offensive, capturing the fortress of Minden on 10 July. Believing Ferdinand's forces to be beaten, Contades abandoned his position and advanced to meet the allied forces in battle. The decisive action of the battle came when six regiments of British and two of Hanoverian infantry, in line formation, repelled repeated French cavalry attacks. The allied line advanced in the wake of multiple failed French cavalry charges, sending the French Army reeling from the field. This battle saw the British and their allies achieve a decisive victory over the French forces and it has since been commemorated annually by certain British Army regiments. These include the Royal Anglian Regiment, the Royal Regiment of Fusiliers, the Royal Welsh, the Princess of Wales's Royal Regiment, 12 (Minden) Air Assault Battery, 12th Regiment Royal Artillery, 32 (Minden 1759) Battery, 16th Regiment Royal Artillery, 3rd and 5th Battalions, the Rifles and the North Saskatchewan Regiment [Reserve Canadian Army].

The Minden Rose tradition originated from the actions of British soldiers during the battle. According to legend, as the British infantry advanced through the fields towards the French positions, they picked wild roses and placed them in their hats and coats. This act of bravery and defiance has been immortalised in the annual commemoration of the battle.

On Minden Day, soldiers traditionally wear a rose in their headdress to honour the memory of those who fought in the battle. The rose serves as a symbol of courage, resilience and the enduring spirit of the regiment, linking current soldiers with their predecessors.

Officers who have not previously attended the Royal Regiment of Fusiliers Officers' Mess Minden Day dinner are presented with a rose to be eaten. The names of those who have done so are then written in the mess's records.

The traditions of military units contribute not only to their morale, identity, values and training but to their fighting ability. Strong morale allows you to deal with hardship and fear. For the UK armed forces, it is the warfighting component we prize above all else.

From their rituals, they learn about their past, their culture, their character and why they are successful. The embodiment of these principles is the Chelsea Pensioners. Their frequent presence at civilian events is an opportunity for all, from every walk of life, to be reminded of this.

Their excellence is based on habit. When so much habit, training and togetherness have been lost during the pandemic, we should look to our armed forces as a model of how to reinstil it. That drumbeat, those habits, are what creates excellence. Excellence is never an event; it's a habit.

Our greatest military successes and leaders have had their provenance in defeat. All commercial success has, too. Ask any entrepreneur. Perhaps one reason politics so often fails to achieve excellence is that it does not permit failure. Perhaps another is that in Westminster these days, little seems to endure, even between administrations of the same political hue – as demonstrated by the Conservative Party in the last fourteen years. I think the public sense this. They want Britian's values to be vivid enough to create efficiency and continuity in all their political leaders.

Military customs remind everyone that people come and go, but the ethos remains. Units with a strong culture and morale are more likely to survive under conditions of duress.

The traditions and customs of our armed forces, steeped in history, remind us that our actions are not just about the here and now. They are for generations to come. They are keepers of the flame. Their actions on the battlefield today will assist those yet to be born who will inherit their colours.

CHAPTER EIGHT

WHY BRITAIN'S TRADITIONS MATTER

This chapter summarises and answers the question: why do our traditions matter? We explore the role of traditions at the heart of a modern nation. In a world of increasing instability and change, are traditions about to become even more important? For example, might they encourage investment or help to improve underperforming public services? Why has there been a resurgence in local festivals, customs and the creation of 'new' traditions? What are the things that are quintessentially British? How do our traditions make change easier? How has our history conspired to bring us to this point? When viewed in historical context, how do these times compare? Could it be that this most traditional of countries is about to emerge as one of the most reliable, most forward-looking and most long-term dependable countries on Earth? As we face a crisis of confidence, where nothing seems to work and the challenges ahead appear terrifying, could Britain be best placed to succeed in the future?

Frank Gibbons: I wonder what happens to rooms when people give them up, go away and leave the house empty?
Bob Mitchell: How do you mean?

Frank Gibbons: I don't know. I was thinking about you going away from next door after all this time and me and Ethel going away, too, pretty soon and wondering what the next people that live in this room will be like. Whether they'll feel any bits of us left about the place.
Bob Mitchell: Here, shut up. You're giving me the willies.

NOËL COWARD, *THIS HAPPY BREED*

Frank Gibbons has been with us all the way through this book. He is the central character in Noël Coward and David Lean's 1944 film *This Happy Breed*. He is not a famous man. No one knows him except his family and friends. He is not educated. He is not wealthy. He is a father, a husband and a combat veteran. He is a man subject to events rather than the cause of them. He meets triumph and tragedy and does a pretty good job of dealing with both. He is a keen gardener, likes a drink, is proud of his country and is deeply suspicious of fanatics.

We seldom hear from the Frank Gibbons of this world. The media prefers us fed on a diet of the marginalised, the opinionated, the ill-informed and the habitually angry. In the fight for attention, we're not interested in the routine, the mundane or the reliable. We need the adrenaline spike of the extreme.

Gibbons wonders what happens when people depart, whether something of them remains as a residue. Well, it does. But it's nothing to do with the supernatural. They live on in our traditions. Gibbons may be long dead, but he's with us still. Even today, he would recognise and support our traditions. He wouldn't say they were better or worse than other country's traditions, but they most definitely are ours. He would still be proud. He isn't starry-eyed or jingoistic, but he nurtures a much quieter but equally profound love of country.

So, why are British traditions so important? For the following reasons.

1. THEY PROMOTE STABILITY AND HELP US NAVIGATE CHANGE

We think these are uncertain times, but a consistent theme for our ancestors was the fragility of life. Some of our earliest traditions were based on superstition, prayer, humility and gratitude as an entreaty to good fortune. We talk of uncertainty today, but we're not facing an existential threat from crop failure or the arbitrary death and destruction of wartime Britain. But even if we were, we'd still cling to our routines, habits and traditions. A common sign placed on wrecked shops and properties during the Blitz was 'business as usual during alterations'.

Our traditions establish and celebrate patterns of behaviour. Our laws are really nothing more than ingrained and codified habits. Some laws are established entirely by behavioural precedents such as the 'ten-year law' in planning and the rights of way on footpaths, for instance.

The purpose of science and law is to shift the balance in favour of certainty and away from risk. It's been so hugely successful that it has partially become the provenance of the risk itself. In recent years, the pace of technical change has accelerated and stability has been undermined. Some politicians wish to accelerate change still further by piling instability on top of uncertainty. The responsible ones, however, try to mitigate risk with stability. They try to make things predictable. They are careful and calibrated and, of course, go unnoticed for that. They know the enemy of investment is instability. They value tradition, reliability and trust. This takes decades to build but can be lost in days. Once it's gone, it's hard to get back. Wars can be started in days. Peace takes years.

At its core, Britain is underpinned by royal traditions. For the best part of 1,000 years, our regnal line has remained unbroken. It was around before our grandparents' time. It will be around even after that of our grandchildren. It has stood the test of time. For that reason, the British monarchy still commands respect and attention. Sir Keir Starmer's negotiations with the new US President in February 2025 were hailed as a triumph, partly because the Prime Minister was armed with a personal invitation from the King. We understand the magic of royalty. We learned that the hard way, from our history.

There is something worth reflecting on here. In the nearly 1,100 years since Æthelstan, the grandson of Alfred the Great, who is first recorded to have styled himself *Rex Anglorum*, or 'King of the English', we have only once experimented with republicanism. It's worth recounting what happened.

In 1649, denying the power of Parliament and insisting on the Divine Right of Kings, Charles I was put on trial for treason in front of a hastily established High Court of Justice in Westminster Hall. It was a show trial by the Parliamentarian side, which had won the Civil War, and the guilty verdict was inevitable; so too was the King's execution outside the Banqueting House on Whitehall on 30 January.

Then, for all practical purposes, there was no King. The Prince of Wales, who would eventually reclaim the throne as Charles II, was in exile in The Hague. What should happen now? Within a week, the Parliament of Scotland had proclaimed Charles II to be King but would only let him come into the country if he agreed to establish the Presbyterian religion throughout the British Isles. In England, the Rump Parliament – all that was left after in-fighting and purges of the Parliament summoned in 1640 – did away with the monarchy, the House of Lords and the Privy Council, set up a Council of State as an executive and declared the Commonwealth of England.

The republican experiment was a mess. Fighting continued between England and Scotland until 1652, the precious union of the crowns temporarily broken in practice if not in theory, and Cromwell's army spent four years brutalising Ireland, with 15 or 20 per cent of the population dying of war, famine or disease. In 1653, Cromwell eventually did what Charles I had threatened to do a decade before. He brought armed men to Westminster and dissolved the House of Commons, telling them: 'You are no Parliament!'

By the end of that year, Cromwell had become Lord Protector for life and was being addressed as 'Your Highness'. He summoned a new Parliament, then dissolved it in 1655. Before he died three years later, he passed on his position to his son. However, a year after Cromwell's death, a new Parliament declared that Charles II had been the lawful King since the death of his father in 1649.

The 29th of May is still celebrated as Oak Apple Day (or Restoration Day, or Royal Oak Day, or Shick Shack Day, or Yak Bob Day) and was the end of the republican experiment. It had lasted eleven-and-a-half years and had seen war, mass slaughter, displacement, autocracy, military dictatorship and failing institutions. We haven't tried it again.

The royal traditions remain the gold standard, providing a moral and ethical framework that guides our behaviour and decision-making. The rituals, ceremonies and festivals carry profound symbolic meanings that reinforce important values, such as continuity, belief, respect, reverence and responsibility.

It's often said that management does things right. Leadership, however, does something different. It does the right things. In a similar way, royalty is there to 'do' some things, but it is mainly there to 'be' something. Royal values are crucial for fostering ethical leadership and governance. They are essential for addressing the complex issues of the future, many of which have an ethical dimension. There are many leaders with ability but only the best show evidence of 'the J-word' – judgement. What's right is not always what's profitable. There has to be a greater understanding of the bigger picture.

The tradition of Remembrance Day, held at 11 a.m. on the 11th of November, is one such example. It always has a royal component, not only to honour those who served in the armed forces but also as a reminder of the importance of duty, service and sacrifice. These are the elements that make up the moral component of the military ethos.

This is the most important factor, not just in military combat units but in every civilian organisation and community. This duty, service and sacrifice obliges us to vote, defend free speech and take responsibility. This is why in offices, high streets and football grounds, our annual two-minute silence is still observed.

Even the veterans who gather for these memorial events have their own traditions. After the march past, a regular staple meal is a curry and a beer. You don't need to be a monarch to have memories or traditions.

There is something else. Think of the Cenotaph, Sir Edwin Lutyens's starkly magnificent monument in the middle of Whitehall, unveiled by King George V in 1920. It was completed for the second anniversary of the armistice which saw the fighting of the First World War end and it has been central to our collective acts of commemoration ever since. It doesn't carry the names of the generals and admirals who led our forces, or the men who won medals in combat. It simply says: 'THE GLORIOUS DEAD.' Every sacrifice, by every rank of every service, in every war. They all count.

The importance of royal traditions grows greater with change, offering a sense of predictability and structure in a bewildering world. They mark the passage of time and provide a rhythm to life, which can be comforting and grounding. The British calendar, for example, is punctuated by various royal events but it is not dominated by them.

Royal weddings are examples of how traditions help us deal with change. These events are not only significant for the Royal Family but for the nation as a whole. They serve as a reminder of the importance of family, unity and continuity. The pomp and ceremony associated with royal weddings also highlights a sense of pride and identity and the rich cultural heritage of our country. By celebrating these traditions, we are reminded of the values that bind us together as a society, which are essential for social cohesion and stability.

Royal traditions often embody practical knowledge and skills that remain relevant. For example, the meticulous planning and execution of state banquets can offer insights into effective event management and protocol. This matters. When Queen Elizabeth II died, it was a huge shock and a major change in the lives of most of us. However, the procedure and process then took over and guided us through it. This is essentially the training and programming to be able to deal with change.

The monarchy serves as a unifying symbol that transcends political and social divisions. Royal events and ceremonies are not just relics of the past. They embody the culture, practice and ethics needed to face the future with confidence.

Once you have stability, then everything else becomes possible. In many ways, the British just don't have a choice. Whether we like it or not, we are defined by our traditions. It's not a matter of debate. You can say you hate all the traditions but to everyone around the world, it's what we're known for. And what's wrong with that?

So often in Britain, the process of institutional change is itself a ritual. The State Opening of Parliament, for example, is a tradition that dates back centuries and symbolises the constitutional monarchy's role in the governance of the country as Parliament changes. It is the only regular occasion when the three constituent parts of Parliament meet. The sovereign, the House of Lords and the House of Commons: the King-in-Parliament.

The ceremony involves the monarch delivering a speech outlining the government's agenda for the coming year. This tradition not only reinforces the importance of the monarchy in the political system but also serves as a reminder of the country's democratic values and the rule of law. By maintaining this tradition, we are reminded of the importance of accountability and transparency in governance, which are crucial for a stable and prosperous future.

2. THEY BRING IDENTITY AND COHESION TO OUR COMMUNITIES, REGIONS AND GENERATIONS

In researching this book, it became clear how much affection there is for our traditions. Right the way across the country, ancient customs are being pursued and new ones are still being created. Why is this relevant beyond a quaint idea of Britishness, which many would regard as old-fashioned and outdated? Is there any clear, independently measurable evidence to show the impact of tradition on the efficiency and success of organisations and institutions? In short, yes there is. Management and leadership experts write about little else. There is an entire canon of work on the beneficial effects of rituals and traditions on community culture and employee engagement.

Understanding the profound role that rituals and traditions play in shaping culture is not just a 'nice to have'. It could contribute to those elusive twin government obsessions of productivity and sustainability. It is well documented that the UK suffers from a persistently low rate of productivity. Some studies find that those with stronger cultures have a 30 per cent increase in employee engagement, which can increase productivity.

When colleagues feel connected through shared traditions, the likelihood of an effective contribution increases. Rituals, even those as simple as celebratory lunches for project completions, can create a sense of belonging. According to a report from management consultancy Deloitte, companies with cultures of this sort have been shown to outperform their peers by up to one-third in revenue growth.

It's not just commercial organisations either. When you look at healthcare teams, it's just the same. A study published in the *Online Journal of Issues in Nursing* found: 'Nurses who experienced higher levels of gratitude reported lower levels of burnout and higher job satisfaction.' In addition, healthcare workers who practised gratitude had stronger relationships with their colleagues and felt a greater sense of community within their organisations.[1] The healthcare professionals incorporated what they called 'gratitude rounds' – a ritual where staff members express appreciation for one another.

Now some might say the notion of gratitude is all a bit 'snowflake'. Why do we need to say thanks to people who are just doing their job? Well, because times have changed. When we're struggling to get staff back into the office on a regular basis, why not make it a place where they can be recognised and praised by their community? They won't get that working from home.

Courtesy and fellowship are in our nature and our behaviour. When Sir William Blackstone wrote his *Commentaries on the Laws of England* in the 1760s, he described the English as 'a polite and commercial people'. We were, by and large, and we remain so.

The significance of rituals and traditions extends beyond mere participation; they serve as tools for communication and the alignment of values. Through practices that reflect the mission and core values, we can convey expectations and aspirations.

And this is where we can become much more efficient, by teaching organisations about the importance of tradition. Put another way, they need to be taught how to tap into the enormous goodwill of those they serve. It isn't just about money. Most don't go into public services for money. They do so to be part of a team, doing something good in the community. It's a case of Matthew 19:21: 'You will have treasure enough in heaven.'

As we said previously, look at the number that registered their names to help the NHS during Covid. The initial 250,000 target was smashed with more than 750,000 volunteering.[2] But they were stood down without even being thanked, because the sad truth is that the NHS is a bureaucracy we love that doesn't love us back.

How do we know this? Because all bureaucracies primarily serve themselves. Despite caring and dedicated staff, the NHS has lost sight of the needs and ambitions of those it serves. This is because it has lost its local roots and connections. Doctors don't know their patients and their problems like they used to. We are inspired by the hard work of the staff, so why can't we help them? Many communities raise money for services, but that's often as far as it goes. Why is this? It could well be a lack of resources. But what if we redirected spending on DEI initiatives to volunteering schemes or setting up traditions and recognition for staff?

The organisation has at least been collectively awarded the George Cross, the highest civilian gallantry award, recognising its exceptional service, particularly during the Covid pandemic. Former NHS England chief executive Amanda Pritchard and May Parsons, a matron who delivered the world's first approved Covid vaccination, received the honour on behalf of the organisation from Her Majesty Queen Elizabeth II at a ceremony in Windsor Castle in July 2022.

The BBC, the Post Office and local government are also organisations with little tradition or recognition beyond that which has grown among their teams. They hold a special place in our hearts, but again, it is not reciprocated. From the culling of the 'UK Theme' to the inclusion of Bob Vylan in its Glastonbury coverage, Britain's affection for the Beeb remains unrequited. It was local communities that valued Mr Bates and his postmaster and postmistress colleagues more than their employer did. We sift and sort all our recycling for local government only for it to be burned in giant incinerators.

All these organisations have few traditions. There are no march-pasts, no Thanksgiving Day, no medals, no buildings, no vehicles named after their greats. The police and fire services, for instance, all have medals. So do other civilian organisations like the Merchant Navy. Medals and parades are a thank you, but they are also there to inspire the rest of us.[3]

Organisations with traditions are like people with discipline – they continue to perform well even when placed under duress. You can call

it drill, devotion or duty, but in the military, it is used to turn train-
ees into a team. This was clearly illustrated by a 2023 YouGov survey,
which asked Britons about twelve key public services. The ones with
the poorest perceptions are the ones with the least core ethos, tradition
and discipline.[4]

These teams and identities are there across the nations because our
forebears created them. The historic counties of England were administrative areas established by the Normans and based on earlier
kingdoms created by the Angles, Saxons, Celts, Jutes and Romans.
There were twenty-one of them. Our counties, cities and towns retain
a strong sense of themselves. Despite almost perpetual local government reorganisation, the county structure of the UK persists. They are
the basis upon which Lord-Lieutenants and High Sheriffs, the King's
representatives, are still appointed. These appointments are still made
by the Privy Council.

Since the Tudor dynasty, the Lord-Lieutenants have looked after the
local militia. Even in those days, special devolution deals were in existence, with some areas having additional powers. Yorkshire, of course,
had to be awkward. From 1660 onwards, each of Yorkshire's three ridings had its own Lieutenant. In London, things were headed up by the
Lord Mayor. The Sheriff's Act of 1887, the Militia Act of 1882 and the
Lieutenancies Act of 1997 are the key pieces of legislation in this area.
In 1889, elected county councils, as we would recognise them today,
were established under the Local Government Act of 1888. Parliamentary constituencies based on ancient county boundaries remained in
existence as late as 1918.

Counties and councils have come and gone in recent years. The
boundaries of geographical counties, shrieval, lieutenancy and administrative counties have changed continually. But people have generally
associated their sense of place with the ceremonial counties defined in
the Lieutenancies Act and what their postal address indicates. The past
remains all around us, both as a reassurance and a constraint.

The Post Office eventually altered many of its postal counties in accordance with the 1965 and 1974 reforms, apart from Greater London and Greater Manchester. Initially, it was deemed too costly to do so. In 1996, counties became obsolete in the function of directing mail and in 2000, postal counties were removed from the Royal Mail address database. Yet most people still write the county on the envelope. This was in part due to the inability of the Royal Mail to update all of its software. So, in some parts of the country, it was still relevant and, indeed, encouraged to include the county.

There is a movement to revive historic county boundaries. In 2013, the government recognised and acknowledged their continued existence. Road signs to mark historic boundaries were encouraged, along with the addition of historic county names on street and road signs. Flying of county flags was encouraged – all thirty-nine English counties have registered flags. Areas such as Yorkshire have long been abandoned as units of local government for administrative purposes but remain widely recognised for cultural reasons.

So much of identity is about our sense of place, time and nature. It's in our geography, the fact we are an offshore island, the seasons, our climate, flora and fauna and the rhythms of the year and of life all around us. What mattered to our ancestors was etched into the landscape. You can see it in the topography, stone circles and the druids that still meet there in mid-summer. It is in our monuments, gardens and forests.

You can also see it in our pastimes. Although roughly 85 per cent of Britain lives in an urban area, gardens are a special tradition connecting us to the soil. We have more gardens per person than any other country on Earth, with 8,000 square miles devoted to British gardens. This is more than all our national nature reserves put together. In Greater London alone, there are around 3.8 million front and back gardens, with 2.5 million trees in them. An estimated 27 million people enjoy gardening as a hobby – 42 per cent of the population. There were around 144,000 professional and landscape gardeners in the UK in 2022.

The vast majority of us live in urban areas despite it being only 8 per cent of the space. We hanker after nature, with 330,000 allotment plots and vast waiting lists for them. This is reflected in the membership of conservation societies. With 1.2 million members, the RSPB is the largest nature conservation charity. However, the National Trust is the largest membership organisation of any in the UK, with 5.38 million members.

You can see it in our weather. You can see it in the traditions of trades and travellers. In church flowers, saints' days, water sources, village fetes and in kisses under the mistletoe. So many of our traditions are connected with the land, sea and the seasons. So much with our sense of place like the boundary ridings, walks, audits and proclamations from the town hall steps. They enable families and communities of all generations to participate together in a common cause.

3. THEY SHOW THAT CHANGE, DONE TRADITIONALLY, CAN BE EFFICIENT AND POPULAR

Our traditions provide a template for how we should manage change. Let's take the London black cab, for example. The traditional colour came about because black paint was the cheapest and most practical option after the Second World War, making it the standard colour for the Austin FX3 taxi.

Its design has its roots in the horse-drawn Hansom carriages of the nineteenth century (developed by architect Joseph Hansom in 1834). These early vehicles were designed to be robust and capable of navigating the narrow and often uneven streets of London. It is still required to have a turning circle of just twenty-five feet, which allows it to navigate the tight corners and narrow streets. This was originally so that cabs could manage the tight turning circle at the Savoy Hotel. Sir Stephen Fry has owned and driven several black cabs, while the flamboyant financier Nubar Gulbenkian had two Austin FX4s, saying: 'They can turn on a sixpence, whatever that is.'

Accessibility has always been a key consideration in the design. Modern cabs are designed to be wheelchair-accessible, with features such as ramps and swivel seats to assist passengers with mobility issues. The wide doors make it easier for all passengers to enter and exit the vehicle comfortably.

But even the modern version would still be recognisable to someone from a hundred years ago. The high roof remains a practical feature because it allows passengers to enter and exit the vehicle with ease, even if they are wearing a top hat, which was a common accessory when the design was first introduced. And yet, it is a modern electric vehicle with air conditioning, Wi-Fi, satnav, USB charging ports and advanced safety systems. But it looks just like what went before.

There are still few vehicles that can seat five people face-to-face and be driven by an expert. Before London cab drivers can get their licence, they need to pass a test known as 'The Knowledge'. This examination process is considered one of the most challenging in the world and is a mandatory requirement to become a licensed taxi driver in London.

Similarly, with the double-decker London red bus. Largely unchanged from its original 1954 design, the 'Boris Buses' were directly inspired by it. Half of all British bus journeys happen in London. Incidentally, there are more Tube train journeys than overland journeys in the whole of the UK.

As iconic as the black cab or the double-decker bus is the Metropolitan Police officer. Even their unusual custodian helmet is an example of modernisation in a traditional form. It looks just like its predecessor but has been updated to include modern requirements and materials. While uniformed officers in certain specialised roles may be exempt for practical reasons, the majority of those on foot patrol continue to wear it. During the 1970s and 1980s, officers were expected to conduct public order and crowd control in the standard helmet. The cork construction offered little protection against thrown missiles, so the construction of the helmets was changed. Visually, they remained the same, but they are now made out of a hard-wearing plastic material and covered in felt. Internally, they were padded with foam fitted into the helmet with a webbing style. Two chin straps were added, a thin leather strap for normal duties and a public order strap with a chin cup to securely hold the helmet in place.

In England and Wales, only around 5 per cent of police officers are authorised to carry firearms. This means that even today, the vast majority of UK police officers are not armed on a regular basis. This isn't accidental. When Sir Robert Peel established the Metropolitan Police in 1829, he was careful that the new law enforcement officers should be clearly civilians rather than military. They wore blue uniforms rather than the red characteristic of the army, with top hats to underline the civilian look, and carried truncheons but no firearms.

The message of our traditions is that we prefer our future to fit with our past. This also explains our love for renovating old buildings. The Tate Modern and Battersea Power Station are some of the most modern locations in London, but the buildings remain recognisable to anyone who saw them nearly a hundred years ago. Similarly with St Pancras Station and the preservation of the *Cutty Sark* at Greenwich.

For the reasons given here, radical change often fails or doesn't even get started at all because it ignores the principle of incremental change in keeping with tradition. The saga of multiple attempts to reform the House of Lords or the honours system is an example of this.

Modest, popular and sensible reform is shunned in favour of more exciting radical reinvention, which then proves too threatening, controversial or difficult. The result is paralysis.

Margaret Thatcher's reforms were radical and delivered at high speed. She had a plan but also a narrative. The measures were anchored in traditional British values of self-reliance, charity, agency, Christianity, pride and love of country.

In Britain, modernisation requires a sense of tradition. It also requires a sense of humour.

Although pomp and circumstance dominate our national traditions, a sense of jeopardy hovers above most state occasions. They can be tense affairs. People get nervous. Strange things happen. Sometimes, no matter how well organised, things go wrong. They did at the coronation, but no one noticed and if they did, they didn't say. Overall, it went right.

Public representation at these events is a personal honour and a duty, but you should never forget that the event is about how other people feel. A measure of the suitability of representation is a person's ability to conduct themselves appropriately when in public view. Even when doing something unusual. There's nothing normal about carrying an eight-pound ceremonial sword for fifty-one minutes and then passing it on to present the Jewelled Sword of Offering to the King. It may be smaller and lighter than the Sword of State, but it still would have been disastrous to drop it. There were, after all, only 2 billion people watching.

As a result of the tension, humour is never far away, especially once the event is over. After the coronation at Westminster Abbey, everyone changes back into their scruffs. One minute, you're on telly all over the world. The next you're filling up in a petrol station and buying a tin of meat for the cat.

It's important to be the same person that does both. This is the real test of any form of representation. Can you remain the same person when you are in the public eye? Politicians are not extraordinary people. They are just ordinary people in extraordinary situations. Some find the juxtaposition of these situations difficult.

Too many think that public representation is coming up with all the right answers. Sometimes, though, there's no right answer. It could be different depending on the circumstances. Ambiguity lies in wait for all leaders. The provenance of certainty – so popular in these rapidly moving times – can only be mediocrity. We don't need a red cat or a blue cat. We need a cat that catches mice.

That's what constituents want. They don't want all the answers in the pub quiz. They want to be understood and they want practical help. They don't want a lecture on political dogma. It's the same at the international level. The room belongs to those who can make something happen. The measure is the three 'R's: responsibility, reliability and relatability. These are the foundations of trust.

A sense of humour and a sense of humility are both pillars of the national character. They indicate judgement, timing, terms of reference and intelligence, and they are a measure of behaviour under duress. It's another paradox. Humour is something we take seriously.

There isn't one of our national traditions that doesn't in some small way bring a smile to the faces of onlookers and participants alike. Even at the most solemn occasions, such as the seventy-fifth D-Day commemorations, the veterans were the first to crack a joke afterwards. It is in this way that these wonderful men pay tribute to their fallen colleagues. They gave their lives so that others could live, so survivors do so with gratitude.

4. THEY ARE THE BEDROCK OF OUR ARMED FORCES BECAUSE THEY MEMORIALISE COURAGE

If there's anything we're known for around the world, it's our calmness under stress. No one does this better than the British military. We admire the ability to keep going, to keep striving, despite setbacks, despite loss. The secret to this is our habits, routines and traditions. We make carrying on look like a mere matter of fact.

Persistence wins more battles than power. This is the test of a fighting philosophy. It is not how well it fights in success. It's how well it rallies in defeat. Quatre Bras and Ligny were both battles fought with inconclusive outcomes, just days before the decisive outcome at Waterloo. In December 1941, two British battleships, HMS *Prince of Wales* and HMS *Repulse*, were sunk by the Japanese. Shortly after, Singapore fell in the worst British defeat of the Second World War. Japan was still defeated.

There are many times in history when the cause looks lost. In February 2022, Ukraine was written off by most of the foreign ministries of the Western world as a lost territory. Over three years later, it is still fighting bravely.

It's been the source of so many victories in history from Agincourt to Waterloo to the Battle of Britain and the Falkland Islands. An outnumbered force suffers setbacks but keeps going. Thus, a part of our tradition is not our raw aggression; it's our determination to carry on and get the job done. A stubborn refusal to give up can often be the source of so many victories. You can't beat people who won't be defeated. Churchill captured this aspect of British tradition and tenacity perfectly:

> We shall go on to the end. We shall fight in France, we shall fight on the seas and oceans, we shall fight with growing confidence and growing strength in the air, we shall defend our island, whatever the cost may be. We shall fight on the beaches, we shall fight on the landing grounds, we shall fight in the fields and in the streets, we shall fight in the hills; we shall never surrender.

One of the archive films of Churchill's funeral captures the emotion in the faces of the crowd that came to pay their respects.

WINSTON CHURCHILL TRIBUTE

https://www.youtube.com/watch?v=87Xkr8z3lEo

It's why we excel in so many of our special forces. It's not the size of the dog in the fight. It's the size of the fight in the dog.

If we really understand who we are, we should realise that stamina and staying power is one of the most important assets Britain has. Why do we know this? As Sir Christopher Wren wrote inside St Paul's Cathedral: *Si monumentum requiris, circumspice.* This translates to: 'If you seek his monument, look around you.'

The lesson of history is clear. We've defended our island countless times and we must prepare to do so again. We must be able to defend ourselves. All is in jeopardy without military strength, but it can come in many forms. It's not solely about kinetics. Britain is home to many of the best universities in the world. Modern warfare is about brains as much as brawn. Britain has historically excelled in the ingenious arts of cryptography, intelligence and counterespionage.

All the evidence shows that military expenditure can be the making of a revitalised economy. Strength and success walk hand in hand. Our traditions are not past; they are prologue and current commentary.

Traditions create resilience and reliability. These two qualities are what make us good allies.

Traditions, though, are not always old. They are being created all the time. An example is in Royal Wootton Bassett in Wiltshire. For many years, it had close links with the former RAF base at Lyneham. In October 2011, the town was granted the 'royal' prefix in recognition of the role the town and its people played in the repatriation of UK servicemen and women killed as a result of war. A spontaneous tradition grew up to honour the funeral corteges that came through the town from the airbase. In February 2016, this tradition was extended to thirty-eight British victims of a terrorist attack on a Tunisian Beach.

Similarly, during Covid, the National Covid Memorial Wall was created. It consists of 240,000 red and pink hearts, one for each of the casualties of Covid in the UK. It was not created by the NHS but by campaign groups like Covid-19 Bereaved Families for Justice UK.

Why does this happen? Because British people need and want to participate. This is a hidden superpower of ours. Our values are illustrated when answering the call to volunteer. You can see evidence of this everywhere in Britain. In 2023/24, 54 per cent of adults in England (about 25 million people) volunteered at least once in the last year. This is because they love their institutions and clubs, and this is a valuable resource, provided that those organisations understand their convening power.

As much as traditions remind us of our current values, some traditions have disappeared because they no longer do so. For example, in the eighteenth century, there was a custom in England known as 'wife-selling'. This involved a man publicly auctioning off his wife to the highest bidder, often in a marketplace or a pub. It was sometimes seen as a humorous way to escape an unhappy marriage. There is evidence that it last happened in the 1920s in the town of Barnoldswick in Lancashire. Incidentally, Barnoldswick (or Barlick, as it's known by locals) is famous for being the only town in England and Wales that has half the letters of the alphabet and doesn't repeat any of them. It's also home to some of the finest people on the planet.

Where traditions no longer reflect our values, they go by the wayside and rightly so. In the sixteenth century, a London law forbade wife-beating after 9.00 p.m., but only because the noise disturbed people's sleep. A few traditions centred around animal abuse are also thankfully history. The good people of Pembrokeshire and Suffolk seemed to have something against Britain's smallest bird, the wren. Wren Day is celebrated on Saint Stephen's Day on 26 December. This used to involve hunting a wren, which would then be tied, alive, to a pole or pitchfork. The poor creature would then be paraded for the purpose of raising funds. The tradition continued late in Suffolk, and in Pembrokeshire there was a similar Twelfth Night custom, the Cutty Wren. This tradition is celebrated in the folk song here:

https://www.youtube.com/watch?v=WJzHBQIlJwk

The bird was placed in a little house of paper with glass windows and hoisted on poles, again for fundraising purposes.

Our traditions are like our history. They are not static. They are open to interpretation and used to promote modern values.

5. THEY GIVE BRITAIN A UNIQUE CULTURE AND ALLOW US TO FACE THE FUTURE WITH CONFIDENCE

Our traditions and our way of life are the great counterweights to unsettling change. How do they do this? By reminding us of what is ours – our land, our village, our authority, our church, our pub, our fishing waters, our heritage, our way of life, our rights, our sports and our food.

These all say much about who we are. How can we summarise them? Save for the Remembrance services, they involve making merry, eating and drinking, usually in large quantities. The overwhelming conclusion when reviewing the traditions is that we take the business of fun seriously. It says something about who we are that we are all so ready to participate in these traditions, many of which are frankly bizarre.

The traditions are quite frequently violent beyond the point that any public body would usually authorise, such as cheese rolling or shin kicking. This, of course, does not stop them from happening. They frequently have a connection to the seasons of the year or some link with the land, local history, a pub or a church. They remind us of how intimately tied to the land our ancestors were.

Pubs and churches are the bookends of British rural life. There are so many landlords and landladies who are the heart of our communities and traditions. One such landlady is Sue Beavis at The Three Horseshoes in Elsted, Sussex, which is a traditional country pub within the South Downs National Park. There's no music, she doesn't serve chips and if you use a mobile phone in the bar, you'll be sent out into the garden. She is a hard-working, long-suffering inspiration to everyone that knows her.

This book pays specific tribute to pubs. They are essential to so many villages and neighbourhoods. They are important for our traditions. They are central to our sanity. Just like churches, pubs are places of reflection, reconciliation, refuge, congregation, inspiration and holy spirits. They are vital to our maintenance, as an essential part of who we are in our right minds. There's simply nothing else like them on Earth and they're a national treasure. Some of them are even taking on the role of post offices and village stores and/or being taken into community ownership. Although many pubs have closed, our youngest generation, Generation Z, is going to the pub not because they drink more but because it's an authentic experience and a real-world respite from their digital existences.[5][6]

Pubs and churches (there are roughly the same number of each in the UK depending on how you measure them) gave rise to our traditional rights of way. Our footpath infrastructure is a unique feature of

Portraits of the Household Cavalry Mounted Regiment, created by British photographic artist Ripley. This series of twelve large-scale portraits was the official coronation present from the Household Cavalry to HM King Charles III. The top portrait, entitled 'The Squadron Leader of The Blues and Royals', was reconfigured by Ripley for the cover of this book.

TOP LEFT Penny as a child, beside the Royal Yacht *Britannia* in Portsmouth Dockyard.

TOP RIGHT At Fratton Park, home of Portsmouth Football Club, the scene of the largest and fastest ever community buy-out, which Penny helped lead.

BOTTOM With Boris Johnson, campaigning to leave the EU during the 2016 referendum campaign. © PA Images / Alamy

TOP Penny and colleagues in the Royal Navy, pictured heading from Royal Naval Reserve shore establishment HMS *King Alfred* to Bramble Bank in the Solent to pull a tug of war beside the annual cricket match.

MIDDLE At Dartmouth, undergoing Royal Navy officer training.

BOTTOM Penny with veteran clearance divers in her honorary Navy role, which is affiliated to MCM2 Squadron and Navy bomb disposal.

TOP LEFT Penny as guest of honour at the San Carlos dinner in 2019, commemorating the achievements of the Falklands taskforce. Major-General Julian Thompson, who commanded 3 Commando Brigade during the Falklands War, is on her left.

TOP RIGHT With British D-Day veterans in Normandy at the seventy-fifth anniversary of the landings.

BOTTOM LEFT Taking a selfie with Falklands veterans and their giant hip flask.

BOTTOM RIGHT Penny with Battle of Monte Cassino veteran Colonel Otton Hulacki.

TOP Penny with the First Sea Lord and the then Duke of Cambridge, during her time as Secretary of State for Defence, at a service at Westminster Abbey to commemorate the Continuous At Sea Deterrent policy. © Daniel Leal / Getty Images

MIDDLE LEFT Briefing UK armed forces.

MIDDLE RIGHT Penny at Apsley House, representing the UK government at the 650th anniversary of the Treaty of Peace, Friendship and Alliance between Portugal and the UK.

BOTTOM With Prince William and Prince Harry, launching the UK's crackdown on the illegal wildlife trade.
© Tolga Akmen / Getty Images

Penny with the then Prince of Wales, touring British Overseas Territories hit by Hurricanes Irma and Maria.

TOP Penny at the Accession Council, informing the Privy Council and the world that HM Queen Elizabeth II had passed away, alongside Prince William, Queen Camilla, Prime Minister Liz Truss and the Archbishop of Canterbury.
© WPA Pool / Pool / Getty Images

BOTTOM Penny at the King's coronation, as his first Lord President of the Council. © WPA Pool / Pool / Getty Images

Some of the hundreds of drawings depicting Penny holding the Sword of State, sent to her by young girls and Brownie groups after the coronation.

our ancient landscape. Just about every church and pub has a footpath leading to or from it. Some even predate humans as animal tracks. These were the first two places that needed to be linked up. You might think it odd that British footpaths get a mention in a book about traditions. They are, though, the physical signs of our traditions, liberties and habits. So many traditions are about walks to, from and around the church.

The parish system is itself 1,000 years old and again has stood the test of time. Special mention here also goes to Save the Parish. This is a grassroots movement working across the nation to ensure the poorest communities are not abandoned. After all, they do a lot of local good as the basic building block of our democracy. Their contribution can be as small as maintaining footpaths, negotiating rights of way and using local knowledge on planning issues. By returning the billions of Church Commissioners' assets to the funding of ordinary parish ministry, the Church can reignite a passion for the parish across the nation among thousands of communities.

So many footpaths were first rights of way, established for agricultural workers in the fields to get to churches. After the Acts of Enclosure of the sixteenth to the nineteenth centuries, some of the rights changed and much common land was fenced off. Some 4.5 million acres – about one-seventh of England – were enclosed between 1750 and 1850, with around 200,000 miles of hedges planted during this period. The legend of the Enclosure Acts was popularly summarised as 'To he that hath, shall be given. From he that not, shall be taken away' as a cynical corruption of Matthew 13:12. But even this did not diminish the ancient rights of way.[7]

Our forebears knew the importance of these. They go back to the case of 'Re: The inhabitants of St James, Taunton' in 1315, which stated that rights of way persist despite demonstrable evidence that the paths have not been used for years. No other country has these rights enshrined in so many years of custom and practice. Indeed, walking is one of the great British traditions to be indulged in before or after a Sunday roast. Somewhere along the line, there will be a pub.

So many of our customs and traditions seem to involve eating, drinking and making merry, but so many of them also originated as games or contests in pubs with societies and controlling bodies. Pubs were where we invented (many different versions of) skittles, bar billiards and shove ha'penny, among many others. Believe it or not, these games were once the subject of a TV programme fronted by former England cricketer Fred Trueman. The *Indoor League* was a pub games competition series that was produced by Yorkshire TV. It's arguably the programme that gave the tradition of darts its first TV outing. The show was cancelled forty years before the current British darts wunderkind Luke Littler was even born.

THE *INDOOR LEAGUE*

https://www.youtube.com/watch?v=G2QRnF1KtiM&t=30s

We love games. We invent them, play them, export them and govern them. The British have invented so many sports and games – archery, badminton, baseball, basketball (oh yes), bobsleigh, boxing, bowls, croquet, cricket, curling, darts, football, golf, hockey, horse racing, netball, polo, rounders, rugby, snooker, squash, table tennis, volleyball and water polo, to name a few. Of course, the British didn't invent punching people in their faces, riding a horse or kicking a ball, but we were the ones who wrote the rules for it.

One man made so much of this possible. His name was Edwin Budding, a mechanic repairing the textile mills of Stroud in Gloucestershire, who in 1830 invented the cylinder lawnmower. Inspired by cross-cutting machinery used for trimming wool, he created the first model, primarily intended for mowing grass in sports grounds and large gardens.

The Industrial Revolution allowed people to move around more easily. Where there were many local rules for games, there needed to be a standardised rule book. As more people moved around the country and the empire, there was a greater need for boarding public schools. Sport became a key part of the curriculum at these schools. It not only promoted health and fitness but prepared them for military service and taught them about teamwork, preparation and a sense of fairness. All of these were seen as good qualities to oversee the future of the empire. A classic example of this was Haileybury College in Hertfordshire, which originated from the East India Company's need for a college to train young men for service in India.

India contributed directly to our identity and language with words like avatar, bungalow, chutney, cot, dinghy, dungarees, guru, gymkhana, juggernaut, jungle, loot, punch, pyjamas, shampoo, thug and veranda. The word curry originates from the Tamil word *kari*, which means sauce or relish for rice. There are over 8,000 curry houses, employing 80,000 people and contributing £3.5 billion to the UK economy. There are more than 11,000 Chinese or East Asian takeaways in the UK. In 2023, the UK had nearly 48,000 takeaway and fast-food restaurants. Our identity is in our food, too.

Pubs were important for hydration in the Middle Ages. Beer was safer than water to drink, as it undergoes processes like pasteurisation to reduce harmful bacteria and extend its life. Beer was often mixed with water to make it safe for children to drink – this was known as 'small' beer.

A pint of beer typically has around 180 calories, which is about twice the energy content but half the alcohol of a glass of wine. It also enters the bloodstream more slowly. Beer could be consumed throughout the day for hydration, whereas wine was typically enjoyed with food. So, the British grew used to drinking all day; perhaps that's why we're able to Keep Calm and Carry On with a sense of humour. You see more people laughing than crying in pubs. The term 'Dutch courage' is linked to the Dutch use of gin, particularly among troops fighting alongside their allies in the Low Countries during the Napoleonic wars.

It was because of this all-day habit that we have British pub hours. During the First World War, too many munitions workers (many were women working in factories) were over-indulging. Their marked increase in alcohol consumption on the home front led to the passage of several laws making the sale of alcohol stricter. It was decided to close the pubs after lunchtime. We still have the remnants of those licensing laws more than a century later, and it took a Royal Commission and around a dozen Licensing Acts to roll most of them back.

These days, it's more likely to be tea and biscuits that define our tradition. The UK may be known for its tea culture, but recently coffee has overtaken it as the preferred hot beverage in the UK. A 2023 Statista global consumer survey revealed that 63 per cent of Britons regularly drink coffee, compared to 59 per cent who drink tea. But the truly world-class aspect is biscuits. We eat more biscuits than anywhere else on Earth. On average, we munch on three a day, which works out at 204 million each day across the UK's 68 million population. Over the course of a year, that works out at 1,095 biscuits each, an astonishing 8.5 kilograms or about 103 packets of biscuits per year for the average household.

Here's where tea was vital to the Industrial Revolution. The tea-break tradition, a pause for refreshment, emerged when employers provided workers with tea and a break to boost energy and morale during long shifts. The tea break became a significant part of British industrial culture, with employers often providing tea to employees. The practice was also influenced by the temperance movement, which promoted tea as a healthier alternative to alcohol.

The Sunday roast tradition can be traced back to medieval England. Some say it started in 1485, during the reign of King Henry VII. In this time, the royal guards, also known as Yeomen of the Guard, earned their nickname 'Beefeaters' because of the large quantities of roast beef they ate. These guards would usually cook the meat every Sunday morning before attending mass. After church services on Sundays, it became a tradition in villages to congregate around communal ovens, where they would roast the meat from the week's hunt. It's associated with families getting together. In polls, people consistently rank it as one of the most important traditions. Eating a meal after church is common in most of Europe, but the Sunday roast variant developed uniquely in the British Isles. The French nickname for the English remains *les rosbifs*. American visitors are habitually confused by the prospect of the traditional British family getting together and sharing a joint.

There are many places to enjoy a Sunday roast, but Newcastle's Blackfriars restaurant and banquet hall is said to be the oldest in the UK, having been established in 1239. The oldest in London is Rules, established by Thomas Rule in 1798, on Maiden Lane.

Bangers and mash is another favourite. Sausages (snorkers – old English for piglets) got the name 'bangers' as they were filled with water due to food shortages during the First World War, which caused them to explode when cooked.

Fish and chips is a famous British dish, but it's not that recent nor that British. The first fish and chip restaurant was opened in 1860 by an Ashkenazi Jewish immigrant, Joseph Malin, who came to London's East End from Europe. The dish was so important that it was not rationed during the Second World War. Churchill recognised the morale-boosting importance of the 'chippy' during a difficult time.

In a similar way, the full English breakfast is another staple. The British eat breakfast like it's their last meal on Earth. For those who eat it too frequently, it often is. We take the full English breakfast so seriously that there is even an English Breakfast Society. This describes itself as 'a learned society of fellows, dedicated to the history and heritage of the traditional English breakfast'.[8]

British traditions are habits that remind us who we are and what's important to us. They are bound into seasons, places, occasions and the rhythms of life. The more unstable the times, the more they grow in importance. Our traditions matter both as a mark of our historic pride and as a part of our faith in the future. It sounds illogical to say that ancient traditions prepare us for the future, but they do. They provide us with a strong sense of continuity, stability and identity. Whether we like it or not, our traditions are what make us. They are deeply rooted in history and still offer valuable lessons and frameworks that help us navigate the complexities of modern life.

You might well ask, how does hurling yourself down Cooper's Hill in pursuit of cheese prepare us for modernity? Well, apart from being exactly the sort of thing that Wallace and Gromit would do, the spectacle and the laughter alone remind us that communities can be fun. The fact that they were never designed for anything serious speaks volumes about our customs. There is an enormous sense of humility when people are just getting together to do something absurd.

Of course, we could turn our back on traditions. We could say there's no role for remembering our values or the past. Who cares about our culture? Isn't it all lies? There's plenty more attention-getting content available on the internet. On a routine visit, for instance, you can find all sorts of casual violence, pornography, racism, lies and extremism. All of the worst, most grotesque characteristics of humanity are being broadcast to millions of people. Consuming this in quantity will have an effect. It will contribute to a steady erosion of our communities and faith in humanity.

Our British traditions are of greater value than anything from the social media world, which is being showered down on us from who knows where.

Our traditions stand for the best qualities in us – there is a real sense of fun, decency, history and community. Apart from the consumption of alcohol, they are healthy. They do no harm. On the contrary, they can do a great deal of good. They bring people together. They are usually offline and outdoors. They may be old-fashioned, even quaint and idiosyncratic. They may even be utterly escapist. Yet in a world of multiplying new fears, both real and imagined, and with constant change all around us, they serve as an antidote.

In *Greater*, we laid out the need to modernise Britain. Here, we have described how that should be done. Our traditions hold the key to unlocking the future. With 1,000 years of heritage and success, it would be arrogant and madness to turn our back on these hard-fought lessons. Stability and reliability are about to become so much more important to the world, as our allies become overtaken by intoxicating novelty. This will be exciting and radical for a few. To the many, though, it will result in fear and insecurity if everything we've known is torn up in this process. This is because excellence is a habit built up over time, not a one-off event. Temporary novelty can never eclipse a lasting legacy. Utopian dreams are very powerful but illusory. We can't have what we want. We must want what we have. And we've been given so much.

We have something precious. It was given to us by our antecedents. They realised how important it was. We should not betray either our heritage from the past or our inheritance in the future by turning our back on it.

I said at the opening of this book that the coronation changed me. It made me want to know more about our heritage and traditions. I also said that I started from a position of loving Britain and its culture. After a year of researching and writing this book, I discovered many more traditions, both royal and rural. They are, by measure, boisterous, alcohol-fuelled, even absurd – yet I also found many that were solemn, moving, inspiring and reflective. They say a lot about who we are. How could I summarise this?

We remember the past. For us, it's many layers of the past.

We embrace individualism, even eccentricity.

We forget that we have enjoyed 1,000 years of uninterrupted sovereignty.

We've lost confidence.

We've been negative for too long. And that achieves nothing.

We like fairness. When something's really wrong, we actually do something.

We're sceptical about politicians. Lord knows there's enough reason.

We agree on many values.

We love humour, community, compassion and hard work.

We love saucy Dorset nobs. Enough said.

We love a game. And we've invented most of them.

We love the rules. If only to break them.

I would recommend seeing as many of these traditions as possible. No, I'm not about to throw myself off Cooper's Hill chasing a chunk of cheese, but I can't help admiring those that do.

In writing this book, we have catalogued what happened since 2000 – 9/11, the banking crisis, Brexit, Covid, Her Majesty Queen Elizabeth II dying, five PMs in six years, European war, the cost-of-living crisis, technical change, uncensored social media, polarisation, the return to power of President Trump. Many of these are centrifugal forces that throw us to extremes. That's why the traditions and the community relationships matter. They are centripetal. They bring us back together. We serve something bigger than ourselves and our personal views.

At other times, they do something more simple. They remind us of who we are and give us the confidence to face the future again. They make us laugh, eat and drink with our community. They allow us to draw breath and break bread. In the words of John Greenleaf Whittier in his hymn 'Lord and Father of Mankind', they 'reclothe us in our rightful mind'.

I said at the start of this book that I've always loved this country. I must confess that researching these traditions and customs has changed that view.

Now, I love it even more.

CALENDAR OF OUR CUSTOMS

This is just a flavour of British customs and traditions. Those in search of more detail should read *The English Year* by Steve Roud. This section is a wider look at the whole of Britain and at the relevance of these traditions to our national as well as local life. It seemed appropriate to organise the traditions by calendar month, though many of our greatest treasures are with us daily, even hourly.

The basis of everything is the importance of the land – when to sow, when to reap, when to gather and store. So much of our calendar is and remains agricultural and seasonal, which began with Easter or the spring equinox (Ostara) and the coming summer solstice (Litha). This must always have been a time of great relief to our forebears after a long winter. The return of the good weather was always a time of high spirits, as it remains to this day.

May Day is still celebrated with morris dancing fairs and ribbon-festooned maypoles. Some villages, like Ickwell Green in Bedfordshire, still have a May Queen. And Jack in the Green still occasionally makes an appearance.

The backbreaking work of the harvest was celebrated by a great party afterwards. At London St Martin-in-the-Fields, it was traditional for pearly princesses to take vegetable bouquets as offerings. The Pearly Kings and Queens Association is a charitable body still in existence and they've held a harvest celebration at St Martin-in-the-Fields every year since the 1950s.

Thanks is a consistent theme. Well dressing still takes place in

Derbyshire and Staffordshire from May to September, where wells are blessed and then dressed with elaborate panels of clay and flower petals.

It is not just the seasons and festivals that are a focal point. Even weekdays have superstitions and these vary from county to county. For those in Hertfordshire, a sneeze on Wednesday means the postman will come. In Devon, don't start any new projects on a Friday, if you want success. In Norfolk, if it's raining on a Sunday, it means bad weather all week. This isn't that helpful, as that could pretty much be guaranteed to be said about any day at any part of the year in any part of the country.

Traditions are built up around everything, including food. Depending on where you are in the country, the humble Christmas cake can be a harbinger of doom. Do not be tempted to scoff the lot on Christmas Eve if you live in Lincolnshire. If you do, bad luck is inevitable. If Scottish Bannock or fruitcake breaks in the middle, someone's going to die. Stirring the cake anticlockwise is frowned upon except for Stir-up Sunday, the last Sunday before the season of Advent, when families mix and steam their Christmas pudding. The name comes from the opening words of a collect prayer in the Book of Common Prayer, which often begins with an address to God, such as 'Almighty God' or 'O Lord, our heavenly Father'. When the Christmas pudding is stirred anticlockwise, it symbolises the wise men travelling from East to West.

There is dressing up as the Green Man, pouring cider over the tree roots and hanging cake from its branches. The places to see this include Woolsthorpe Manor in Lincolnshire, where Isaac Newton's apple tree is still alive and growing. It can be seen in modern orchards as well, such as Cotehele's Mother Orchard, which consists of more than 300 trees and 125 different varieties of apple trees, planted between 2007 and 2008. These include the Cornish Honeypinnick, Limberlimb, Pig's Nose and Lemon Pippin.

The varieties grown in the Mother Orchard have been bred to survive the south-west's mild and damp climatic conditions over the last 250 years. The orchard's intention is to provide a set of 'mother trees' that can be used for the selection of future varieties for domestic and commercial use.[1]

Consuming alcohol is a recurring theme throughout much of British folklore. I am particularly fascinated by the custom of 'tooling'. The aim was to raid the beer casks of your neighbours under the pretence of searching for misplaced tools. Men would visit farmhouses, claiming that their axe, scythe, billhook, bodging lathe or fishing rod might be hidden behind the pile of beer casks in the shed. Although this tradition is not widely known, it is still practised in many parts of the UK.

Superstitions are highly local, too. On New Year's Eve, traditions around first footing still exist, predominantly in Scotland and the north of England. This was based around consequences for a particular person or item of goods being the first across the threshold in the new year. In Westleton in Suffolk, the lights were turned off in many households on Christmas Eve to stop poltergeist activity.

Variances continue between professions as well as places. It was bad luck to whistle on board a ship because it could summon a strong wind that could sink the boat. Or down a mine, where it was believed whistling could conjure up evil spirits. This is a bone of contention, apparently. Some miners held fast to the theory that whistling could dispel evil spirits and protected the whistle. However, if you were an arable farmer in Cornwall and if the wind dropped while you were winnowing the wheat, a whistle was said to guarantee the breeze to return.

Often, traditions whose origins date back centuries are retained only in one or two places – a time capsule from an otherwise forgotten piece of history. Other areas celebrate widely observed festivals in a particularly unique way. For example, at Little Moreton Hall in Cheshire, traditional All Hallowtide activities still take place. This is celebrated on 2 November as a time to remember deceased spirits, saints and martyrs. It's a time to feel close to loved ones who have passed away.

I hope you enjoy and explore these wonderful, eccentric and moving events as much as all the participants do.

SPRING

MARCH

St David's Day

St David's Day is 1 March, celebrating Wales's patron saint. David is the anglicised version of St Dewi, the sixth-century monk and bishop. The day is marked across the UK, but particularly in Wales. Flags, dragons, daffodils, entertainers, male voice choirs and national costumes are the order of the day. Cardiff has celebrated with a big parade since 2004.

In Lanark, South Lanarkshire, Whuppity Scoorie takes place. This event celebrates the arrival of spring. In the early evening, children will gather outside the local church. They will have fashioned large paper balls, attached to long strings. At precisely 6.00 p.m., they circle the church three times in a clockwise direction, swinging the balls above their heads. This ritual is believed to ward off evil and ensure a bountiful harvest, with their efforts being rewarded in return.

WHUPPITY SCOORIE

https://www.youtube.com/watch?v=_ufdIe4ovM8

The UK Wife-Carrying Races

In Dorking, in early March, you can find the Wife-Carrying Races. This stems from a Scandinavian tradition, which ensured that the menfolk were able to carry off women from the villages they were intending to raid. Couples race over an obstacle course together. These days, couples don't have to be married and same-sex couples are welcomed.

Every March, couples must negotiate a 400-yard obstacle course. The winners do it in the shortest time. The 'husband' has to carry his 'wife' (as long as they weigh over 50 kilograms) in recognised holds. These include the piggy-back, fireman's lift and the popular Estonian Hold technique, which requires the 'wife' to hang upside down on the carrier's back. Winners receive a cash prize and, surprise surprise, a barrel of beer.

https://www.youtube.com/watch?v=2wfCkOTqBBg

St Piran's Day

St Piran is the patron saint of Cornwall. This day is celebrated across many parts of the region on 5 March, including Bodmin, Truro, Marazion, Launceston, Falmouth and Perranporth. At the beach in Penzance, locals welcome St Piran. He then heads into the town centre to continue the celebrations with a parade and performances, followed by an event at the cathedral.

Newark Penny Loaf Day

Newark Penny Loaf Day, held on the nearest Sunday to 11 March, sees civic leaders give out bread to local charitable causes, honouring the charitable legacy left by Hercules Clay. A resident of Newark-on-Trent during the Civil War, Clay narrowly escaped death when a fire damaged his home – an event he had foreseen in a dream. The charitable dole is his expression of gratitude for his survival. His Bible is still used in this annual service.

Thriplow Daffodil Weekend

For the last fifty years Thriplow, a village in Cambridgeshire, has celebrated the arrival of spring by honouring the daffodil. The fete, held in mid-March, features morris and molly dancers, a maypole and a variety of other attractions. The community takes great care in ensuring that thousands of daffodils, in all their varieties, bloom throughout the village.

The Betty Morley Dinner

The founders of Brasenose College, Oxford, were the first of many benefactors to make provision for celebrations to ensure that they were remembered. Richard Sutton allowed for a modest worldly festivity after the annual commemorative rites for him in the Chapel: 'The Principal and Scholars and their successors shall have ... 13s 4d to increase their fare that day.'

Other benefactors followed suit and by 1635 there were thirteen such celebrations every year, each in honour of a different benefactor. The largest was that of Elizabeth Morley, the widow of a prosperous London draper. She was the first after the founders to endow Brasenose with land. It was also an each-way bet. She intended to ensure that the principal and fellows prayed for her soul. There was also to be an annual commemoration on 26 January, with a dinner. The warden of New College was appointed to oversee the proper execution of her wishes and to attend the celebrations. An annual dinner is still held in mid-March and the warden still attends to receive his fee.

St Patrick's Day

St Patrick, the patron saint of Ireland, is celebrated across the UK and the world on 17 March. His feast day is perhaps more closely associated with lively festivities, drinking copious amounts of Guinness and having a good old knees-up, than any other saint. The parade and events in London are perhaps one of the best-known. The procession starts in Piccadilly and weaves through Trafalgar Square down Whitehall.

St Cuthbert's Day

A special service is held at Durham Cathedral on 20 March, where St Cuthbert is buried. On his feast day, the congregation is invited to visit his tomb. There is also a procession from Finchale Priory, where pilgrims carry the Banner of St Cuthbert to his resting place.

The vernal equinox, also known as the spring equinox, also occurs around this day and is celebrated across the country. Druids typically lead a procession, perform blessings and scatter seeds to encourage an abundant harvest.

Cranmer Day or Thomas Cranmer Commemoration Day

On 21 March, Oxford marks the martyrdom of Thomas Cranmer, Archbishop of Canterbury, who was executed for heresy by the Catholic Queen Mary I. A wreath is laid at his memorial following a procession.

The Kiplingcotes Derby

This is a horse race run on the third Thursday in the East Riding of Yorkshire. It has taken place since 1519 and is thought to be England's oldest annual horse race. Everyone is welcome to participate. The terrain is hard-going over four miles. Rules state that if the race is not run one year, it must never be run again.

Oranges and Lemons Service

At St Clement Danes church in London, also on the third Thursday, an annual service is held to commemorate its connection with a well-known nursery rhyme. The churchyard used to reach the river where tolls on fruit being brought into the capital were levied. Known as the 'oranges and lemons' service, it has been running since 1919.

The Tichborne Dole

On 25 March, an ancient tradition called the Tichborne Dole takes place in the village of Tichborne in Hampshire. Locals are entitled to claim a gallon of flour from outside Tichborne House. Any tenant of the property must agree to these terms. The tradition stems from the twelfth century, where a dying Lady Marbella Tichborne requested to leave a charitable legacy. Her husband said she could have all the corn from the land she could walk (or crawl) around while still holding a lit piece of wood from the fire. She managed twenty-three acres before the torch went out (known as 'the crawls' to this day) and cursed anyone who dare not continue her wishes.

Hawick Reivers Festival

Hawick lies at the heart of what was once a 'no man's land' between England and Scotland, before the formation of the Union. From the late thirteenth to the early seventeenth century, it was inhabited by Border Reivers (raiders), known for their fierce loyalty and often engaging in skirmishes and battles. Today, a festival held in late March celebrates their bellicose ways. There are processions, including a torchlit one, sports, entertainment and a market.

Whitby Goth Weekend

Whitby, where it is said Dracula first came to England's shores, has been hosting the bi-annual Goth Weekend for a number of years. Bram Stoker stayed in Whitby in the summer of 1890 to recover from a gruelling theatrical tour of Scotland. In the public library, he found a book published in 1820 by William Wilkinson, the Levant Company's former agent in Bucharest, called *An Account of the Principalities of*

Wallachia and Moldavia. He copied into his research papers the footnote: 'Dracula means devil. Wallachians were accustomed to give it as a surname to any person who rendered himself conspicuous by courage, cruel actions or cunning.' His use of Whitby as the arrival point of the *Demeter*, Dracula's ship, was probably inspired by an actual shipwreck. In 1885, the Russian ship *Dmitry* foundered on Tate Hill Sands off Whitby.

The Dalemain World Marmalade Awards

At Dalemain House, an eighteenth-century mansion in Cumbria, they choose late March to celebrate marmalade. Early forms of the jam were made with quinces and had Portuguese origins. This first-known English recipe, using oranges, is from 1677 in a book held at the Cheshire Record Office. It was eaten in the evening, but the Scots decided to start consuming it in the mornings. One hundred years later, that was the norm across the UK. Legend has it Mary Queen of Scots used it as a sea sickness cure, with the name marmalade coming from the French words for sea and ill, *mer* and *malade*. During the celebrations, there is a boil-off to find the best recipe.

The Boat Race

The annual Oxford–Cambridge University Boat Race was first held in 1829. It runs over four miles of water from Putney Bridge to Chiswick Road Bridge. It draws massive crowds along the banks of the River Thames. Seen as a posh event, it is relentlessly mocked. Over at the Spitalfields City Farm at the same time, and to a slightly smaller crowd, the Oxford versus Cambridge Goat Race sees animals go horn to horn to be crowned King Billy and pick up an edible trophy.

APRIL

April Fool's Day

On this day, it is the custom to prank one's friends, but only until noon, because after that it would just be plain silly. In Scotland, April Fool's Day was traditionally known as *Huntigowk Day*, meaning hunt the cuckoo (or the fool). The traditional prank involved asking someone to send a message to someone. The individual reading the note would be in on the prank and would respond with a new note. This would continue for as long as possible, or until the pubs opened, whichever was sooner.

A similar sort of custom was employed in some workplaces for new starters. They would be sent to the stores for a 'long weight/stand' or to the chief engineer for 'a bag of tappet clearances' or to textile mills for tartan paint.

In 1686, the writer John Aubrey referenced 'Fooles Holy Day'. This was the first reference to the day in Britain, and in 1698 several people were fooled into going to the Tower of London to see lions being washed.

In recent times, most media, in particular the BBC, has prided itself on creating the best April Fools. In 1957, *Panorama* reported a bumper spaghetti harvest grown on trees and plantations in Italy. In 1976, it was reported that Grimond Library – a fictional library which was the subject of a BBC nationwide investigation – was being built upside down due to a copying error. In 1979, viewers were introduced to Tramp the sheepdog, who could drive.

SPAGHETTI TREES IN ITALY

https://www.youtube.com/watch?v=8scpGwbvxvI

THE UPSIDE-DOWN GRIMOND LIBRARY

https://www.facebook.com/watch/?v=386339601739076

TRAMP THE CAR-DRIVING SHEEPDOG

https://www.youtube.com/watch?v=ogRODRXJtjQ

The Countess Pillar Dole

Head westward from Penrith in Cumbria on the A66 and you will pass the Countess Pillar. It was erected in 1656 by Lady Anne Clifford to commemorate the last time she met with her mother in 1616. She also established a dole of bread and cash and to this day, on 2 April every year, the dole is distributed to the needy at the foot of the pillar.

International Pillow Fight Day

On the first Saturday in April, at various locations around the UK including London and Hull, pillow fights are held. Apparently, an international pillow fight day was inspired by the film *Fight Club* but has now become a tradition in its own right. This seems typically British both in its thinking and its observance of the first rule of Fight Club. Damn.

The Grand National

In early April, the Grand National takes place at Aintree, a few miles outside Liverpool. The horse race was founded by William Lynn, who owned the Waterloo Hotel and leased land in Aintree from the Earl of Sefton. Again, not to be outdone by the toffs, there is an alternative steeplechase on offer in Bideford. The Sheep Grand National takes place on the same day. The course is rather shorter, at 250 yards, and the field less crowded. About six sheep, each with a knitted jockey strapped to its back, navigate a series of sheep-themed jumps.

The Quill Pen Ceremony

On 5 April, or close to this date, on particular anniversaries, a service takes place where the quill pen in the hand of John Stow's stone effigy is replaced with a fresh one by the Master of the Merchant Taylors' Company, the Lord Mayor or the Alderman. Stow authored the great Survey of London and is buried at St Andrew Undershaft on St Mary Axe, London. Built in 1532, it survived both the Great Fire of London and the Blitz, rare for a building in the City of London. A church has existed on the site since 1147, dating it to Norman times. Its curious name derives from the shaft of the maypole that was traditionally set up each year opposite the church.

St Andrew Undershaft is also of note due to having had one of London's few surviving large stained-glass windows, installed in the seventeenth century, but this was destroyed in the Baltic Exchange bombing in 1992.

Badajoz Day

On 6 April, in 1812, British forces successfully stormed the Spanish castle and city of Badajoz. Instead of a union flag being hoisted up the flagpole, Lieutenant James MacPherson used his scarlet jacket. Today, a group of soldiers from the Mercian Regiment march to Castle Green in Nottingham to repeat the act and to commemorate the victory.

Tartan Day

The Declaration of Arbroath was signed on 6 April 1320 and was commemorated by Tartan Day. This involves haggis hurling and hunting. This tradition has since lapsed in the UK but can still be observed in areas with large Scots communities.

Battle of Barnet Day

Although the Wars of the Roses were between the houses of York and Lancaster, a decisive engagement was fought near London. On Sunday 14 April 1471, Easter Day, the two sides clashed near Barnet, then a small Hertfordshire town north of London. Both sides of the Battle of Barnet are commemorated, with wreaths laid at the battle monument. A medieval festival takes place, featuring a reenactment of the battle where Edward IV (York) was victorious.

Royal Maundy

The Royal Maundy is another ancient royal ceremony dating back to the thirteenth century for members of the Royal Family to distribute money and gifts. The tradition has its origins in the Bible and is based on the commandment, or mandatum, that 'ye love one another' (John 13:34) that Christ gave after washing the feet of his disciples before Good Friday.

Henry IV began the practice of relating the number of recipients of gifts to the monarch's age. It subsequently became customary for the monarch to perform the ceremony.

In the eighteenth century, the act of washing the feet of the poor was discontinued and in the nineteenth century, money allowances were distributed in place of the various gifts of food and clothing.

Today's recipients are as many elderly men and women as there are years in the sovereign's age. They are chosen due to the Christian service they have given to the church and community. At the ceremony, which takes place annually on Maundy Thursday, the monarch hands to each recipient two small leather string purses. One is a red purse, containing money in lieu of food and clothing. This is a set of specially minted coins, consisting of four denominations: one penny, two pence, three pence and four pence, making the total value of a full ten pence. The other, a white purse, contains silver Maundy coins consisting of the same number of pence as the monarch's age. Because of their rarity, they can become highly valuable.

Maundy money has remained much the same since 1670, the coins traditionally being struck in sterling silver. A Maundy set still consists of four small silver coins, but in 1971, at the time of decimalisation, the face values of the coins were changed from old to new pence.

The World Marbles Championships

The Greyhound pub, located at Tinsley Green near Gatwick Airport in Sussex, hosts an annual competition on Good Friday, attracting players from all over the world. Marbles is an ancient and skilled game in which competitors aim to knock forty-nine marbles from a marked circle using their own 'tolley' (another marble); two teams of six players take part in each heat and the winning team is the one whose tolleys stay in until the end. The tradition of a competition here reputedly goes back to Elizabethan times. Marbles of all sizes and colours are on sale at the event.

https://www.youtube.com/watch?v=1CfSAclqkh8

The Bacup Britannia Coconut Dancers

Easter Saturday brings forth the Bacup Britannia Coconut Dancers, who are clog dancers that perform across the town and surrounding areas with blackened faces. The original reason for the darkened faces of the 'Nutters' (a common local surname) is unclear, but as the application of blackface is often considered offensive and racist, the group is controversial.

Some say the custom was brought to the area by Moors who settled in Cornwall in the seventeenth century, became miners and then moved to work in quarries in Lancashire.

Their name refers to the wooden 'nuts' worn at their knees, waists and wrists, which are made from the tops of bobbins. These are protection for the hands and knees, essential in mining work.

https://www.youtube.com/watch?v=1NMkdDHFwgA

The Musselburgh Racecourse Corgi Derby

First launched in 2022 to mark Queen Elizabeth II's Platinum Jubilee, the Corgi Derby was created to celebrate the breed that was the late monarch's favourite. She owned over thirty corgis during her reign, keeping at least one from 1933 to 2018. Her corgis became a symbol of the monarchy and were often featured in official photos and artwork. Pembroke Welsh corgis are not just pets but have also played a role in Welsh folklore, where they are believed to be fairy steeds. Although a recent tradition, corgi owners come to the course to put their dogs through their paces.

https://www.youtube.com/watch?v=olaJkuH9pSk

World Coal-Carrying Championships

Easter Monday brings a comparatively recent tradition, which was created in 1963: the World Coal-Carrying Championships.

The women's race starts from the Royal Oak and continues to the finish line at the Maypole Green in Gawthorpe village. Women carry twenty kilograms of coal, but the men carry fifty kilograms. The world records for this intense challenge are mercifully short – both around four minutes.

https://www.youtube.com/watch?v=ArPCLH-a3Hg&t=73s

Culloden Day

The Battle of Culloden, in April 1746, was a pivotal engagement in the Jacobite Rising. This saw the forces of Prince Charles Edward Stuart (Bonnie Prince Charlie), attempting to reclaim the throne for his family, face a British Army led by the Duke of Cumberland, son of King George II. Every year, on the nearest Saturday to 16 April, a service is held at the Memorial Cairn to remember the fallen of the 1746 Battle of Culloden. This was a historic clash and the last battle on British soil.

Prayers are offered, some in Gaelic, and wreaths laid by clan families to commemorate their ancestors.

Damson Day

Lyth Valley in Westmorland, Cumbria, has been well-known for its damsons and its Damson Day. Festivities are timed to coincide with the blossoming of the trees. The event was created to highlight the rich heritage of the damson, although many other artisan producers are present at the event.

https://www.youtube.com/watch?v=R-qV_3RVOIU&t=8s

Kate Kennedy Procession

In St Andrews, the Kate Kennedy Club stages an annual pageant in mid-April. The Spring Procession traces its roots to ancient, medieval, pagan and Christian spring rites, with fifers commemorating 'Cath Cinneachaidh'.

Legend has it that in the fifteenth century, the beautiful niece of Bishop James Kennedy, Lady Katharine, visited in the spring of her life and the spring of the year. Idolised by all, a festival grew up and it became the Kate Kennedy Procession. Each year, it celebrates the great characters from Scotland's history.

World Dock Pudding Competition

Dock Pudding is a distinctive West Yorkshire savoury dish from the Calder Valley – where they have an annual World Dock Pudding Competition, held on the third Sunday of the month. It is made from dock leaves, nettles, oatmeal, onions, butter and seasoning. The flavour is 'somewhere between spinach and asparagus' and it is often eaten with bacon dishes. This is, of course, accompanied by a traditional brass band. A visit to the Traditional Yorkshire Recipes website is highly recommended, if for no other reason than to gaze upon the ingredients of Queer Times Pudding.

https://traditional-yorkshire-recipes.info

Barmote Court Day
Wirksworth in Derbyshire is home to the last remaining Great Barmote Court. Established in the twelfth century to regulate lead mining, the court still convenes on the third Wednesday of April.

St George's Day
St George is the patron saint of England and events held to celebrate him on 23 April are on the increase across the whole of the UK. Expect morris men, mummers, beer and roast beef. Salisbury in Wiltshire hosts plays about the saint and the dragon he slew, along with a procession featuring a host of mythical characters.

In Lichfield, Staffordshire, St George's Court sits on this day. The mayor and local dignitaries gather to humiliate and fine others. The more absurd the charge and the reasons behind the fines, the better.

William Shakespeare's Birthday
William Shakespeare's birthday is also on 23 April. In his hometown of Stratford-upon-Avon, they celebrate his birth on the Saturday nearest

this date. A procession of his well-known characters heads to his tomb at Holy Trinity Church, where he is given a new quill.

The Battle of Dunbar Commemoration

The first Battle of Dunbar, a key event in the Wars of Scottish Independence, ended in victory for King Edward I of England. This historic battle is commemorated each year on the nearest weekend to 27 April, with reenactments across the weekend.

Trevithick Day

The residents of Camborne celebrate Richard Trevithick, a pioneer of steam power, honouring his significant contributions to the Industrial Revolution. Festivities are held on a Saturday late in April and consist of dances, first by the Bal maidens (from the Cornish word *bal*, meaning mine). These were female manual labourers working in the mining industries of Cornwall. At one stage, there were more than 50,000 of them. There is a large parade of steam vehicles, a fairground, flowers and stalls.

The Cuckoo Fair

In Heathfield, Sussex, or Heffle as it was known, they hold the annual Cuckoo Fair late in April to mark the arrival of spring. The tradition dates back to 1315 when the Bishop of Chichester got permission to hold a market. A cuckoo was released as part of the festivities. These days, a pigeon usually performs the role.

Marsden Cuckoo Day

In Marsden, West Yorkshire, they also celebrate the arrival of the cuckoo. The story goes that the people of Marsden attempted to capture the bird to bring eternal spring to their village but failed. Today, among the various celebrations such as duck racing, the highlight is a cuckoo parade through the streets.

Beltane

Beltane celebrations often begin on 30 April, historically observed primarily in Scotland and Ireland. Marking one of the four divisions of the Celtic year, the festival continues to be celebrated in some places. Traditionally, people visit a local holy well to make offerings of cloth strips, with the belief that as the cloth rots, so too will their ailments.

The Clootie Well Ceremony

At the Black Isle village of Munlochy, the service takes place at the renowned Clootie Well (a holy or sacred spring). The site has been described as an important part of Highland history and culture, attracting visitors from across the world. But some say the practice has got out of hand, with hundreds of non-biodegradable fabrics festooning tree branches and trunks.[1]

The Beltane Fire Festival

At Calton Hill there is a modern revival of Beltane festivities, featuring bonfires, torchlit processions, Green Men and May Queens. Meanwhile, at Glastonbury, you can expect blessings given at the White Spring, maypole dancing and a procession of dragons.

Butser Ancient Farm near Petersfield in Hampshire hosts several annual celebrations marking ancient customs and the changing seasons, including Beltane (1 May), a pagan Gaelic fire festival that celebrates the transition from spring to summer. Unlike the modern astronomical definition of seasons, which places the start of summer at the June solstice, Beltane is based on the traditional agrarian calendar. This calendar observes the beginning of summer from the evidence of nature itself – increased warmth, the blooming of plants and the fertile earth ready to sow crops. Beltane falls about halfway between the spring equinox (Ostara) and the coming summer solstice (Litha).

The Christian holiday of Easter, which celebrates the resurrection of Jesus, is named after the Anglo-Saxon goddess of spring Eostre, also known as Ostara. The holiday celebrates spring at its peak and the coming summer. Beltane also sometimes goes by the name May Day. For pagans, this holiday is associated very strongly with fertility.

BELTANE/BELTAIN FESTIVAL AT BUTSER

https://youtu.be/Z4EOzNFfDso?si=Dkuga3yMmce-pYcV

Fritillary Sunday

In the meadows of Ducklington, near Witney, the rare snake's head fritillary flower thrives. Oxfordshire residents celebrate by walking among the flowers in the meadows and enjoying traditional May festivities, such as morris dancing and music, on a Sunday late in April.

The Whitebread Meadow Charity Auction

On a Monday late in April in Bourne, Lincolnshire, an unusual property auction takes place to settle the grazing rights for Whitebread Meadow. Bidding takes place against the backdrop of a children's race over 200 yards. The winning bid is the highest made before the winning child finishes. The event now raises funds for charity.

Beating the Bounds

Every five years, in April or May, Beating the Bounds takes place at Bodmin, Cornwall. This is an ancient service checking local property boundaries to ensure people were not encroaching on each other's land. After an eighteen-mile hike around the local parish, a silver ball is thrown into the Salting Pool. Attempts are made to recover it for reward. A hurling match is also held and funds raised for good causes.

Court Leet Day

The Assize of Bread and Ale was a thirteenth-century version of the Food Standards Agency. It was a court that inspected the wares of local producers to ensure the consumer was getting a fair deal. Alcester in Warwickshire still has one such court, held on a Saturday in April or May. Dignitaries visit local traders and sample their wares. Those that pass the test have a sprig of flowers placed above the door.

The Tudor Pull

The Tudor Pull is a rowing event upon the River Thames, held on a Sunday in April or May. It involves taking a special piece of regalia, a waterpipe named the Stela, to the Tower of London via royal barge. The row starts at Hampton Court Palace. The Stela Ceremony, where the object is handed over, takes place inside the east gate of the Tower of London.

https://www.youtube.com/watch?v=o_Jiswe67zw

The Maldon Mud Race

In the 1970s, a clever local from Maldon, Essex, fuelled with a bit too much ale, came up with the idea for a mud-based charity fundraiser. The Maldon Mud Race requires its contestants to make their way through the mud of the Blackwater Estuary. The English language is ill-equipped to describe this, so here's some video.

https://www.youtube.com/watch?v=I1bMtdv3AWI

The Bluebell Service

At this time of year, bluebells are out in abundance. Britain has more than half the world's bluebells. For the past century, a special service has been held on a Sunday in April or May in Swithland Wood, Charnwood Forest, Leicestershire, to honour this British flower. Prayers are offered and hymns sung in an amphitheatre deep in the woods.

Garland Day

A church-decorating service takes place at Charlton-on-Otmoor, Oxfordshire, twice a year. A garland is paraded through the village and then placed on the rood screen. Later in the day, the May Queen is crowned and a party held.

The Asparagus Festival

The Vale of Evesham in Worcestershire is well-known for its fruit and vegetable production, particularly its asparagus. At this time of the year, some time between April and June, the local community celebrates the wealth it has brought them. The spring bank holiday weekend usually coincides with the asparagus auctions at the Fleece Inn in the village of Bretforton. After a concert by the Bretforton Silver Band, locally grown asparagus is auctioned off to the public. Traditionally, large sums of money are bid.

MAY

Well Dressing

Throughout the month of May, the tradition of well dressing takes place across the country. Also known as well flowering, it's a tradition in which wells, springs and other water sources are decorated with designs created from flower petals. The custom is most closely associated with the Peak District of Derbyshire and Staffordshire. This custom dates back more than 200 years. It's estimated that between May and August, over 100 well dressings take place across the UK.

May Day

1 May is celebrated with morris dancing. Morris dancers are groups of six or eight participants that perform a traditional English folk dance, carrying wooden sticks and dressed in bells, that involves rhythmic stepping. The dance is often performed at seasonal festivals and events, banishing the dark of winter and celebrating the warmth and fertility of summer or the harvest.

Morris dancing was first recorded in documents from the fifteenth century. Some say it is connected to dance traditions from the druids, others that it comes from dances in English royal courts. Others say it comes from the word 'Moorish' because dancers used to paint their faces in black (today, only some still do and the tradition of blackening their faces may originate as a form of disguise – see mummery, discussed later).

Dancing at dawn is often followed by a fry-up. Maypole dancing and May fairs are common across the UK. There is also an old custom of parading a Jack in the Green, a tradition that was revived in the 1980s. Deptford puts on a good show. Wessex morris men dance at dawn next to the Cerne Abbas Giant (a hill figure). Accompanying them is the Dorset Ooser. The origins of this mythical, devil-like mask lie deep within ancient folklore. He is a giant who dances and is paraded by the morris men. These days, he ends up down the pub for a full English.

On May Day morning, up until the early nineteenth century, London's milk maids would dress in their best and wear garlands of flowers and silver. In Islington, this tradition has been revived by the all-female New Esperance Morris. At the ancient Castle Mound at Laxton in Nottinghamshire, the Rattlejag morris dancers welcome in summer. In Minehead in Somerset, two enormous hobby horses, the Sailors' Horse and the Town Horse, have toured the town in the evening of the last day of April for centuries. Padstow in Cornwall has a similar event, except the wooden horses are known as the Old 'Oss and Blue Ribbon 'Oss.

THE RATTLEJAG MORRIS DANCERS

https://www.youtube.com/watch?v=gCx-myJWnms

The choir of Magdalen College, Oxford, climbs to the top of the tower to sing a Te Deum each May morning to the crowd below. The tradition dates from 1509, when its tower was completed. Over at the medieval gatehouse, or Bargate, in Southampton, the choir of King Edward VI School used to climb to its battlements and sing to the crowd below. These days, morris dancing takes place in the evening.

MAGDALEN COLLEGE CHOIR SING THE HYMNUS EUCHARISTICUS

https://www.youtube.com/watch?v=8Vp7dxbhVFo

Riding of the Bounds

Later in the summer, traditional boundary-riding customs take place in the Borderlands. Since 1438, this ritual ensured that the Scottish–English border was being properly maintained. In Berwick, they undertake this ritual every May, on the Saturday of the May Day bank holiday. It starts with a ride from Barracks Square to the Guildhall, followed by a fifteen-mile patrol along the boundary led by a piper.

The Spalding Flower Parade

Over in Spalding, Lincolnshire, an area reliant on bulb producing, they celebrate an annual flower parade. This consists of tulip-covered floats, marching bands and a flower queen.

Wath Bun Throwing and Festival

Wath, North Yorkshire, hosts the Wath Bun Throwing and Festival over the May Day bank holiday weekend. This usually features morris maypole dancing alongside the throwing event. The vicar will read out the last will and testament of Thomas Tuke, who in the nineteenth century left a legacy to distribute loaves to the needy. The vicar then climbs the church tower and throws bread rolls to the crowd below.

https://www.youtube.com/watch?v=Yjcuv6BvGTs

Ely Eel Day Parade

Ely in Cambridgeshire is named after the eels living in the rivers and tributaries around the city. On the Saturday before the May Day bank holiday, an eel parade is held, led, naturally, by a giant eel. As well as the traditional May Day entertainments, there is an eel-throwing competition. Toy eels rather than live ones are used today.

https://www.youtube.com/watch?v=i9F6fgxZ4Z4

The Blackawton International Festival of Worm Charming

The Sunday before the May Day bank holiday, head to Blackawton in Devon for the International Festival of Worm Charming. Entrants register at the local pub and are invited to join a procession, during which a worm song is performed and a toast to the worms takes place. Contestants head to a secret field where their mission is to gather as many worms as possible within a metre-square plot in fifteen minutes.

https://www.youtube.com/watch?v=Vgud6FMYBG4

Dorset Knob Throwing

The Dorset knob is a small baked pastry, similar to a rusk. Legend has it that at the end of each day, bakers would mix leftover dough with butter and sugar to make into small round portions. The Dorset knob is quite dry and is often eaten with butter or cheese. Traditionally, they are dipped in tea or cider but can also be eaten with honey and cream, known in Dorset as 'thunder and lightning'. The knob-throwing event, which started in Cattistock, proved so popular that it had to be incorporated into the Cattistock Countryside Show, held near Chilfrome.

The Bolster Giant

At Chapel Porth cove near St Agnes, Cornwall, there is a commemoration and celebration of a local giant, Bolster. Legend has it that among his many misdemeanours, he ate children. There is much merrymaking and then a large fight on the cliff tops, where Bolster meets a sticky end.

https://www.youtube.com/watch?v=8v4yKUqFwls

Beltane at Thornborough Henge

At the prehistoric site of Thornborough Henge in North Yorkshire, the turn of the season is marked with mummers, dancing, drumming and the obligatory Beltane bonfire.

Calstock May Reels

The giant theme continues into the May Day bank holiday weekend. Calstock's May Day Revels stem from the legend of the rivers Tamar and Tavy. It's a sad story, which tells of the consequences of having a lie-in. The water nymph Tamara had two suitors: the giants Tavy and Torridge. Her father made the giants fall into a deep sleep and turned her into a stream. When Tavy woke, he chose to become a stream too. The rivers Tavy and Tamar flowed out together to the Plymouth sound. Torridge woke late and tried to follow, having also opted to become water. He took a wrong turn and ended up flowing north to Bideford, never to see Tamara again. During the parade, the giant Tavy knocks on the first-floor windows to call out residents to join the flow. After the festivities, Tavy boards his boat and sails away down the river Tamar.

Jack in the Green

Over in Hastings, on the south coast of England, the festivities are centred around Jack in the Green, a chap covered in a garland. After a party, poor Jack is killed up by the castle to free the spirit of spring. This ancient tradition died out in the nineteenth century but was revived fifty years ago. In recent years, the City of London has joined in. Whitstable, on the north coast of Kent, also has a notable Jack in the Green event.

https://www.youtube.com/watch?v=uElWHewU1vk

Rochester Chimney Sweeps Festival

In Victorian times, chimney sweeps only had one day off a year and it was on 1 May. In Rochester in Kent, both events are combined into something Dick van Dyke would have been very at home with. More than sixty morris dance groups perform over the bank holiday weekend, while other chimney-related festivities involving the Moggies (lucky chimney sweeps) take place.

https://www.youtube.com/watch?v=RIXBWcAImfo

The Clun Green Man

At Clun in Shropshire, the Green Man does battle with an ice queen, known as the Battle of the Bridge. For summer to be a good one, the Green Man has to win. The fight is eked out over the whole weekend, with early skirmishes, trash talk and possibly a weigh-in. If that weren't enough, there is also duck racing.

http://www.clungreenman.org

Ickwell Morris Dancers

Perhaps the oldest May Day celebration belongs to Ickwell in Bedford-shire, centred around a permanent maypole on the green.

Lewes has held a traditional garland ceremony since Victorian times.

https://www.youtube.com/watch?v=rFQSHcQvmos

The Black Prince Flower Boat Procession

This annual event takes place in the villages of Millbrook, Kingsand and Cawsand in Cornwall. The procession is based on an old tradition where apprentice boat builders would build a small boat and if it was seaworthy, they could continue their studies. The best boat was carried through the streets. The party ends with the boat being launched at Cawsand beach.

Mayor Making Day

In Reach, Cambridgeshire, an ancient charter fair goes back to the reign of King John. Over in Rye, where records date back to the thirteenth century, they elect their mayor on May Day. Rye is part of the Confederation of the Cinque Ports, formed to protect the coast from attack. Volunteers don period uniforms. The new mayor and their team swear allegiance to the monarch. Coins are then thrown from a town hall window.

The Hereford May Fair

The historic May Fair at Hereford, held the Tuesday following the bank holiday, has been celebrated for over 900 years. It includes a unique custom to kick off proceedings. The mayor offers the bishop twelve-and-a-half bushels of wheat to mark the resolution of an old conflict. The wheat is paid to the bishop to compensate for the loss of rights over the festival.

St John of Beverley's Feast Day

The nearest Thursday to 7 May marks the Feast Day of St John of Beverley, a Northumbrian bishop from the late seventh to early eighth century. He is associated with many tales of miracles and intercession in battle. His day is commemorated by the choir of Beverley Minster and the residents of Harpham parish. The local holy well is adorned with yellow flowers.

Gawthorpe Maypole

The village of Gawthorpe in Yorkshire is famed for its annual Maypole celebrations, held on the first Saturday in the month.

Meanwhile, on the same day, in Bristol, Jack in the Green is dispatched again, this time on Horfield Green.

Helston Flora Day

This is one of the oldest-surviving May customs and involves a day-long dance around the town on 8 May. Usually, they have their own special tune to dance to.

https://www.youtube.com/watch?v=68m5wpcMScA

Guildford May Day

In Guildford, the Pilgrim Morris hold spectacular celebrations with their own Jack-in-the-Green character, known here as the May Bush. Their Maypole is known as the Summerpole. The Pilgrim Morris are accompanied by a zebra who abuses passersby. Think Rod Hull's Emu in horse form.

Knutsford Royal May Day

This celebration is so renowned and vibrant that it has been granted royal status, following the participation of the Prince and Princess of Wales in the late nineteenth century. Their unique custom is 'sanding', where the town's pavements are decorated with patterns and pictures of coloured sand for the day.

https://www.youtube.com/watch?v=ZUsj5imEbZ4

Spaw Sunday

At Midgley, Cragg Vale and Penistone in Yorkshire, there are celebrations honouring local water sources on the first Sunday in May. It's known as Spaw Sunday. Blessings are said and the wells decorated. At Midgley, events are rounded off with a bacon and dock pudding breakfast. At Cragg Vale, tradition dictates that worshippers drink the well water mixed with liquorice.

This day is also known as Cowslip Sunday. This has recently been revived at Lambley in Nottinghamshire, and festivities involve drinking cowslip wine.

Penzance May Horns

In Penzance, Cornwall, there is the Blowing of May Horns, held on the first Sunday of the month. Trumpets and tin whistles are blown by revellers dressed in green and white. Their procession to Penzance starts at dusk at a pub in Newlyn. En route, a character called Old Ned dies and is repeatedly revived. Do not attend if disturbed by the blowing of horns.

https://www.youtube.com/watch?v=DbQFa_HjidA

Whit Sunday

This day has celebrations and festivities in many places, the Manchester Whit Walk being one example. These are powerful and moving occasions for Christians and the wider community.

https://www.youtube.com/watch?v=AHzpx-dlquo

Randwick Wap

This is a revived ancient cheese-rolling festival in Gloucestershire, held on the second Saturday in May. The Wappenshaw, or Wap for short (from the Old English for 'weapon show'), was originally a gathering and review of troops, formerly held in every district. The Wap is believed to date back to medieval times. The object was to satisfy the military chiefs that the arms of their retainers were in good condition and that the men were properly trained. Sadly, this spring show was banned in the late nineteenth century by the court at nearby Whitminster due to 'debauchery'.

Revived in the 1970s by the late Reverend Nial Morrison, the simple blessing and procession of the day has become an event. The blessing of the cheese, and food in general, can be traced to the origins of most of the world's religions, when primitive people first asked blessings for a successful hunt or harvest and then gave prayers and offerings before eating the meal. Pre-contest larks involve a Wap Mayor and Queen parade. A mop-man clears the way by dousing the crowds with water. The mayor is then dunked in the duckpond. Cheeses are then rolled down the hill and consumed. Traditional Wiput cake, a unique local delicacy, is on sale in the Wap tent.

https://youtu.be/n-R2lOxKHMU?si=nNRVOWaDdlrAAFkj

Punch and Judy Day

This is Mr Punch's official birthday. Samuel Pepys's diary contains the first-ever recorded Punch and Judy show in 1662 in Covent Garden. It is marked by a special service at St Paul's Church, Covent Garden, on the second Sunday in May, during which Mr Punch usually makes an appearance in the pulpit. Following this, performances take place across the area.

The Byzant Ceremony

On a mid-month Sunday, the ancient Byzant Ceremony takes place in Blackmore Valley in Dorset. Dating back to 1364, the custom celebrates the gaining of a reliable water supply from neighbouring Enmore. There is a procession, where a mace is carried. Flower posies called 'Tussie Mussies' are handed out to carry on the walk.

On the same day, the Gold Hill Cheese Race takes place to celebrate the centuries-old tradition of cheese production in the local area.

Chestnut Sunday

On the nearest Sunday to the 11th, Bushy Park near Hampton Wick, the second-largest of London's Royal Parks, celebrates the blossoms of the chestnut trees planted 300 years ago. This tradition has been going since Victorian times.

Stow Horse Fair

On the second Sunday of the month in the Cotswolds, there is a traditional fair for Gypsies and travelling people to meet up and trade. The charter granting permission was issued in 1476. It began as a sheep fair but is now exclusively for horses.

The Hoop Trundle

On a Friday mid-month, the Hoop Trundle is held in Ely. It commemorates pupils of King's School being granted permission to play games in the cathedral grounds.

The Battle of Lewes Commemoration

On 14 May 1264, the Battle of Lewes was fought between Henry III's nobles under Simon de Montfort and those loyal to the King. The King was forced to give representative rights to the rebels. On or near the 14th, Lewes stages a large-scale battle reenactment to commemorate the event.

Moulton May Festival

Moulton in Northamptonshire holds its traditional May festival around this time, which includes a chariot race. Bradford-on-Avon's Green Man Festival is also held mid-month. Around this time, tulips are out in force and Wakefield celebrates their appearance with its Tulip Festival.

The Scorton Antient Silver Arrow Competition

The Leeds Royal Armouries house a silver arrow, which is the centrepiece of one of the oldest sporting events in the world. The Scorton Antient Silver Arrow is an archery contest, dating back to the late seventeenth century. It takes place at the hometown of whoever won it the preceding year.

https://www.youtube.com/watch?v=ebkrW1WokMQ

Cyclists' Memorial Sunday

A Sunday service is held mid-May at Meriden in Warwickshire to commemorate the contribution that cyclists have made to serve their country in times of war. Meriden is home to the Cyclists' War Memorial.

Levellers' Day

On the Saturday nearest to 17 May, the Levellers, a radical republican political group, are celebrated and commemorated at Burford in Oxfordshire. Hundreds of Levellers were imprisoned and their ringleaders executed. Flowers are laid at the church in memory of those who died.

Newbiggin Boundary Marking

On the third Wednesday of the month, an annual boundary-marking walk is held in Newbiggin, Northumberland, which was a significant port town. It is the freeholders that take part and they give out food as they walk the boundary.

Kitchel Throwing Day

The following day, in Harwich in Essex, is Kitchel Throwing Day. This is another event where buns, this time spiced, are thrown from the upstairs windows of the town hall. It is also the annual Mayor Making Day, where the newly elected mayor and mayoress ceremonially throw the small, sweet fruit buns called 'kitchels' from the Guildhall balcony to a crowd of children. This has been going on for a few hundred years, even during the war, when rationing determined that apples, not buns, were thrown.

https://www.youtube.com/watch?v=YdVoWzcP6oo

The Royal Horticultural Society Chelsea Flower Show

The RHS Chelsea Flower Show (formerly known as the Great Spring Show, dating from 1862) is an annual garden show held over five days during the third week of May in the grounds of the Royal Hospital Chelsea in Chelsea, London. It's been held in this location since 1912 and is attended by the monarch on prize-giving day. It is one of the largest generators of revenue in the UK event calendar. The RHS says the show brings in nearly £5 million in income each year. This includes sponsorship income from the show itself and television rights.

This is one of the most popular events in London's social calendar. It is limited to 57,000 people each year and all tickets are sold in advance. The Charity Gala Preview on the Monday night begins at 7 p.m. and finishes at 9 p.m. but for two hours attracts some of the most famous and wealthy people in the country. Although celebrities, royalty and wealthy business leaders attend, one of the greatest fascinations of the evening is the number of experts on every type of plant imaginable. They come from all over the country to discuss everything from asters to Zaluzianskya.

Ceremony of Dicing for the Maid's Money

In 1674, John Howe, a Puritan theologian, published *A Treatise of Delighting in God* and left a bequest of money to invest. The annual profits earned would provide a gift to a worthy maidservant. His legacy is celebrated in Guildford today by dicing for the maid's money. Domestic workers throw dice. Those with the lowest score win the prize.

The Weighing of the Mayor

On the third Saturday of May, the Mayor of High Wycombe is weighed on the first day of his office. He will be weighed again a year later, when he hands over his chains to his successor. This was done to make sure that he hadn't profited too much from his year of service. Tradition has it that if weight has been gained, the crowd will break into some good-hearted booing. Such tubby mayors may wish to spend the following Sunday at Hampshire's Watercress Festival in Alresford. As well as festivities and charitable distribution of the salad, there is the World Watercress Eating Championships.

https://www.youtube.com/watch?v=8ysgeSN9dqw

St Bede's Day
On 25 May, Durham Cathedral holds a special service in honour of the eighth-century historian Saint Bede. He spent his life as a monk at Monkwearmouth and latterly at Jarrow, where he was buried. He now rests in Galilee Chapel at Durham Cathedral.

Clovelly Seaweed Festival
Around this time, the Clovelly Seaweed Festival is held. This celebrates the culinary, aesthetic and health benefits of this group of aquatic plants.

Bun Day in Bedworth
Late in the month, on a Friday, another bun-themed event takes place in Nuneaton and Bedworth in Warwickshire. Sticky buns are distributed to local schoolchildren to mark the generosity of Nicholas Chamberlaine, a priest in the Church of England. He founded large numbers of alms houses across the area in the seventeenth century.

Blessing of the Sea
On a Monday late in the month, Sea Blessing ceremonies used to take place in many coastal towns and villages. Some services survive, including the blessing of the fleet at Brixham in Devon.

The Penicuik Hunter and Lass Festival

This takes place in the town of Penicuik in Midlothian on the last Saturday in May. It is centred around riding. Founded in 1936, it commemorates Robert the Bruce granting the town of Penicuik to Randolph de Clerc as a reward for slaying a deer that had continually evaded the hunt.

Hunting the Earl of Rone

On the spring bank holiday, Combe Martin in Devon celebrates Hunting the Earl of Rone. Its origins lie in the seventeenth century, when the Earl of Tyrone was shipwrecked. The earl is hunted by uniformed grenadiers all weekend and eventually caught on the bank holiday Monday. During the chase, he is frequently shot and revived by a hobby horse. At sunset, at the final shooting on the beach, he is not revived and is cast into the sea. As if it couldn't get any more bizarre, he wears ships' biscuits around his neck during the entire event.

https://www.youtube.com/watch?v=66Eyov2jnnA&t=65s

The Atholl Gathering

At Blair Castle in Pitlochry, Scotland, the Atholl Gathering takes place in late May. The Atholl Highlanders are the only private army in Europe. They meet and present awards for skill and long service. New recruits wear juniper in their Glengarry caps. The traditional Highland Games take place, as well as a tug of war. You could write several books about the Highland Games themselves, an event which is sporting, cultural and historic. In Grant Jarvie's excellent book *The Highland Games: The Making of the Myth*, he says:

The Purpose of the Highland Gatherings … is for the laird and clansman, crofter and shepherd to meet on equal terms and keep alive the best sporting traditions … the past, whether it be real or reinvented, refers to a number of specific practices such as dancing traditional reels, tossing the caber, throwing the hammer and the traditional grand march of the Highland pipers.

This illustrates something true of all tradition – it doesn't matter whether the past is real or not. The point of tradition is to remember, honour and celebrate our *current* traditions. This can be quite contemporary, in fact. Scottish identity remains a current political issue and so some see the traditions in that context.

Indeed, many local traditions have a political point. The May Tree Fair takes place at St Germans in Cornwall. It sees the election of a mock mayor and mayoress at the local pub.

The Uffington White Horse
The White Horse in Uffington, Oxfordshire, is a prehistoric hill figure formed from deep trenches filled with crushed white chalk. This chalk hill figure, located on the downland of Berkshire, is cleaned at this time of year to maintain its bright whiteness.

Yorkshire's Barwick-in-Elmet hosts its Maypole on spring bank holiday Monday. Its claim to fame is that it is the tallest in the UK. A young man attempts to climb to the top as part of the festivities.

https://www.youtube.com/watch?v=Hp_WpGMVyN8

The Hooden Horse

A traditional form of the hobby horse, this gets an airing in May in Charing and the neighbouring village of Westwell in Kent. It prances and nibbles those it meets.

https://www.youtube.com/watch?v=d3rvejc1Pto&t=78s

The Court of Arraye

This is an inspection of the armed forces and takes place at this time of year in Lichfield, Staffordshire. The tradition has been going for centuries and involves the mayor checking on the city's ability to defend itself. The inspection is accompanied with festivities and the crowning of the Bower Queen.

Tetbury Wool Sack Race

Spring bank holiday Monday is also when the Tetbury wool sack race takes place in Gloucestershire. The event celebrates the wool trade and involves competitors heaving sixty pounds of wool up and down a very steep Gumstool Hill.

https://www.youtube.com/watch?v=aVNN_ORE3ks

Oak Apple Day

29 May has become known as Oak Apple Day and Worcester is one of the places where it is celebrated. The city was loyal to the Stuart cause. Charles II famously hid in an oak tree to evade capture and his supporters wore oak sprigs as a sign of thanks for his good luck. This day was not only the King's birthday, but it was the date he entered London after the restoration. Northampton was a Parliamentarian town but was reconciled with the King on his return to the throne. They too now celebrate Oak Apple Day, due to their monarch's generosity when the town suffered a huge fire. Neot in Cornwall hosts the most lavish Oak Apple Day celebrations of all.

The Cotswold Olympics

On the Friday after the spring bank holiday, the Cotswold Olympics take place, dating back to 1612. Some of the events sound rather brutal, including a contest to kick each other in the shins. It ends with a bonfire and a torchlit procession from Dover's Hill back to Chipping Campden.

https://youtu.be/j_24qbipoZs?feature=shared&t=135

Neville's Cross Day

On a Saturday near 29 May, the Battle of Neville's Cross is commemorated. It took place outside Durham's walls in 1346, between the armies of Scotland's King David II and England's Edward III. There is a service and bell ringing to remember the part these activities played in the English forces' preparations for battle.

Fownhope Heart of Oak Society Annual Club Walk

In the nineteenth century, insurance schemes started to pop up across the country, organised through friendly societies. Rural workers would pay subs, for which they would be assisted if they fell on hard times. Fownhope in Herefordshire has an association dating back to the eighteenth century. Its members celebrate this society's existence at this time of the year with an annual walk. There is a procession with members carrying decorated sticks and banners, along with morris dancing, music and a hog roast.

The Grovely Ceremonies

Outside Salisbury Cathedral on 29 May (Oak Apple Day), the Grovely Ceremonies take place. This tradition dates back to 1603 and involves villagers from Great Wishford proclaiming their ancient rights to Grovely Wood by shouting: 'Grovely, Grovely, and all Grovely.' The origins of this custom date back to the reign of Elizabeth I, who issued a charter enshrining the rights of the villages of Great Wishford to collect wood. To commemorate this, activities take place, such as waking everyone up by banging tins and playing trumpets, a procession into the Grovely forest, decorating houses with bunting and bows from the woods and carrying branches to the cathedral for the morning service.

St Walstan's Feast Day

St Walstan is the patron saint of farmers and agricultural workers. His feast day falls on 30 May. His shrine is located at Bawburgh Church, where two white oxen carried his body on a cart for burial. The original shrine was destroyed in 1538 and his remains were burned and scattered. On the nearest Sunday to 30 May, he is commemorated by a procession from the church to the well in the orchard nearby.

The Corby Pole Fair

Every twenty years, a charter fair is held at Corby, Northamptonshire.

Its traditions date back to 1585, when Elizabeth I granted them a charter to hold the event. Known as the pole fair, it used to involve a greasy pole which people attempted to climb. This fell foul of health and safety officers in more recent times. This has not spoilt the fun, which is all set to music by the Corby Silver Band, formed especially for the event in 1902.

Dwile Flonking

This is a drinking game reputed to have origins dating back several centuries. There is considerable evidence that it was invented down the pub in the 1960s. It has the full bingo card of the traditional English game. Ridiculously complicated rules and play accompanied by songs and beer. Put simply, teams take it in turns to hit each other with a beer-soaked cloth.

https://www.youtube.com/watch?v=UBamCWdx6gI

World Toe Wrestling Championship

If that isn't quite your sport, you could head to Derbyshire and try toe wrestling. The International Toe Wrestling Competition is held at Bentley Brook Inn, Fenny Bentley, in Ashbourne. It has been held for more than fifty years. Competitors from as far away as the US, China and India will be flexing their feet for the championships. Two contestants battle on a special podium with two walls either side, locking toes and trying to push their rival's foot or toe to the opposite wall.

https://www.youtube.com/watch?v=UFh_BSxjVJQ

World Custard Pie-Throwing Championships

Or perhaps head to Coxheath in Kent for the annual World Custard Pie-Throwing Contest. The recipe for the pies is a secret, but they are said to contain flour and water. Crowds of people arrive at the Coxheath recreation ground to see the teams go head-to-head. There has even been a team that flew from Japan to compete.

https://www.youtube.com/watch?v=BS_Ooo4z03A

World Pooh Sticks Championships

The River Windrush at Witney in Oxfordshire plays host to the World Pooh Sticks Championships. Five hundred sportsmen and women of all ages take to a bridge near St Mary's Cogges to drop their twigs. Spectators watch the coloured twigs float along the five-metre course to the rope finish line. Tactics vary between players – some aim for the sides of the stream, while others propel their sticks into the middle.

https://www.youtube.com/watch?v=62fNw6BeDt8

The Annual Tortoise Fair

If you are more of a spectator, around this time of year there is the Annual Tortoise Fair at Corpus Christi College, Oxford. This includes tortoise racing, with several other colleges having their own stable of reptiles.

https://www.youtube.com/watch?v=urW6rY6MkaY

The Brightlingsea Blessing of the Waters

Brightlingsea in Essex is the venue for a traditional blessing associated with Rogationtide, the Sunday before Ascension, held in late May or early June. Dignitaries of the Cinque Ports, in full regalia, attend a brief service onboard a ship. They then lead a flotilla along the Brightlingsea Creek to West Ness to reclaim the waters and assert the rights of local people to use them. This is the salt-water equivalent of boundary marking.

Hollycombe Festival of Steam

Hollycombe, near Liphook in Hampshire, has Britain's largest collection of working steam engines. The festival, held on 31 May, offers a look at how the Victorians and Edwardians used steam as an instrument of work and play, featuring a number of popular fairground sideshows of the period. The interaction and proximity of the steam engines is one of the greatest attractions. The imaginative layout and use of the steam engines means that it can be seen as a normal fairground, with steam-driven rides such as the Golden Gallopers, Steam Swingboat and Steam Chair-o-Planes.

https://www.youtube.com/watch?v=Rq-aAJuMfMU

The Ceremony of the Lilies and Roses at the Tower of London

The Presence Chamber in the Tower of London is an octagonal room with a vaulted roof of stone, where medieval kings held court. Henry VI came to a violent end here when he was imprisoned and then murdered in 1471, allegedly while at prayer in the oratory on the night of 21 May, the Vigil of the Ascension. In 1923, a marble tablet was laid in memory of Henry and since then, lilies have been placed there by students of Eton College upon the evening of each anniversary, commemorating Henry as their founder. Since 1947, the lilies have been supplemented by roses, a token of King's College Cambridge, the other college founded by Henry, as the legacy of his reign. When we remember people, we remember values.

There's more to Henry's background. Three weeks before his murder, his only son Edward was killed at the Battle of Tewkesbury on 4 May, after which his wife, Margaret of Anjou, was taken prisoner by the Yorkists. Seventeen years earlier, King Henry had suffered a breakdown, and he declined into mental illness through the rest of his life, unleashing a power struggle within the kingdom that was only resolved by his death.

Held in private, at dusk, to the accompaniment of a choir, this is a quiet ritual of remembrance. It begins with a procession outside the Queen's House on Tower Green, led by the Yeomen Warders. It then winds up a narrow staircase of worn steps from Water Lane to cross a stone bridge and enter the austere octagonal chamber, where a single shaft of sunlight traverses the room. The ceremony includes warders with their maces, the chaplain and the governor of the tower, the provosts of Eton and King's Colleges in their dark gowns, the young scholars with their sheaves of lilies and roses and the choir in their red vestments.

Cooper's Hill Cheese Rolling

Overlooking the Severn Valley in Gloucestershire is a hill in the village of Brockworth. Every spring bank holiday, people assemble on one of the steepest pastures in Britain. The aim is simple. Around 200 participants chase down a hill after a nine-pound wheel of Double Gloucester cheese. The first over the finishing line, 200 yards away at the bottom, is the winner. People are frequently injured. It is now deemed so dangerous that it is no longer official. This doesn't stop its popularity. The event has hundreds of years of tradition behind it – some say 600 years. It is held by the people of the village, but participants now come from Australia, Belgium, Canada, Egypt, Germany, Japan, New Zealand and the US.

The physics are frightening. Nine pounds of cheese travelling 200 yards down a 50 per cent gradient, acquires 1,800 joules of kinetic energy, moving at approaching 100 miles an hour. Getting in the way of that will spoil your day. Just for comparison, an average human generates around 40–50 joules of kinetic energy when jumping into the air, assuming a typical jump height of 16–20 inches and an average body weight of seventy kilograms. For this reason, in recent years, organisers of the event have used a lightweight foam version of the cheese.

It doesn't stop the enthusiasm or the entrants. In 2023, a Canadian, Delaney Irving, won the ladies' race but only learned of her victory when she recovered consciousness in the medical enclosure. A total of six competitors ended up in hospital following the event.

https://www.youtube.com/watch?v=bx9I9n41La8

SUMMER

JUNE

June is packed with summer sports, and the riding season in the borders continues. There are events to mark the summer solstice, well dressings and rushbearings (notable ones at Warcop and Barrowden). Rents are paid in seasonal roses and mummers perform stories from the Bible. There is a spectacular mummers' performance every four years in the City of York.

Two large events in the Royal calendar take place this month. In the second week of June, the Trooping of the Colour takes place to mark the monarch's official birthday. The second event stems from one founded by King Edward III in 1348 – the Order of the Garter. It is the most senior British order of chivalry. Mid-month, the Garter ceremony is held at Windsor Castle. The Knights and Ladies Companion are hosted by the monarch and process to St George's Chapel for a special service accompanied by the bands of the Grenadier Guards, the Household Cavalry, Windsor's military knights and the Yeomen of the Guard.

THE GRENADIER GUARDS MARCH

https://www.youtube.com/watch?v=oemeSg3CEVo

Leicester Damask Rose Ceremony

Roses are a big theme in June and a number of events mark their use as a form of payment. On the 24th, Leicester has a damask rose ceremony, which has been going since the 1600s. A rose and four old pennies are paid as a type of quit-rent, a gift in lieu of money, for a pub on Loseby Lane in Leicester.

The Clopton Rose Ceremony in Hadleigh

A similar event takes place in Hadleigh. A single red rose is the rent presented by the mayor to the parish council for use of the Guildhall and local lands. This marks a rent that was paid to the Clopton family. After the rose has been exchanged, it is placed on the tomb of William Clopton, to whom the original debt was to be paid.

The Knollys Rose Ceremony

A third rose-themed payment takes place in London. In 1381, a footbridge was erected between two properties on Seething Lane, close to the Tower of London. The owner, Lady Constance Knollys, had not sought permission to do so and was fined one red rose for the offence. The commemorative custom was created by the Company of Watermen and Lightermen of the River Thames. They carry the rose in a procession to Mansion House, in order to pay the fine to the Lord Mayor.

Summer Solstice

The summer solstice takes place over 20–21 June. The most famous celebration takes place at Stonehenge on Salisbury Plain. It is an ancient service harking back to pagan times. There are other services around the country. Another large event is at the stone circle at Avebury, also in Wiltshire.

Cornish Midsummer Fires

On the 23rd, the Cornish Midsummer Fires take place. These have their origins in ancient customs but have been going in their current form since the 1920s. A chain of beacons is lit from a point near Land's

End across to the Devon border. Before doing so, herbs and flowers are cast into the flames of the first fire while Cornish prayers are said.

World Crazy Golf Championships

If crazy golf is your sport of choice, then Hastings is where you should head. The World Championships take place during this month. The contest is over eighteen holes and silly outfits are encouraged.

Ossett Beercart

On the first Saturday of the month, in Yorkshire, the Ossett Beercart is held. This is a morris dancing event where the dancers pull carts carrying beer kegs. They process around the town, stopping to perform dances. On reaching the town hall, the barrels are unloaded. Proceeds from the day are donated to local charities.

The Great Knaresborough Bed Race

A mid-month event is the Great Knaresborough Bed Race. Teams of six, in fancy dress, push beds over a three-kilometre course around the town to raise funds for local good causes. Part-way through, the competitors are required to transport their beds over the River Nidd.

Swaton World Egg-Throwing Championships

On the last Sunday of the month, over in Swaton near Sleaford, Lincolnshire, the World Egg-Throwing Championships take place. The main challenge is straightforward. A couple chuck a raw egg at each other over an ever-increasing distance until the egg smashes. The duo who manage to hurl it to each other the farthest wins. Side events include a contest to hurl eggs at a human target and 'Russian roulette'. Think of that scene in *The Deerhunter*, except instead of a loaded pistol there is a box of eggs, one of which is raw and the rest hardboiled. Contestants must take it in turns to select an egg to smash against their own heads.

https://www.youtube.com/watch?v=1El1uzjsdOo

Lilias Day

Lilias Day has been celebrated in the village of Kilbarchan in Renfrewshire, Scotland, for over 300 years. There was originally a fair to commemorate the saint after which the village was named, St Barchan. In the 1700s, the day was renamed in honour of the local laird's daughter. It includes a large historic pageant, with figures taken from Scottish history.

Eaglesham Fair

There are many historic summer fairs that take place over the month of June. The fair at Eaglesham has been a fixture in the local calendar for over 400 years. An integral part of the event is the ancient race for a Kilmarnock Bunnet (which is a traditional part of Highland head dress). There are other challenges, including a pie-eating contest.

Wybunbury Fig Pie Wakes

Pies are also the centre of attention at the village of Wybunbury in Cheshire. Early in June, there is a competition to see who can roll a fig pie the furthest. The origins of this event date back 200 years.

https://www.youtube.com/watch?v=5wzzx5W2lZ8

The Rochester Dickens Festival

In Rochester, a festival celebrating the life and work of Charles Dickens is put on twice a year. There is a grand parade where locals dress as characters from his works. The second event is held at Christmas.

Thaxted Morris Men Weekend

The weekend after the spring bank holiday, the Thaxted Morris Men in Essex hold one of the biggest morris meetings in the country, which lasts all weekend.

Neston Ladies Day

In Cheshire, on the first Thursday in June, the Neston Female Society holds its Ladies Day. The society was founded in 1814 and was one of many at the time. The day begins with the march of their members, adorned with flowers as they head towards the annual general meeting.

Appleby Horse Fair

In the first week of June, there is a huge horse fair on Fair Hill on the River Eden, Cumbria. Largely visited by the travelling community, their horses are ridden down to the river to be washed and displayed.

According to the BBC, market traders at the annual fair are asked to check their goods are genuine and safe. Counterfeit goods sold during the 2024 Appleby Horse Fair included alcohol, tobacco, vapes, perfumes, cosmetics and electrical products.[1]

https://youtu.be/K_rpu-rZq_E?si=hldS6aQpo4EMXPVY

Newtongrange Gala Day

On the second Saturday of the month, Newtongrange in Midlothian, Scotland, holds a gala, which has been going strong for 200 years. Two local children are selected to be the king and queen and are accompanied by others that form the court. There is a procession around the village before the couple are crowned. Villagers decorate their houses for the occasion.

Mazey Day

On the second Saturday of the month, Mazey Day takes place at Penzance amid the Cornish festival of Golowan. Highlights include a costumed procession, a dance by serpents and a skull-headed hobby horse.

https://youtu.be/Sn8J9iYWAiE?si=MLioHeAKbxY9cq04

Saint Barnabas' Day

On a weekday near 11 June, an event takes place in Hampshire inspired by the naturalist Gilbert White, who lived in the county in the village of Selborne. This day is Saint Barnabas' Day and White was reported to have constructed a bower (a shady place) in a local wood to mark the occasion. Inspired by this, local children and conservationists have reconstructed the bower in Woolmer Forest near Liphook. It is blessed and an extract from Gilbert White's journal is read out at the site.

Bromsgrove Court Leet Fair Day

Bromsgrove's summer fair was granted a charter by King John in 1199. As part of the fair, on the Saturday closest to mid-month, the Town's

Court Leet, which preserves local customs, tests the produce of local traders to check it is up to standard.

Middlewich Folk and Boat Festival

Middlewich holds an annual Folk and Boat Festival, connected with the canal boat heritage of the area.

https://www.youtube.com/watch?v=Hg1THuWHWqo

Bawming Day

On the third Saturday of the month, the village of Appleton Thorn, Warrington, puts on an event called 'Bawming the Thorn'. At the village centre is a hawthorn tree, which is decorated and then serenaded by local schoolchildren. The Bawming Song is sung to the tune of 'Bonnie Dundee' and the chorus is:

> Up with fresh garlands this Midsummer morn,
> Up with red ribbons on Appleton Thorn.
> Come lasses and lads to the Thorn Tree today
> To Bawm it and shout as ye Bawm it, hooray!

The custom lapsed a couple of hundred years ago. It was revived in the 1930s.

Gorebridge Gala Day

If your preferred method of transportation is mechanical not equine, then head over to Gorebridge. On the third Sunday in June is an annual gala celebrating the children of the village. A king and queen are crowned and lead their members of the court around the village by motorcade.

The Ashmore Filly Loo

Near to 21 June, Ashmore in Dorset is home to the wonderfully named Filly Loo. This event marks the longest day and much of its activity centres around the village pond. There is a horn dance by torchlight.

https://www.youtube.com/watch?v=kt3zFvrx7Bs

Chester Midsummer Watch Parade

Late in the month, costumed parades take place in Chester and have done for hundreds of years. Unicorns, dragons, giants and angels are among the cast.

https://www.youtube.com/watch?v=UzY9RjPTGog

Loanhead Gala Day

On the last Saturday of the month, Loanhead, Midlothian, hosts a century-old event to celebrate its children. The local children dress up as courtiers to a queen. As well as dressing up, the children also decorate their houses with ribbons and flowers. There is a coronation and a procession.

https://www.youtube.com/watch?v=txZNRvcpKUA

Pixie Day

Near the 24th of the month, Ottery St Mary holds Pixie Day. Folklore has this village as a former home of the fairies. They decided to leave after humans and their loud church bells decided to move in. Before they left, they did apparently try to take the bellringers hostage, but they later escaped. That was the final straw. Pixie Day commemorates this lore and has its origins in the fifteenth century.

https://www.youtube.com/watch?v=_2x2TpOBay4&t=659s

Abram Morris Dancers' Day

On the last Saturday of the month, the Abram Morris Dancers, a group based near Wigan, perform at their annual day of celebrations. If they fail to do so for a period of time, they forfeit their rights to the ground upon which they dance.

Wakes Day

The Oddfellows were established in 1810 and are a national organisation still going strong. They exist to provide friendship and support in communities. On the last Saturday of the month, known as Wakes Day, the Parwich branch in the Derbyshire Dales holds a unique Oddfellows procession.

https://www.youtube.com/watch?v=GvlZM8Zoht8

Wakes Weeks

The Wakes holiday started as an unpaid holiday when the Lancashire mills and factories were closed for maintenance. Each town took the holiday on a different week in the summer, so that from June to September each town was on holiday a different week. This also staggered bookings at popular nearby seaside resorts like Blackpool.

Cornish Rebellion Day

On the 27th, at Bodmin and St Keverne, services are held to remember the Cornish rebellion of 1497. The rebellion was a response to the raising of taxes by Henry VII to fund a campaign against Scotland. Cornwall suffered particularly because the King had recently stopped the legal operation of Cornish tin mining. It may have attracted rebels to Cornwall. Perkin Warbeck, a later pretender to the English throne, based himself there.

SERVICES AND THANKSGIVING IN JUNE

In 1728, Ann Nepton set up a trust upon a piece of property to make an annual payment to the poor people of Barking in Essex. The property eventually passed to the Company of Poulters. The land was acquired by the North London Railway company in 1862 and in 1865 by the Great

Eastern Railway company. The Company of Poulters still administers Ann's legacy. Money is distributed and prayers are said at her tomb.

At the church in Selston in Nottinghamshire, the vicar preaches a Sunday service from the fifteenth-century tower. The origins are said to lie in a decision in 1907 by the then vicar to preach to traveller families that might be passing by the church. Nearby Selston Green was a controversial campsite for traveller families as late as 2020.[2]

On the first Tuesday of the month, an event known as the Bubble Sermon is organised by the Stationers' Company at St Bride's Church. This was part of a request in the will of an eighteenth-century member of the company. The Bubble Sermon is also known as the Richard Johnson Service and commemorates Richard Johnson, a benefactor of the company. The theme is based on the Latin phrase *Vita Humana Bulla Est*, meaning 'human life is a bubble'. The service includes a sermon on this theme, often with a performance of 'I'm Forever Blowing Bubbles' by the St Bride's Church choir.

The Gate to Southwell Festival in Nottinghamshire is a custom dating back to 1109, although the service today is a modern revival of an ancient tradition. It centres around funds raised to build Southwell Minster. The funds were known as the Southwell Pence and led to the minster being completed in 1201.

At Welcombe in Devon, the local church is dedicated to St Nectan, who was killed by cattle rustlers that he was trying to convert. St Nectan was a fifth-century holy man who lived in Stoke, Hartland, in the Brythonic-speaking county of Devon (at the time). The legend says that the rustlers decapitated him, but despite this, he picked his head up and walked back to his well before collapsing and dying. From that time, miracles began at St Nectan's tomb. Wherever his blood fell, a foxglove sprung up. On the Sunday nearest his feast day of 17 June there is a service, procession and decorations made from foxgloves.

St Alban is England's first martyr. He was executed by the Romans for sheltering Christian priests. In the town that bears his name, they remember him on a Saturday near his feast day, 20 June. Puppets tell the story of his life as they process to the Cathedral.

Saint Winifred's feast day is 22 June. Her shrine is at Holywell, Flintshire. Legend has it that the well was created by pure spring water that poured from her neck after her head was severed by a man she had rejected (seems to be a theme here). She then came back to life and lived out her days as an abbess. It has been a place of pilgrimage since 1115, making the site one of the oldest continual pilgrim destinations in the UK. On this day, Holywell commemorates her by processing to the well, venerating her relics and blessing the sick and infirm.

Jankyn Smyth was a significant figure in Bury St Edmunds in the fifteenth century. He left a bequest for a mass to be held each year on the anniversary of his death. This is now held on the last Thursday of the month. The charity he started as payment for the mass still continues and provides beer and cakes after the services for anyone in receipt of alms.

Youlgrave is one of a number of villages to hold well dressings during the month around the feast day of St John the Baptist. The village has an ample water supply, which has never dried up.

Many churches celebrate Midsummer, the patronal feast of St John the Baptist, on 24 June near the summer solstice. At Bishop's Castle in Shropshire, there is a summer fete on this day, complete with rush-bearing and morris dancing.

On this day, an outdoor sermon is held at Magdalen College, Oxford, to mark the feast day of St John the Baptist. St John's Quadrangle in the college has an outdoor pulpit for such purposes. The college stands on the site of a hospital named after the saint.

The Hepworth feast and plague commemoration takes place towards the end of the month. It marks the end of the terrible plague of 1665. This type of event used to be commonplace in many villages and parishes. Now only a few survive.

It used to be a common custom for churches to organise walking days for their parishioners. At Warrington, a huge walking event survives, with many thousands of people joining in for a walk about the town.

RIDING CUSTOMS

In West Linton, Peeblesshire, a border riding custom takes place, led by an elected couple known as the 'Whipman and his Lass'. As well as a horse ride, there is one for bicycles and another for wheelbarrows.

In Hawick, early in the month, another riding tradition takes place. As well as marking the boundary, it serves to remember the 1514 capture of the English flag by a local boy. The ride starts early after the party have been fortified by the taking of snuff and breakfast. Once the riders return, accompanied by a fife and drums band, a proclamation is read, after which a ball takes place.

Another border riding event takes place between the 6th and the 12th in Lanark. It is called Lanimer Week and features a parade high in pageantry and the crowning of the Lanimer Queen. The event originated in the twelfth century and has continued each year to this day uninterrupted.

Mid-month, Linlithgow celebrates Marches Day, another boundary-marking event, as it has done for many hundreds of years. The village is woken up at 5 a.m. with a loud parade of flutes and drums. The procession walks the boundary fuelled by fortifying alcohol.

On a Friday mid-month at Selkirk, a boundary riding is followed by the Casting of the Colours, which commemorates the return of a single surviving soldier after the Battle of Flodden in 1513, where his colleagues were slain. A procession returns to the town after the ride-out accompanied by pipers and a band. The riders dismount and carry their standards to the marketplace. The Burgh Flag (the colours) is then presented back to the village for safe keeping.

THE BURGH FLAG CEREMONY

https://www.youtube.com/watch?v=ANcR8hjRMAg

If Selkirk is one of the largest events, Yetholm is perhaps the smallest community to take part in a ride-out. The Yetholm events date back to the thirteenth century. They ride to the Stob Stanes, standing stones on the hilltop near the border with England, where according to tradition, Gypsy Kings were crowned.

Mid-month during riding season in Lanarkshire, at the town of Biggar, the Fleming Queen is crowned. This takes place to remember Mary Fleming, who was a Scottish noblewoman from the area and attended Mary Queen of Scots, as well as being her childhood companion and cousin.

The Lockerbie Gala and boundary riding is also held at this time of year. This ride-out is led by the 'Cornet', the 'Cornet's Lass' and a standard bearer.

Guid Nychburris Day is another boundary-riding event, which takes place on the third Saturday of the month. Local characters of note are the Pursivant, who meets the riders at the start of their quest, and the Queen of the South, who is crowned after the ride is done and a proclamation read.

Another border-riding event takes place at Melrose. This usually takes place on a Monday at the much more civilised hour of 6 p.m., with riders returning after a few hours.

BATTLES

On 14 June in 1645, the Battle of Naseby was fought. The Parliamentarian victory is marked by battle reenactors, commemorating the occasion at the village.

On the following day, the final battle of the War of the Roses was fought in 1487 in Nottinghamshire. The Tudor's decisive victory is remembered by a battlefield walk on this day.

24 June 1314 was the Battle of Bannockburn, held near Stirling, where Robert the Bruce won victory over English forces. On the anniversary of the battle, wreaths are laid to remember all who fought.

The Highland Games at Ceres are the oldest in Scotland and are held on this day too. Their charter was granted under Robert the Bruce in 1314 to mark the local contribution to the Battle of Bannockburn and the games opens with a lament for them. A unique aspect of these games is the throwing of the Ceres Stane, another enormous rock.

The World Nettle-Eating Championship

The World Nettle-Eating Championship is held at the Bottle Inn pub in Marshwood in Dorset. This tradition began as an argument between two farmers at the pub (seems a common theme). Both claimed the tallest stinging nettles. One said he would eat the leaves of his nettles if he was wrong. Stalks of stinging nettles are cut into two-foot lengths and competitors have an hour to eat as many leaves as they can. Whoever has the highest number of bare stalks at the end wins. It is an ordeal, as the nettles don't just taste disgusting but also sting the mouth and throat.

https://www.youtube.com/watch?v=8a26VgzjFg8

JULY

Battle of Marston Moor Commemoration

On the nearest Sunday to 2 July, the Battle of Marston Moor commemoration takes place. The conflict happened on this day in 1644 between the Parliamentarians and the army of the Scottish Covenanters, the Royalists under Prince Rupert and the Marquess of Newcastle with his Whitecoats. The Parliamentarian victory saw the King lose control of the north. Isaac Foot MP, father of Michael, Dingle, Hugh and John, used to say: 'I judge a man by one thing, which side would he have liked his ancestors to fight on at Marston Moor?'

Whalton Baal Fire

Who needs Independence Day when you have Baal Fire? This is an annual bonfire that takes place in Whalton, Northumberland, outside the local pub on 4 July. It has been going for hundreds of years and used to involve people leaping through the fire and burning a corn dolly. These days, a corn dolly is still made to symbolise fertility, but she escapes the flames.

https://www.youtube.com/watch?v=reEjPeB6vP4

Rushbearing

On the first Saturday in July at Ambleside, Cumbria, a religious service called rushbearing takes place. These services used to be commonplace across the country. Floor rushes were collected by the community and replaced in the church. Ambleside is one of the only remaining events of this kind. Flower-covered structures are paraded through the town to the tunes of a brass band. Proceedings are followed by a fell race later that day. Great Musgrave also has a rushbearing on the same day.

Hole in the Hedge Ceremony

In Annan in south-west Scotland, a 600-year-old boundary-marking event takes place. A unique aspect of this event is the 'hole in the hedge' ceremony. To commemorate a boy searching for villains, a young lad is shoved through a hedge. As well as alcohol, snuff-taking is also encouraged at the event. The finale of the proceedings is the ceremony with pipes and drums.

https://youtu.be/K4AwMW1P8yg?feature=shared&t=255

Sma' Shot Day

Over in Paisley it is Sma' Shot Day, named after the thread used to make Paisley shawls. The first Saturday in July was a holiday for those in the weaving trade. It was given this new name and new meaning after the workers won a dispute against the factory owners.

Riding and Heritage Day

In Bodmin, across the first weekend in July, there is a Riding and Heritage Day. Rather morbidly, celebrations on this day were to commemorate the hanging of an unpopular mayor in the fifteenth century. These days, the focus has moved to the hunting of the Beast of Bodmin. Festivities include Cornish wrestling and a riding service on Sunday commemorating St Petroc.

The Hat Fair

Originally a buskers' event, the Hat Fair in Winchester is the UK's longest-running festival of street theatre, comedy and music, which is held during the first weekend in July.

Procession of the Madonna Del Rosario

On the first Sunday of July, there is the Procession of the Madonna Del Rosario in Manchester's Ancoats area. It has been held every year since 1890, except in times of war and during the recent Covid pandemic. A procession is headed by a group of men carrying the Madonna. It's followed by women in Italian dress and children, some of whom are dressed for their first Holy Communion.

The Love Feast

Over in Alport Castles in the Derbyshire Peak District, a much less glamorous service is taking place. Alport Castles is not a medieval structure. It's actually the largest landslide in Britain, where the resulting debris has formed a series of castle-like rock formations. The Love Feast is an annual custom held on the first Sunday of the month. It is a simple service to commemorate the non-conformist tradition in Derbyshire.

Chelsham Kelly Service

The service on this day at Chelsham in Surrey celebrates local boy Thomas Kelly. He became Lord Mayor of London in 1837. He left a bequest to provide bread for the poor of the village, which is still distributed to this day following the service. Flowers are placed on his grave, as well as on the graves of his parents.

The Oxenhope Charity Straw Race

If you're tiring of so many religious services, then the Straw Race at Oxenhope in West Yorkshire may be more to your taste. This is the ultimate pub crawl, in which two teams compete over two-and-a-half miles while carrying a bale of straw. The rules state they must stop at particular pubs along the way and drink a pint of beer.

https://www.youtube.com/watch?v=YaSsYb2fTKE&t=60s

Helpston John Clare Cushion Ceremony
John Clare, the English poet, is celebrated on a Friday close to his birthday on 13 July 1793. It is known as the cushion ceremony, named after the flower garlands placed on his grave at Helpston in Cambridgeshire.

Bradwell Pilgrimage and Padley Martyrs' Pilgrimage
Early in the month, the villagers of Bradwell, Essex, keep an ancient pilgrimage alive by walking from their church to the historic Chapel of St Peter-on-the-Wall. At Padley near 12 July, they also undertake a walk to commemorate the death of two Catholic priests. Nicholas Garlick and Robert Ludlam were discovered at Padley Hall during a raid in 1588 and executed for being ordained priests, a crime deemed treasonous at the time.

Kilburn Feast
At Middleham Castle in Wensleydale, North Yorkshire, they celebrate a former resident, Richard III. Down the road in Kilburn, a huge horse fair used to take place on the Sunday after 6 July. This has now become the Kilburn Feast, which includes a male Lady Mayoress fining the locals for minor misdemeanours. Fines are paid and kisses bestowed by the heavily lipsticked mayoress.

Duns Summer Festival

In the Scottish borders, Duns celebrates summer with games (two teams used to be made up of married men versus bachelors) and boundary riding. The Summer Festival was set up in the mid-twentieth century and is a week-long celebration starting on the first Sunday of the month, with a wide selection of traditional events. On the Tuesday, a cavalcade led by the reiver makes its way to the summit of Duns Law for a service commemorating General Leslie and the Covenanters' encampment here in opposition to King Charles I in 1639.

https://www.youtube.com/watch?v=yvNz_7x-57g

Rose Petal Day

Rose Petal Day takes place in Salisbury on an early Sunday in July close to the 7th. This was the date in 1220 when St Thomas Beckett's remains were moved to his new tomb in Canterbury Cathedral. At St Thomas's Church, they remember this by casting rose petals from the tower.

Jedburgh Callants Festival

Originally called Jethart, the Jedburgh Callants Festival dates from the mid-twentieth century. This consists of traditional ride-outs and wreath-laying at the Morebattle war memorial. One ride follows the route taken by Mary Queen of Scots to visit her adviser, James Hepburn, 4th Earl of Bothwell, at Hermitage Castle. Mary was in Jedburgh in the Scottish borders, likely on business, when she learned that he had been wounded in a skirmish near his property. Mary rode on horseback to Hermitage Castle, a journey of about twenty-five miles across difficult terrain. On the return journey, Mary's horse stumbled, throwing her into a bog and she contracted a fever. Mary later married Bothwell.

Battle of Northampton Commemoration

On 10 July 1460, the Battle of Northampton took place during the Wars of the Roses. The Northamptonshire Battlefields Society reenacts the action, which ended in a Yorkist victory and the capture of Henry VI by the Earl of Warwick.

Tewkesbury Medieval Festival

The second weekend of the month sees the largest medieval festival take place at Tewkesbury in Gloucestershire. There are tours of its famous battlefield and reenactments of the fight, the storming of the Abbey and execution of the Lancastrians.

St Swithin's Day

Legend has it that when St Swithin's bones were moved, he showed his displeasure by bringing about heavy rain and floods. From the ninth century onwards, it has been believed that if the weather is bad on St Swithin's Day, 15 July, it will continue for the next forty days and nights.

Black Cherry Fair

In Chertsey, Surrey, the Black Cherry Fair, named after the local cherry harvest, has taken place in the abbey fields on the second Saturday of the month almost every year since 1440.

Durham Miners' Gala

In Durham, on the same day, the Miners' Gala celebrates trade unions. It is a celebration of community, international solidarity and working-class life. This is a traditional political event, attended by leaders of the Labour Party.

Rushbearing

At Farndon, Grasmere and Newchurch on this day, there is a rush-bearing service at the local church to mark when new rushes would be strewn on the floors.

At Old Weston, they prefer straw on their church floor and mark when it would have been changed on St Swithin's Day.

Pontefract Liquorice Festival

Pontefract was once a centre of liquorice cultivation and holds an annual festival on the second Saturday of the month to celebrate the plant.

https://www.youtube.com/watch?v=hhhtRUEQkXw&t=203s

Witcham World Pea-Shooting Championships

If you are tiring of the tennis at Wimbledon, over at Witcham in Cambridgeshire there's a pea-shooting contest on the same day.

https://www.youtube.com/watch?v=2X3c5rhDooc&t=5s

Grindon Hedgehog Rolling

In Grindon, Staffordshire, hedgehog rolling is the sport of choice. The hogs are actually fir cones and are swept along using 'besoms', a sort of broom.

British Pedal Car Grand Prix

In Ringwood in Hampshire, it is a Pedal Car Grand Prix that pulls in the crowds on this day.

https://www.youtube.com/watch?v=qn7PJYUj-uk

More ridings out take place in the Scottish borders, including at Wigtown and over in Kelso. More still take place later in the month, at Littleborough and Langholm. At the latter, there is a spectacular gallop at Kirk Wynd and a proclamation called the 'fair crying'. This is delivered by a man with impeccable balance standing on the back of a horse.

Crow Fair

In Moulton in Cheshire, the Crow Fair is held. This was established during the Great Depression of the 1920s and 1930s and was a way of raising funds. Unemployed men would dress as crows and dance for money. Perhaps this inspired *The Full Monty*. Scarecrows decorate the village, real birds are released and a local dressed as a scarecrow features in the dancing.

https://www.youtube.com/watch?v=A-XzsEtfDBM&t=9s

Dunmow Flitch Trial

Over in Essex, the Dunmow Flitch Trial happens every four years. This event celebrates marriage. It sees couples proving to a specially convened court that they have been happily married for a year and a day. The couple who makes the most convincing case wins half a cured pig. It is said this tradition dates back to 1104, when the prior of Little Dunmow blessed a couple who were in disguise. They turned out to be powerful landowners and donated the land to the Church on the condition that this custom was established.

Chester Mystery Plays

In Chester, every five years in mid-July, a series of Mystery Plays are performed. This tradition stems back to medieval times, with these plays being performed around the feast of Corpus Christi. They were suppressed during the Reformation and fell out of favour, but they were revived in the mid-twentieth century. York and Lincoln also have similar events on a similar cycle. In the run-up to the events there is the reading of the bands, where the performers seek a licence to perform from the mayor.

The Vintners' Annual Procession

In London, the Worshipful Company of Vintners parade in Tudor dress, carrying fragrant nosegays from their hall to St James Garlickhythe. The tradition dates back to earlier, less sanitary times, with a wine porter sweeping the procession's path clean as they go.

St Peter's Fair

In Holsworthy in Devon, in the middle of July, an annual bequest is carried out. In the nineteenth century, the Pretty Maids Charity was founded. Annual interest from the bequest is given each year to a deserving woman who meets certain criteria. As well as the bounty, the Pretty Maid gets to open up St Peter's Fair.

Pilton Green Man Festival

At Pilton in Devon, a festival is held mid-month celebrating the Green Man.

The Annual Cart Marking Ceremony

At the Guildhall in the City of London, an annual Cart Marking Ceremony takes place. As a forerunner to the DVLA, vehicles are branded to show they have permission to operate in the capital. The branding is carried out by the Worshipful Company of Cartmen and dates back around 500 years.

Doggett's Coat and Badge Race

In 1715, the oldest rowing race in the world was founded by Irish actor Thomas Doggett. As well as performing, he also helped manage several London theatres. It is known as Doggett's Coat and Badge because those were the prizes given to the victor. In his will, Doggett left specific instructions for the continuation of the race. The contestants were newly qualified watermen or lightermen. It still follows the original course of four miles and seven furlongs, beginning at London Bridge and ending near Cadogan Pier. It is currently managed by the Worshipful Company of Fishmongers. A report of the 1864 race makes for some amusement:

> The original conditions were that the race should be rowed all the way against the tide, but during the last few years the rule has been so much infringed that the competitors have been enabled to save the tide nearly all the way up. This deplorable decision to go with the flow obviously marks the start of the subsequent sustained decline in the British national character.

St Boswells Fair

This horse fair, held at the green in St Boswells, Melrose, is attended by many Gypsy and traveller communities. It dates back several hundred years and was originally a livestock fair. It falls close to 18 July, in celebration of the saint's day.

Ashburton Court Leet
In Ashburton, Devon, elections take place at this time of year for the Ashburton Court Leet. Duties include bread weighing and ale tasting, making them an early forebear of the Food Standards Agency.

London Procession in Honour of Our Lady of Mount Carmel
The procession in honour of Our Lady of Mount Carmel takes place in mid-July. It has been running annually since the 1880s and claims to be the first outdoor Roman Catholic religious event held in England since the Reformation. The event starts with the release of doves, followed by a procession through Clerkenwell to celebrate the Italian diaspora in the area.

The Cleikum Ceremony
In the third week of July, the Cleikum Ceremony takes place. It is held at Innerleithen as part of St Ronan's Border Games. St Ronan is believed to have challenged the devil to a fight, defeating him with his trusty staff. The legend is brought to life alongside a flower parade, games, hill races, tugs of war, a torchlit procession and fireworks reenacting the devil being burned.

Royal Swan Upping
Royal Swan Upping is a centuries-old royal event that takes place annually on the Thames. The ceremonial practice dates back to the twelfth century and involves the counting and marking of swans. The event was held to determine whether the swans belonged to the Worshipful Company of Vintners, the Dyers' Company or the sovereign. Today, over five days in the third week of July each year, the swans are weighed, given health checks and tagged by swan markers who are

dressed in full livery. Although the event is steeped in history, it is now a blend of tradition, conservation and community engagement.

https://www.youtube.com/watch?v=KUFB_mHotoo

The origins of Swan Upping can be traced back to Henry III, who declared that all unmarked mute swans in open water belonged to the Crown. This decree was primarily due to the value of swans as a delicacy at banquets and feasts.

Swan Upping begins at Sunbury and ends at Abingdon, covering approximately seventy-nine miles of the River Thames. The participants, known as Swan Uppers, are dressed in traditional uniforms and travel in six wooden boats. The Swan Uppers represent the Crown and two livery companies: the Vintners' Company and the Dyers' Company. Each group has its own distinct uniform, with the Queen's Swan Marker and Swan Uppers wearing scarlet jackets, while the Vintners' and Dyers' Swan Uppers wear blue and white.

The primary purpose of Swan Upping is to conduct a census of the swan population on the Thames. The Swan Uppers row along the river, stopping at various points to catch and mark the swans. The process involves carefully capturing the swans, checking their health and marking them with identification rings. This helps in monitoring the swan population and tracking their movements. The data collected is important for conservation efforts and ensuring the well-being of the swans.

Swan Upping also serves as an educational event. The Swan Uppers visit local schools along the route to educate children about the importance of wildlife conservation and the history of the event. This outreach helps foster a sense of community and encourages a new generation to take an interest in nature.

Swan Upping has faced challenges over the years, including changes in the river's environment and threats to the swan population. Pollution, habitat loss and human activities have all impacted the swans. However, the event has adapted to these challenges, with increased emphasis on conservation and collaboration with environmental organisations.

In recent years, Swan Upping has gained international attention, attracting tourists and media coverage.

Tolpuddle Martyrs' Festival

The Tolpuddle Martyrs are commemorated in Tolpuddle, Dorset, in the third week of the month. At the heart of the events is a Methodist church service in memory of the hardships faced by early trade unionists, including the six farm workers who were sentenced to seven years' transportation to Australia in 1834.

Honiton Hot Pennies Day

Back in Honiton, East Devon, an annual fair dating back to the thirteenth century takes place. A large flower-covered pole is raised with a giant glove at the top, which acts as a signal that no one can be arrested for debt at the fair. This tradition was to encourage people to attend the fair who might otherwise have been afraid of arrest. Pennies are thrown from the upstairs window of the pub where the festivities start. Proclamations are read by the town crier and repeated by the crowd.

Battle of Falkirk Commemoration

On 22 July 1298, the Battle of Falkirk was fought. William Wallace's Scottish forces were crushed by those of King Edward I. On the nearest Saturday to the date of the battle, commemorations take place at the monument in Callendar Park.

The Brinsley Coffin Walk

In Brinsley, Nottinghamshire, a rather morbid service takes place. Prior to the church being built, the locals had to carry coffins three miles across the fields to Greasley for burial. At this time of year, the coffin walk commemorates those times. Pallbearers carry caskets along the route. Today, thankfully, the coffins are empty.

https://www.youtube.com/watch?v=dN-1zGhn-ME&t=103s

Meantime, over in Congham, North Norfolk, it is the season for snail racing.

Carnwath Red Hose Race

If you're looking for something slightly more energetic, try the Red Hose Run at Carnwath, South Lanarkshire, Scotland. This contest dates back to 1508 and, as the name suggests, runners have to wear red socks. It claims to be the oldest surviving foot race in the world. It now takes place during the local agricultural show.

Ebernoe Horn Fair

Ebernoe, a parish in West Sussex, holds the Horn Fair on 25 July, St James's Day. It is so named after the horns taken from a ram roasted for St James's Day. As well as the roast, cricket is played and the horns are recycled as the daily trophy.

St Ives John Knill Ceremony

In 1767, a monument was built on Worvas Hill near St Ives by local benefactor John Knill. He left instructions that services would take place every five years at this steeple and a dole given out. The tradition is still going strong. The event includes dancing and the singing of a psalm.

Herne Hill Three Horseshoes Wheelie-Bin Race

In south London, a more modern tradition is the Herne Hill Three Horseshoes wheelie-bin race. Teams of four consume large amounts of alcohol and then propel each other in a wheelie bin along a 400-yard course and back. The dustbins are usually customised and their owners are in fancy dress, with prizes awarded for costume and conveyance as well as speed. The bins are all damaged and awaiting recycling and are supplied by the local council. There is also live music on site and, of course, plenty of food and drink. Customisation of wheelie bins is actively encouraged, while the contestants themselves are actively discouraged by people throwing things at them.

Throughout the summer at beaches all across the UK, national sandcastle competitions take place.

Church Clipping

Another summer tradition is church clipping, from the Old English *clyppan*, meaning to embrace. Congregations gather to encircle their church and embrace it shortly after Saint Peter's Day. St Peter's Church in Edgmond, Shropshire, claims to have the longest-running event of this kind. It has been an annual occurrence since 1867.

https://www.youtube.com/watch?v=sbMQRIfz7i4&t=5s

The Galashiels Braw Lads' Gathering

This is a traditional borders festival marking the victory over the English. In 1337, a party of English raiders, returning home over the border, stopped to rest in a grove of plum trees. It is said that the troops were overpowered while tucking into the local plums. As part of the commemorations, plums are given by women to the menfolk. The festivities also include the Mixing of the Roses Ceremony, which takes place at the old town cross. This commemorates the marriage of Margaret Tudor to King James IV, as their wedding took place at Galashiels.

The British Lawn Mower Grand Prix

In Sussex in July or August, the British Lawn Mower Racing Association organises the Flymo equivalent of the British Grand Prix. All classes of lawn mower are represented, right up to ride-on mowers.

Bognor International Birdman

Over in Bognor Regis, West Sussex, the Birdman competition takes place. The aim is to become airborne after launching oneself from the pier, relying only on manpower to gain lift. There is a matrix of classes based on how seriously the competitors take themselves. Most participants view it not as a flight competition but as a diving one.

Eyemouth Herring Queen Festival

In Eyemouth, Berwickshire, in the Scottish borders, a herring festival takes place. It celebrates the importance of peak herring season and commemorates an 1881 fishing disaster when 129 men were lost in a storm. During the festival, a Herring Queen is crowned. In 2024, fourteen-year-old Holly Blackie became the eightieth Eyemouth Herring Queen, and this year was particularly special as fifty former queens travelled from all over the world to witness her coronation.[3]

Old Woodstock Mock Mayor

Late in the month in Old Woodstock in Oxfordshire, a custom takes place to poke fun at the expense of neighbouring New Woodstock and its grand town hall. A new 'mock' mayor is elected for Woodstock, who ends up getting dunked in the River Glyme. Candidates make their speeches, then the committee elect their new mayor for the year, forming a procession across Blenheim Park to the New Woodstock Town Hall for dancing with morris men and the real Mayor of Woodstock. The message for politicians is not to take yourself too seriously.

The Caerphilly Cheese Festival

Caerphilly in Wales hosts a cheese festival, focusing on eating cheese rather than rolling it down hills.

The Whitstable Oyster Festival

Over in Whitstable, Kent, the oyster is celebrated with morris dancing, fireworks and decorations made from oyster shells. The festival starts with the landing of the oysters at Long Beach, where the first catch of the season is brought to shore. There is a parade and an oyster-eating competition.

Continuing the mollusc theme, Musselburgh in Scotland hosts the Riding of the Marches every twenty-one years. As well as ride-outs, sports, games and music, celebrations include a commemoration of the town's fishing heritage.

https://www.youtube.com/watch?v=utYyZFtQbD8

Battle of Shrewsbury Commemoration

On 21 July, the Battle of Shrewsbury is commemorated. It took place in 1403 between Lancastrian King Henry IV and Henry 'Hotspur' Percy, heir to the Earl of Northumberland. In Yarrow, they commemorate the turmoil experienced in the seventeenth century with blanket services. It was an area known for its religious dissent. Open-air church services were held because worshippers were banned from gathering indoors and the services were named after the blankets they used for shelter.

Battle of Killiecrankie Commemoration

In the last weekend in July, the Battle of Killiecrankie is commemorated. It was fought in 1689 between Jacobite Highlanders supporting King James II and forces loyal to William of Orange.

Siddington Redesmere Fete

One of the most beautiful summer events takes place at Siddington in Gloucestershire. The Water Lily Queen leads a procession before being rowed across the lake in a swan-shaped boat and then crowned on the shore by the King of Redesmere. The tradition is over 100 years old.

St Benet's Abbey Commemoration

The last event of note in July is a commemoration of the resilience of the Abbey of St Benet at Holme in Norfolk, which was never officially dissolved during the suppression of the monasteries under Henry VIII. It stood alone in defiance.

AUGUST

Throughout August across the whole of the UK, agricultural shows and scarecrow festivals are held. Large scarecrow festivals can be found at Hayling Island near Portsmouth in Hampshire and Kettlewell in the Yorkshire Dales.

Lammas

It is also the month of Lammas or 'loaf mass'. Celebrated on 1 August, it is a Christian celebration of the corn harvest.

Yorkshire Day

Yorkshire Day also falls on the first day of the month. It was created in response to the alterations in county boundaries in the 1970s. A declaration in Latin, Old Norse and English regarding the integrity of Yorkshire is read at each of the four city gates of York. The date was chosen as it was the anniversary of the Battle of Minden.

Yorkshire and Lancashire's differences come directly from their ancient history. While Lancashire was part of the larger Viking settlement area, there's also evidence of Norwegian settlement, particularly along the coast, with some Danish influence in inland areas. Place names including 'by', 'kirk', 'thorpe' and 'thwaite' indicate their Scandinavian origin. Yorkshire also experienced Viking influence, especially in the east and north. A large part of the population in Yorkshire has Viking Y-chromosome ancestry.

While both regions experienced Viking influence, there were some notable differences. For example, Yorkshire has more place names of Danish origin compared to Lancashire, which tends to have more Norwegian-influenced names. Additionally, the settlement patterns in Yorkshire were more focused on the coast and along major rivers, while Lancashire had a more dispersed pattern, with settlements found in less habitable areas.

The National Eisteddfod of Wales

During the first week of the month, celebrations are held, including the border traditions of ridings with torchlit processions and fireworks. The National Eisteddfod is held at this time to celebrate Welsh arts and culture. Its origins go back to the twelfth century, when Lord Rhys hosted a contest for his composers.

Lauder Common Riding

This is one of the longest-established customs in the borders calendar, with records dating back hundreds of years.

St Wilfrid's Procession

On the first Saturday of the month, St Wilfrid is celebrated. He was the Abbot of Ripon and the Bishop of York, and Rippon Cathedral is dedicated to him. On this day, the town celebrates him with a parade and the consumption of Wilfrid tarts, which are apple and Wensley-dale pies.

Bonsall Hen Races

Over in Bonsall, it is time for the annual chicken run. Hens must race over a thirty-foot course. There are several heats and a grand finale. Worms are deployed to get the birds to head in the correct direction.

UK Thumb Wrestling Championships

If you prefer competing rather than spectating, then get yourself along to Beccles to compete as a thumb wrestler. Thumb wrestling is a major event in Suffolk's cultural calendar. The objective is to pin down your opponent's thumb long enough to chant: '1-2-3-4, I win a thumb war!' Alcohol is consumed simultaneously.

On the following day, the pagan community holds a Pagan Pride festival.

The Grand Wardmote

That same weekend is the Grand Wardmote, an annual gathering and competition of the Woodmen of Arden, an archery club based at Meriden. They have their own uniform and use traditional yew longbows.

Egton Bridge Gooseberry Show

On the first Tuesday, the oldest surviving gooseberry show in the country takes place at Egton Bridge, near Whitby. People come from far and wide in the hope of having produced the heaviest gooseberry.

Coldstream Civic Week

The following Thursday is Coldstream Civic Week, another traditional borders celebration dating back to the 1950s. The highlight is a ride to Flodden battlefield, which saw action between King Henry VIII's forces and Scotland's James IV, who was slain in the fight. The ride is spectacular, with around 300 horsemen led by the Coldstreamer, who bears his flag. Wreaths are laid and a short service given for those who fell, accompanied by a lone piper.

Inverkeithing Hat and Ribbon Race

On the first Friday, the oldest road race in Scotland takes place. Men over fifteen years old all compete for ribbons to present to their sweethearts. Hundreds of years old, it takes place at Inverkeithing and is known as the Hat and Ribbon Race.

Brigg Horse Fair

The 800-year-old Brigg Horse Fair at Brigg, North Lincolnshire, takes place around the 4th or 5th of the month.

Black Shuck Festival

On 4 August 1577, Black Shuck, a terrifying demon dog, terrorised the residents of the small Suffolk town of Bungay. Since the dog first materialised at the local church, it has appeared at various moments throughout history in the town and wider region. In 2022, Bungay held its first Black Shuck Festival. Old Shuck, Old Shock or simply Shuck is one of many such black dogs recorded across the British Isles. It is sometimes recorded as an omen of death, but in other instances is described as companionable. The name Shuck derives from the Old English word *scucca* meaning 'devil' or 'fiend', perhaps from the root *skuh*, 'to terrify'. The first mention in print of Black Shuck is by Reverend E. S. Taylor in 1850: 'This phantom I have heard many persons in East Norfolk and even Cambridgeshire, describe as having seen as a black shaggy dog, with fiery eyes and of immense size and who visits churchyards at midnight.'

New Galloway Scottish Alternative Games

If the Highland Games are a little bit too energetic for you, the Scottish Alternative Games held each year at New Galloway are the lowland equivalent. The Gird 'n' Cleek is the main event, involving bowling a large metal hoop using a propulsion rod. Snail racing, archery and throwing stuff over other stuff are other events. And if you do want to work up a sweat, tractor pulling is also very good fun.

Mary Gibson's Mausoleum Inspection

For the last 200 years, around 12 August, Mary Gibson's Mausoleum has been inspected in the churchyard of St Nicholas's in Sutton. It is not quite understood why, but the speculation is she made it a provision of her will.

Over in Lymm, in the parish in Warrington and at Macclesfield Forest, a rushbearing service takes place in the local church, which is dedicated to St Mary. On the same day in Marhamchurch, the village celebrates its creation by St Morwenna. This involves an elected queen of the reveille being crowned by 'Old Father Time', whose real identity is kept secret. The queen then leads the procession on horseback to partying, Cornish wrestling competitions and feasting.

York Assize of Ale

Mid-month at York, the sheriff summons local sergeants to the Mansion House to hear speeches and then go on a medieval pub crawl around the town. At each location, after the procession has tested the quality of the beer, the landlord is presented with a certificate to verify its quality.

Moffat Sheep Races

The town of Moffat in Scotland celebrates its long association with the wool trade by racing sheep, complete with knitted jockeys. This is a comparatively new tradition, established in 2012.

The Burryman

In Queensferry, a local is persuaded to dress up in a costume made from thousands of burdock heads. The outfit is completed with a flowery bowler hat. His task is to walk the streets of the town all day, with offerings of whisky as encouragement. This task takes place during the local Ferry Fair Festival.

Marymass Fair

In Irvine, the Marymass Fair takes place mid-month. Its origins lie in the twelfth century and mark the Christian Feast of the Assumption. The revelry lasts twelve days and has an equine theme. The parade also features a Marymass Queen. In 1563, Mary Queen of Scots visited the town with her attendants, who all shared her name. Ever since, the festival has borne her name.

Staithes Nightgown Parade

Over at Staithes and Runswick Bay, it is time for the nightgown parade. This is organised by the Royal National Lifeboat Institution to raise funds for their lifesaving work. Partygoers wear pyjamas and nightdresses.

Ras Beca

This is an annual running race, which commemorates key moments in Welsh history. It is a five-mile race in the Preseli mountains marking the Rebecca Riots, which took place between 1839 and 1843 to protest about poor living conditions and unfair taxation. The rioters disguise themselves in female clothes and called themselves the Merched Beca, meaning Rebecca's daughters, a reference to the biblical tale. The winners' prize is to destroy the Papingo. A Papingo is a painted wooden pigeon, perched on top of a tower. The society formed in the fifteenth century and today still uses longbows to try and hit their quarry. A similar event was founded in 2016 at Drummond Castle.

Race the Train

If you're looking for something a little more energetic, Race the Train is a challenge that takes place on the Talyllyn Railway. Competitors have to try and beat the steam locomotive on a half-marathon course. The trainline was originally built to transport slate from the local quarries.

https://www.youtube.com/watch?v=h8QcMrV2CPM

Annual commemoration of the Western Rebellion and the Clyst Heath Massacre

Close to the date of the Battle of Sampford Courtenay, on 17 August, the Bodmin Old Cornwall Society organises an annual commemoration of the Western Rebellion and the Clyst Heath Massacre. On Clyst Heath on the night of 4–5 August 1549, the royal army under Lord Grey killed 900 rebel prisoners of war from Devon and Cornwall in ten minutes. These events of the Western Rebellion were part of a popular revolt with roots in economic factors but triggered by the introduction of the Common Prayer Book, written in English. The Cornish population wanted to retain the original Latin, not understanding the new translation. The events are seen as the start of the decline of the Cornish language. There is a parade of 900 flags, each marking one of the fallen at Clyst Heath.

Meanwhile, down the road in Plymouth is the National Fireworks Championships.

Bun Race

Saint Bartholomew's Day is 24 August and it is celebrated in Sandwich, Kent, with a Bun Race. Children race around the chapel of St Bartholomew's Hospital and are rewarded with currant buns in a special service at the ancient hospital. The hospital still serves as an alms house for older people and it was founded to mark a victory over the French in the thirteenth century.

Lee Gap Fair

On the same day, the oldest charter fair takes place in West Ardsley in Yorkshire. Known as the Lee Gap Fair, after the man who helped to keep it running during Tudor times, it's been going for more than 800 years.

The Bramble Bank Cricket Match

Late in August, the tides of the Solent reveal Bramble Bank, a 200-metre-long sandbank, which breaks the surface for only one a day year. It is just big enough to play a cricket match on and so that is what people do. Yacht and adventure clubs rendezvous at the sand bank just as it becomes visible. This tradition started in the 1950s and in more recent years, other sports have been played.

https://www.youtube.com/watch?v=EURArd1M4pY

World Walking the Plank Championships

If you really want to get wet, then the annual walking the plank competition in Queensborough Harbour is probably more your thing. In addition to the spectacular scenes of people plummeting into the sea from a ship moored just offshore, competitors are judged on costume and pirate-themed trash talk.

The Leigh Candle Auction

At Leigh, a candle auction for two pieces of land takes place, the winning bet being the one placed just before the candle burns out. This tradition dates back to the seventeenth century.

Edinburgh Military Tattoo

The Edinburgh Military Tattoo is a spectacular annual event lasting three weeks. Six decades old and featuring massed bands, pipers and drums, there are Scottish regiments and performers from all over the world, as well as visiting military bands. British military bands often tour and the Edinburgh Tattoo has featured across the globe, as well as in its home city.

Robin Hood Festival

At Edwinstowe, in Sherwood Forest, Robin Hood and his merry men all celebrate justice with jousting, falconry and an archery competition. By the way, Nottinghamshire is not the most densely wooded county in the UK – Surrey is, with woodland covering around a fifth of its land area. This means that over 20 per cent of Surrey is covered by trees.

Lincoln Mystery Plays

In Lincoln, the medieval tradition of mystery plays has been revived. In this context, mystery means a trade. Plays are performed usually every four years, in buildings associated with the cathedral.

Rushcart Festival

A service similar to rushbearing takes place in Saddleworth, called the Rushcart. The cart tours local villages and marks the change of rushes on the floor of the local church.

Totnes Orange Races

At Totnes, Sir Francis Drake is remembered in a competition known as the Orange Races. Competitors must propel the orange over a 500-metre course without picking it up or carrying it. This commemorates Sir Francis dropping a basket of oranges on Fore Street and being helped to round them up by passers-by.

The Riding of the Marches

Around 18 August, the Riding of the Marches takes place. This boundary-marking event is over a century old but has its origins much earlier. In addition to the riding, a festival queen is crowned and there is a procession of floats. The event finishes with fireworks and a torchlit procession.

St Austell Giant Pasty Ceremony

If by the third week of August you have worked up an appetite, there is the Giant Pasty Ceremony in Cornwall. An enormous pasty is sailed across the bay at St Austell and then carried through the streets, before being sliced up and distributed. Competitions judging the quality of the pasty and a person's ability to eat it are some of the attractions.

Saint Margaret Hope Horse Children

Across Britain, farming communities hold ploughing matches. At Saint Margaret Hope on Orkney, they run an event where children, not horses or tractors, pull the ploughs. The children are dressed as horses, but it is a serious business, as they set about ploughing a plot of land in an allotted timeframe.

https://www.facebook.com/watch/?v=893473100719586

Highland Games

On 19 August 1745, Bonnie Prince Charlie raised his standard to inspire the Jacobite rising. Near this date the Highland Games commences, and there is also a commemoration of these historic events. The games include tug of war, tossing the caber and throwing the hammer. There are, of course, Highland dancing and piping competitions too.

Cilgerran Festive Week

Cilgerran Festive Week takes place on the River Teifi, where participants race coracles across the water to raise funds for charitable causes.

https://www.youtube.com/watch?v=rJE-oHOCN8Q

Knighthood of the Old Green Tournament

Southampton boasts the oldest bowling green in the world, and on a

Wednesday late in August, the Knighthood of the Old Green Tournament takes place. It dates back to at least the eighteenth century. The winner is declared a knight and barred from future contests.

Beating the Bounds
Late in August, every seven years, Beating the Bounds takes place at Richmond in Yorkshire. This boundary marking involves the water bailiff having to enter the River Swale twice, as Richmond's boundary falls midstream.

Dartmouth Regatta Waiters' and Barrel Races
On a Friday late in the month, Dartmouth hosts a waiters' race, where contestants dash through a course carrying trays of glasses, which are filled with beer at the halfway point. The festivities also include team races, with participants propelling kegs through the streets. As if that weren't enough excitement, the sporting events culminate with the International Supermarket Trolley Grand Prix, adding a unique and entertaining twist to the day.

Bosworth Medieval Festival
The Battle of Bosworth took place on 22 August 1485, won by the first Tudor King, Henry VII. A service is held at Saint James's Church in Sutton Cheney to commemorate Richard III and all that fell with him. There is a battle reenactment and jousting tournament.

Elderslie Wallace Day
Elderslie Wallace Day is 23 August. Sir William Wallace was born at Elderslie and residents commemorate their local hero on the date of his execution.

West Witton Burning Bartle
The following day is West Witton Burning Bartle in Wensleydale,

North Yorkshire. A stuffed figure known as Bartle parades through the village, leering at residents and those passing through. There is a fair amount of ritual shouting and drinking on the way. The ritual dates from at least the 1800s and maybe even earlier. Bartle may have been a local miscreant, condemned to death by local courts. What is clear is that he always meets a sticky end. His menacing procession is brought to a close by him being stabbed, covered in fuel and burned to a cinder.

https://www.youtube.com/watch?v=DuTKD37sk_M&t=21s

Aberaeron Mackerel Fiesta

The August bank holiday marks the end of the summer fishing season at Aberaeron. A mackerel fish effigy is carried through the streets to symbolise its funeral, accompanied by black-clad mourners. At the church, the fish is blessed to ensure good fishing for the next twelve months. How else would the day end but with the giant fish being barbecued on the beach?

https://www.youtube.com/watch?v=cye1JUKKIfI

The Axbridge Pageant

This event is held every ten years. Hundreds of locals reenact scenes associated with the town, some dating back 2,000 years. This community event has been performed regularly since 1967, when a celebration of the town's history was first held in the town square. Since then, it has been held in 1970, 1980, 1990, 2000 and 2010. Due to the Covid crisis, it was postponed in 2020.

Day of Syn

Dymchurch is a parish in Kent and holds the Day of Syn at this time of the year. It is based around a fictional character, Doctor Syn, and his smuggling gang. It's been running for about fifty years to raise money for good causes.

Bog Snorkelling

This is another recent tradition born after a night in a Llanwrtyd Wells pub. The World Bog Snorkelling Championships take place annually in August at Waen Rhydd bog in Wales. Competitors must swim sixty metres along a water-filled trench in a peat bog. There are strict rules – for instance, no conventional swimming strokes are permitted. Participants must use only their legs, flippers and a snorkel.

https://www.youtube.com/watch?v=jVuabhIYHaY&t=3s

Grasmere Lakeland Sports and Show

At Grasmere, a summer sports event takes place. Its foundations were in a sheep fair that took place in the nineteenth century. These days, sports including fell racing, sheepdog displays, tug of war and traditional Cumbrian wrestling take place.

Stalling Busk Flower Festival
On the Sunday of the bank holiday weekend, a service takes place on the shores of Semerwater, not far from Bainbridge in Yorkshire, alongside the flower festival Stalling Busk. There is a legend that a sunken city lies under the lake waters and that on a quiet day, you can hear its church bells ringing below the surface.

Notting Hill Carnival
If you fancy something a little louder, this London carnival has been held annually since the mid-1960s and is one of the largest street festivals in the world, second only to the Rio Carnival. It attracts over 2 million people and 300 food vendors over a 3.5-mile route.

Bourton-on-the-Water Football in the River
On the bank holiday Monday in the River Windrush at Bourton-on-the-Water, a football match takes place and has done for well over a century.

https://www.youtube.com/watch?v=foiZ5MJpvAI

Pershore Plum Festival
Pershore, in Worcestershire is famous for its orchards, which were planted in medieval times. The plum harvest is celebrated on this day. Festivities include a plum procession.

World Gravy Wrestling

A late addition to the August sporting calendar is the annual World Gravy Wrestling Championships in Rossendale, Lancashire. Devised in 2007 by Lancastrians, contestants must wrestle in the gravy for two minutes. Points are scored for fancy dress, comedic effect and entertainment.

https://www.youtube.com/watch?v=QCqqNUcVHVE

Wells Moat Boat Races

Alternative sport is available in Wells, Somerset, in the form of the Moat Boat Races. Teams build rafts and race them up and down the moat surrounding the Bishop's Palace.

The Birnam Highland Games

These games are held on the last Saturday of the month and have been a tradition since 1864. Events include a haggis-eating competition and the Kiltie Dash, which is a standard road race for kilt wearers.

Plague Sunday

On the last Sunday of the month, the village of Eyam in Derbyshire holds Plague Sunday. It marks events in 1665, when villagers decided to cut themselves off to try not to spread the bubonic plague. Each year, Eyam holds a memorial service at Cucklet Delph to remember the victims of the plague and the villagers' selflessness. The service begins with a procession from St Lawrence's Church to Cucklet Delph, where the vicar of Eyam uses the same rock pulpit as Priest William Mompesson. During the plague, villagers gathered at Cucklet Delph, a natural amphitheatre, to hear sermons from Mompesson. During the service, the names of the plague victims are read aloud and many villagers dress in seventeenth-century costumes and act out scenes from the village's experience during the plague. Supplies were left on the boundaries of the village, paid for with coins placed in vinegar, which was thought to act as a disinfectant.

AUTUMN

SEPTEMBER

September is welcomed in with the northern lights in th'illuminations (as the locals call it) in Blackpool. If that were not enough,
the World Fireworks Championships also take place in parallel.

WORLD FIREWORKS CHAMPIONSHIPS

https://www.youtube.com/watch?v=L_YD8fId73o

At the month's close, it is the season of harvest festivals, with services and events taking place across the whole of the UK. Churches and
schools are decorated with produce and collections of food, fresh and
tinned, are held for those in the community who are in need.

Cromwell Day

On 3 September, Oliver Cromwell is celebrated by the Cromwell Association. He died on this date in 1658. He's not remembered fondly
by all, however. In 1647, Christmas was abolished by the English Parliament. The test of a true Irishman is still said to be whether their spit
can reach his statue at Parliament from the nearby pavement.

Battle of Worcester Commemoration

The final battle of the English Civil War was the Battle of Worcester in
1651. An annual commemoration of that event takes place in the city.
Reenactors process from what was the Royalist headquarters during

the conflict up to Fort Royal Hill. A short service is held and muskets fired to remember all who fell.

Gloucester Day

Gloucester Day is 7 September. The date chosen commemorates the raising of the siege of Gloucester in 1643, when the city was saved from Royalist forces. The first parade, led by the Mock Mayor of Barton, processes from Constitution Walk eventually to arrive in Kings Square. In the square, the traditional comic meeting of the Mock Mayor of Barton and the Mayor of Gloucester takes place. The parade then departs for a Thanksgiving Day service at St Mary de Crypt. After this, the parade again makes its way through the city, led by the mayor and accompanied by the Sheriff of Gloucester in full civic regalia. Local community groups take part in the second parade in the afternoon, including the local veteran community.

Flodden Day

On 9 September, the 1513 Club commemorates the Battle of Flodden, which was fought between England and Scotland near the village of Branxton in Northumberland.

Straw Jack Harvest

Early in the month, the Straw Jack Harvest event takes place at Carshalton in the London Borough of Sutton. The Straw Jack is paraded around the town to great revelry. At the end of the event, Jack is cut to pieces and the straw of his innards distributed through the crowd. Traditionally, this straw is burned on a fire in the garden of a local pub.

Largs Viking Festival

In 1263, the Battle of Largs took place, resulting in Scotland's King Alexander III slaying the Norse King Haakon. These events are commemorated early in the month over a nine-day period at the Largs Viking Festival. The finale is the festival of fire, complete with torchlit procession and the burning of a longship on the beach with fireworks.

Crying the Neck

This is a West Country harvest custom, with its origins in pagan times. The last wheatsheaf of the harvest is saved and fashioned into a corn dolly. It is hung in the church until replaced by another the following year. It takes place at various churches, but the services at St Columb and at Madron in Cornwall are two of the most well-known.

Braemar Highland Gathering

Held on the first Saturday of the month, this event features all the traditional activities of the Highland Games, along with lively festivities attended by members of the Royal Family.

Cornish Gorsedd

The Cornish Gorsedd is a celebration of musicians, sportsmen, writers and leaders from different walks of life who have made a contribution to the identity of Cornwall. They are dressed in blue robes decorated with regalia. Those being honoured and new to the event are proposed into the Order of the Gorsedd Council.

Marldon Apple Pie Fair

In Marldon, Devon, there is a delightful English village fete presided over by the Apple Pie Princess. This is a legacy of the nineteenth century, when a local baker supplied the church with a giant apple pie. At the same time in Musselburgh, Scotland, the town's fishing heritage is honoured with a vibrant, fish-themed ceremony, celebrating its long-standing connection to the sea.

Faversham Hop Festival

At this time of the year, hops are celebrated, usually by drinking large amounts of beer. The Faversham Hop Festival takes place late August or in the first weekend of September. Pearly Kings and Queens attend and songs are sung to commemorate the key role east London hop pickers, alongside their Kent cousins, played in the annual harvest. A beer barrel is rolled through the streets, up the aisle of the parish church and onto the altar.

There are more rushbearing and rushcart services at Sowerby Bridge, Yorkshire; Urswick, Cumbria; and Whitworth, Rochdale. A church-clipping event to bring good luck for the year also take place at Wirksworth in Derbyshire, alongside the feast of the Nativity of the Blessed Virgin Mary, to whom the local church is dedicated.

Later in the month, at St Mary's in Painswick in Gloucestershire, puppy dog pie is served to parishioners. Quite why no one is sure, but a local legend has its origins in a tale of two sisters who discovered their men were cheating on them. They served up the disgusting dish as part of their revenge.

Clovelly Lobster and Crab Feast

On the first Sunday of the month, Clovelly in Devon celebrates its seafood with a Lobster and Crab Feast. Funds are raised to support the national lobster hatchery in nearby Padstow. Part of the festival includes the release of baby lobsters into the sea. The hatchery protects baby lobsters until they are big enough to fend for themselves. If local fishermen land a lobster laden with eggs, rather than send it to market, they send it to the hatchery.

Sheriff's Ride

Around 8 September, Lichfield has a boundary-marking custom called the Sherriff's Ride. Lichfield was unusual in that in the sixteenth century, it was given the right to appoint its own sheriff. Riders accompany the sheriff on the sixteen miles that marked the parish lines before returning to the city centre to be met by sword and mace bearers and the dean of the cathedral.

Later in the month, Edinburgh also has a boundary-marking event. The riding of the marches dates back to before the sixteenth century. The ride also commemorates the Battle of Flodden as the route passes by the Flodden Wall, constructed to keep the English at bay. It is one of the largest riding events, with a spectacular procession marching up the Royal Mile to the market cross.

Battle of Stirling Bridge Commemoration

On a Sunday near 11 September, the Battle of Stirling Bridge is commemorated by the Society of William Wallace. The conflict took place in 1297, in the Scottish Wars of Independence, and resulted in a victory for the Scots.

Abbots Bromley Horn Dance

On a Monday early in September, the Abbots Bromley Horn Dance, claimed to be one of the oldest traditions in Europe, is held. Following an early-morning church service, the 'deermen' collect sets of antlers. Dressed in Tudor costume, with a hobby horse and a boy with a bow and arrow, they perform a dance outside the church. They dance through local villages all day, stopping at alehouses for refreshment. At dusk the antlers are returned to the church once more, ready for next year.

https://www.youtube.com/watch?v=vLYnVdYHfCg&t=418s

Last Night of the Proms

The Last Night of the Proms is the grand finale of the BBC Proms season. This is a classical music festival, held annually in mid-September in the Royal Albert Hall in London.

Perhaps the best-ever last night speech was given by Sir Andrew Davis in 1992, who sung it to the tune of 'I Am the Very Model of a Modern Major-General' from Gilbert and Sullivan's 1879 comic opera *The Pirates of Penzance*. This brilliant man sadly died of leukaemia in April 2024.

ANDREW DAVIS LAST NIGHT OF THE PROMS SPEECH

https://www.youtube.com/watch?v=bkh2B7Oifpk&t=5290s

It's a quintessentially British evening but all nationalities are welcome. It features many of the naval songs detailed elsewhere and these two favourites.

ELGAR'S POMP AND CIRCUMSTANCE MARCH NO. 1

https://www.youtube.com/watch?v=R2-43p3GVTQ

JERUSALEM

https://www.youtube.com/watch?v=sERiPuOQyvo

First Fruits Ceremony
In the middle of September, at Richmond in Yorkshire, the First Fruits Ceremony is held, marking the town's heritage as a significant corn market for the north of England.

Hop Hoodening
At this harvest time, hops are also celebrated. Hop Hoodening is the Kent event. There is a special service at Canterbury Cathedral, a Hop Queen and Princesses and plenty of revelry, accompanied by, of course, beer.

Jane Austen Festival
In Bath, they celebrate Jane Austen, with festival-goers in period dress and a costumed ball.

The Newent Onion Fayre
Over in Newent, the Onion Fayre takes place on the second Saturday of the month. It dates from the thirteenth century and now includes an onion-eating competition. Newent is a market town in the Forest of Dean in Gloucestershire. Its annual onion-based extravaganza started after Newent was granted the right to hold two annual fayres by Henry III. Five hundred years later, the September fayre had evolved into a

popular onion-trading event, but when the First World War broke out, it faded into obsolescence. Then, in 1996, a group of local people revived the ancient onion festival and it's since gone from strength to strength. Today, the show features not only onions but also leeks, garlic and chives. It attracts almost 15,000 people each year. The highlight is the onion-eating competition, which sees participants race to consume an onion the size of an apple in the quickest possible time.

https://www.youtube.com/watch?v=Ew1CYgDdUnA

World Black Pudding Throwing Championships
If that brings tears to your eyes, then a game of 'merrills' or 'nine men's morris' might be more up your street. It's an ancient version of noughts and used to be played at Ryedale at this time of year. Perhaps the biggest crowd-puller of all is the fiercely contested black pudding throwing contest. Taking place at Ramsbottom, this is a glorified game of skittles, which sees a black pudding projectile launched at a pile of Yorkshire puddings.

Kinder Beer Barrel Challenge
At Kinder near High Peak, Derbyshire, there is the beer barrel challenge. Teams navigate the hills and swamps across local terrain, carrying a full 72-pint beer barrel.

World Stone-Skimming Championships
Late in September, the sporting season draws to a close with the

World Stone-Skimming Championships on Easdale Island in Argyll, Scotland. Competitors gather at the island's water-filled disused slate quarry to see who can skim their stone the farthest.

Widecombe Fair

Tug of war, ferret racing and many other attractions can be found at this time of year at the Widecombe Fair near Mansfield. The fair's rich history is immortalised in the famous song 'Widecombe Fair', first published in the 1889 songbook *Songs and Ballads of the West*. The song tells the tale of a grey horse, lent out for the journey to the fair, whose unfortunate demise became a beloved part of local folklore. The first verse is:

> Tom Pearce, Tom Pearce, lend me your grey mare.
> All along, down along, out along lea.
> For I want for to go to Widecombe Fair,
> With Bill Brewer, Jan Stewer, Peter Gurney,
> Peter Davy, Dan'l Whiddon, Harry Hawke,
> Old Uncle Tom Cobley and all,
> Old Uncle Tom Cobley and all.

All the characters in the song were said to have been real people, and these days they are represented by character actors at the event.

Meanwhile, at Kew Gardens in London, new students dressed in traditional wooden clogs race over a flat course starting and ending at the Elizabeth Gate.

Pig Face Day

Around 14 September, a boar's head feast is held to commemorate the building of the Church of the Holy Cross at Avening. The history behind the tradition is that Queen Matilda imprisoned Lord Gloucester after he had declined to take up with her before she married William the Conqueror. Wracked with guilt after he died in incarceration, she built the church and funded the feast. Now known as Pig Face Day, the event largely consists of consuming porcine products while well dressed in medieval garb.

Egremont Crab Fair

On the third Saturday of September, the Egremont Crab Fair celebrates crab apples. Its history can be traced back to the thirteenth century, and as well as apples being thrown from the back of a cart going down Main Street, there are equestrian events, vegetable shows, hound trails and wrestling. There are more unusual sports such as pipe-smoking contests, pig's bladder football, horn blowing and gurning championships.

That same weekend, the Scottish Battlefields Trust holds a series of commemorations of the lowland battles. This includes the Battle of Prestonpans in East Lothian, the Battle of Pinkie Cleugh near Musselburgh and the Battle of Dunbar, all celebrated in turn.

John Barleycorn Ceremony

Late in the month a rather gruesome service takes place in Whitby. John Barleycorn, who represents the annual barley crop and the beer it produces, is sacrificed in order that beer will flow in the future. The man-sized corn effigy is slowly and dramatically dissected and eviscerated with a degree of wholly unnecessary, gory detail. Just in case John survives his entrails being spilled out and his genitals removed, he is finally beaten to death, piñata-style.

Back in Lichfield, on 18 September, Dr Samuel Johnson is celebrated, having been born on this day in 1709. Around 25 September, the Battle of Stamford Bridge is commemorated by a reenactment by the Stamford Bridge Society. At the end of the month, the Woolmen's Company organises an annual sheep drive across Southwark Bridge to demonstrate their right to exemption from tolls as Freemen of the City of London.

Pearly Kings and Queens Harvest Festival

Over in Cheapside, the church of St Mary-le-Bow plays host to a cockney knees-up. The Pearly Kings and Queens of London's coster-mongers celebrate their history and charitable works to the sound of the Bow Bells.

At Penryn, another mock election for a Mock Mayor takes place. Drinking and disorder is encouraged.

Malvern Autumn Show

The month closes with the autumn show at Malvern, which boasts the UK National Giant Vegetables Championship and the Allen Valleys Folk Festival. The latter event includes the burning of the Allendale Wolf. This consists of a wool vine-shaped bonfire, which is set alight while the crowd howl at the moon.

THE BURNING OF THE ALLENDALE WOLF

https://www.youtube.com/watch?v=qNXTNpcFamM

Sussex Bonfire

Bonfire season starts early in Sussex, with a whole calendar of events starting in September.

Michaelmas

Michaelmas is 29 September, the feast day of dragon-slaying Saint Michael. Roast goose is eaten and Michaelmas daisies picked.

OCTOBER

Harvest festival and bonfire season continues, as do Blackpool's 'th'illuminations'. Battles are reenacted and ghosts take centre stage. Several customs celebrate the good or poor fortune of our ancestors.

Old Man's Day

On 2 October, the residents of Braughing, Hertfordshire (pronounced Braffing) commemorate the near-burial alive of a local resident in the sixteenth century. Legend has it that on that date in 1571, a sad procession was making its way to St Mary's Church in the village. Among the mourners was the fiancée of farmer Mathew Wall, who, though still in his prime, had been found dead. As the pallbearers walked down the tree-lined Fleece Lane, one of them slipped on the early autumn leaves. When the men took hold of their burden again, they were shocked and frightened to hear banging from inside the coffin. The jolt had woken Wall from his coma or narcoleptic fit and he was thumping on the lid from inside. He went on to marry his sweetheart and to live another twenty-four years, a ripe old age for the time, so the custom is called Old Man's Day.

Twyford Bell Ringers' Dinner

Twyford (the place of two fords) in Hampshire is noted in the Domesday Book. In the early morning of 7 October 1754, William Davis, the local squire, was out riding his horse in thick early-morning mist. As he heard the Twyford bells ringing out from St Mary's Church, he realised they were coming from an unexpected direction and pulled up. As it happens, this was just in time, as he had been heading in the wrong direction and had stopped just on the edge of a deep chalk pit. Had he not stopped, he and his horse would have plunged to certain death. He endowed an annual dinner for the ringers, which is held to this day. The church bells are rung and the bellringers have a feast.

London Beer Flood

On 17 October, the residents of the Holborn Whippet pub remember those killed in the 1814 Meux Brewery disaster at the corner of Great Russell Street and Tottenham Court Road. Also known as the London Beer Flood, it happened when a 22-foot-tall wooden fermentation tank ruptured, releasing nearly a million litres of porter and flooding the streets of St Giles, a poor area of the city. It flooded homes and cellars, killing eight people. The flood was ruled an act of god by the jury and the brewery continued trading for over a century, eventually closing to make way for the Dominion Theatre.

Apple Day

Another recently created tradition is Apple Day, an annual celebration of apples and orchards, held in October. It traditionally falls on 21 October, the date of the first Apple Day in 1990, but events are held throughout the month. By 2000, the day was celebrated in more than 600 events around the country. In Herefordshire, an apple festival takes place at the delightfully named Much Marcle. There is apple tasting, cider-making and a feast of apples. Borough Market in London hosts a special Apple Day celebration, where they showcase 1,000 apple varieties in a display that playfully mimics the Apple Store's design.

Brampton Capon Tree Jacobite Memorial Ceremony

On 21 October 1746, six Jacobite men, Colonel James Innes, Captain Patrick Lindesay, Ronald Macdonald, Thomas Park, Peter Taylor and Michael Delard, were hanged from the branches of a capon tree at Brampton in Cumberland. Capon trees (*Quercus robur*) are the last survivors of the ancient Jed Forest. They are a feature of the turbulent history of the border country between Scotland and England. Each year on this day, a memorial event is held.

The 21st is also, of course, Trafalgar Day, one of the great naval traditions. You can find discussion of the day elsewhere in this book.

Whitchurch Blackberry Fair

Around 7 October at Whitchurch, a Shropshire parish, there is a celebration of creativity, local produce and community spirit. The fair features a parade, live music, street performers, market stalls and the 'Blackberry Procession'.

Nottingham Goose Fair

The Nottingham Goose Fair is held annually around this time on the city's Forest Recreation Ground and is believed to have started around 1284. The name likely came from the large number of geese driven from Lincolnshire to be sold in Nottingham, as roast goose was a traditional Michaelmas treat. Today, the fair features a wide variety of rides, stalls and sideshows, including roller coasters, a giant wheel, dodgems, waltzers and traditional rides like gallopers, chairs and cakewalks.

Quit Rents Ceremony

This traditionally takes place in October each year, usually on or around the second Wednesday of the month. The exact date can vary slightly, but it is always held at the Royal Courts of Justice in London. It is one of the oldest legal customs, where the City of London Corporation hands over two knives, sixty-one nails and six large horseshoes to the Crown. This was payment for land, the exact whereabouts of which has been lost in the annals of time. The payment in kind was made to the King's Remembrancer, whose role it was to collect monies owed. One knife is payment for land in Shropshire. The nails and shoes are for the use of a forge near the Strand in London. At this service, new sheriffs are presented with their warrants.

The King's Remembrancer (or Queen's Remembrancer) is an ancient judicial post in the legal system of England and Wales. Since the Lord Chancellor no longer sits as a judge, the remembrancer is the oldest judicial position in continual existence. The post was created in 1154 by King Henry II as the chief official in the Exchequer Court.

Hull Fair

The Hull Fair is Europe's largest travelling funfair, which goes to Kingston upon Hull, England, for one week around 11 October each year. The fair is open every day between these days except Sunday. It gained its charter in 1279 and has run almost every year since.

Houghton Feast

This annual Michaelmas festival is held over ten days in Houghton-le-Spring, a town between Durham and Sunderland. It was founded in the twelfth century. From the sixteenth century, a whole roasted ox became central to commemorate the generosity of Bernard Gilpin, Houghton's rector at the time. He fed the poor through the harsh winter, from Michaelmas through to Easter. Ironically, he was himself killed by a collision with an ox in the marketplace on 4 March 1583.

King Harold Day

The Battle of Hastings took place on 14 October 1066. After King Harold was slain, his body was brought to the abbey he founded at Waltham for burial. Folklore has it that this was the initiative of his common-law wife Edith Swanneck, who found his body on the battlefield. The Normans did not want his grave marked, but Waltham Abbey marks this day as King Harold Day and flowers are laid on his memorial stone.

Tiddlywinks

The months of October and November are tiddlywinks season. This is an unnecessarily complex Victorian parlour game. Other names for the game include bidens, bombs, boondocks, Bristols, brundels, cruds, gromps, middle for diddles, nurdles, scrunges, squidges, snooves and squops. Games are organised by the English Tiddlywinks Association.

Night of the Hunters Moon

On the nearest Saturday to the full moon, the Night of the Hunters

Moon is celebrated at Wortley, north of Sheffield. It was during a great drought in the early seventeenth century that the squire of the manor of Langsett, Sir Rufus Fox, organised a week of prayers, to be offered by all his tenants and their families, while processing around Langsett Lake. On the third day of these prayers, an oak chest was seen in the mud where the lake had dried up. It was found to contain the *Liber Rufus Clivuslongi*, the Red Book of Langsett. Sir Rufus took the connection between his own name and that of the book, as a mark of a special providence.

Sir Rufus began to translate the book from Latin but had to flee the country due to the antics of his brother Guido Fox (Fawkes). The estate went to his cousin, Sir Russell. The book was lost, but a few of Sir Rufus's translations remain, detailing the dancing and fire ceremonies. The Night of the Hunters Moon involves a special masked fire dance and the Fox Dance is performed at Langsett to this very day. The master of ceremonies is known as Mister Fox.

THE NIGHT OF THE HUNTERS MOON FIRE DANCE

https://www.youtube.com/watch?v=fx_csqsZdcQ

On a Sunday early in October, the figure of St Cuthbert at the church bearing his name in Ackworth is given a garland of a corn sheaf as part of their Harvest Festival.

Throwing the Feat Stone

At Efenechtyd in Denbighshire, Wales, early in the month or near Saint Michael's Day on 29 September, locals demonstrate their strength by throwing the Feat Stone, or Maen Camp, backwards over their heads. This stone, which is a large, rounded 100-pound boulder is housed in the local church. This sport is usually incorporated into a 'clipping service'.

The custom was revived in the early twenty-first century and the stone weighs in at over 100 pounds. After the throwing, homemade cakes are served under the lychgate.

https://www.youtube.com/watch?v=O4FsoBSyIlY

Conkers

October is also conker-bashing season. The first mention of the game is in Poet Laureate Robert Southey's memoirs in 1821. At that time, the weapon of choice was snail shells or hazelnuts. Horse chestnuts started to be used from the 1850s. Conker competitions are widespread across the UK and the World Championships are held in Northamptonshire.

Gopher Bell Ringing

At Newark, the Gopher Bell Ringing commemorates the salvation of a Flemish merchant lost in the dead of a winter night. He was led home following the bells of Saint Mary Magdalen Church. His legacy is that the bells are rung on six consecutive Sundays before Evensong in October and November.

Lion Sermon

On the Thursday nearest to 16 October, at Saint Katharine Cree Church in the Aldgate ward of the City of London, a service celebrates another lucky escape – this time of Sir John Gayer, Lord Mayor of London in 1646. He instituted the Lion Sermon, inspired by his time in the Syrian desert, when a lion passed him without attacking him. He subsequently believed he had had a miraculous deliverance. In gratitude, he endowed the church with a fund to preach a sermon in memory of this event and gave money to charities. He also bought a baptismal font for the church, inscribed with his coat of arms. In 2013, Shami Chakrabarti, director of Liberty, was the first woman in 371 years to give the Lion Sermon. She named the three pillars of Liberty as dignity, equality and fairness.

In Somerset, in the middle of the month and into late autumn, there are a number of processions surrounding the Gunpowder Plot.

In Banbury, coinciding with the folk festival, there is a hobby horse festival, where all things equine take over the town.

BANBURY HOBBY HORSE FESTIVAL

https://www.facebook.com/watch/?v=330630597950084

This is not to be confused with the 'Obby 'Oss festival, which takes place in May in Padstow, North Cornwall, nor the altogether more professional (and thoroughly un-British) Finnish Hobbyhorse Championships.

THE FINNISH HOBBYHORSE CHAMPIONSHIPS

https://www.youtube.com/watch?v=MmgNL6PT7Ts

World Porridge-Making Championship

Around the second weekend of the month, the Highlands of Scotland host the World Porridge-Making Championship, which has been running since 1994. The main prize is the 'Golden Spurtle' trophy and the title of World Porridge-Making Champion for the best porridge made with only oatmeal, water and salt. The competition takes place at the village hall in Carrbridge, in the Cairngorms National Park.

Dorset Pack Monday Fair

At the same time in Sherborne in Dorset, Pack Monday Fair is held, an annual street event starting on the Monday following 10 October (Old Michaelmas Day). It starts with a parade around the local streets, where residents bang pots and pans with the aim of waking up the dead. This group is known as Teddy Roe's Band, after the mason who built the abbey. The band is composed of young people who parade the streets making as much noise as possible with horns, bugles, whistles, tin trays, saucepans and so on. Teddy Roe was the master mason who built the great fan vault in the nave of the Abbey Church. When the work was completed, the workmen packed their tools and paraded in triumph around the town. This neatly explains the procession and the name 'Pack Monday' for the fair itself. The route Teddy Roe's Band marched was changed in the 1960s, after it all got a bit out of hand.

Billingsgate Harvest of the Sea Service

Over in Billingsgate, their harvest festival services have a fishy theme. Given the local market was the centre of London's fish trade, the local church of Saint Mary-at-Hill holds a service celebrating the fishing industry and its produce.

Edwardtide

This celebrates the life of St Edward the Confessor, King of England. Usually considered the last King of the House of Wessex, he ruled from 1042 until his death in 1066. He was succeeded by King Harold God-winson, the last Anglo-Saxon King of England, who was killed at the Battle of Hastings. Edwardtide is held around 13 October, the date when his body was moved to its current resting place at Westminster Abbey. Although the abbey's origins can be traced to a Benedictine monastery founded around 960, the church we see today is largely due to Edward the Confessor, whose shrine lies at the heart of the abbey. St Edward was canonised in 1161 and to this day, pilgrims come to pray at his shrine.

Battle of Byland Anniversary

Some 256 years after the Battle of Hastings, the Battle of Byland was fought during the Scottish Wars of Independence. Robert the Bruce led his men to victory over English forces at Sutton Bank. After 700 years, a monument to those events was built, which sees a weekend of remembrances and recreated scenes from that time.

Battle of Edgehill Reenactment

The Battle of Edgehill was the first major engagement of the English Civil War and was fought on 23 October 1642. The date serves as the biggest battle reenactment in the UK by the oldest reenactment society, The Sealed Knot.

Bolving

If you're at a loose end around the middle of the month, you could go 'bolving'. This involves mimicking the sounds made by rutting red deer stags. You know you're doing well if you get a response from actual red deer stags.

https://www.youtube.com/watch?v=pvHsHePrHRc

Diwali

Diwali happens from mid-October to mid-November, depending on the lunar calendar. In certain years and in certain locations, it has merged with Bonfire Night on 5 November. Areas with a large Hindu or Sikh diaspora hold big celebrations, with Birmingham and Leicester holding some of the greatest.

Stow Horse Fair

The Stow Horse Fair is a traditional meeting place for Gypsies and travellers dating back hundreds of years. Its charter was granted in 1476.

Bampton Charter Fair

On the last Thursday of the month, another ancient fair takes place at Bampton in Devon. Its charter was granted in 1258, but there are records showing an event many decades prior. Expect to see the Bampton Mummers in action and a celebration of the Exmoor pony.

The Punkie Night Song

In the Somerset village of Hinton St George, they have the Punkie Night celebration, a local Halloween tradition on the last Thursday in October. Children parade through the village carrying lanterns, wearing costumes and singing the traditional Punkie Night song led by a Punkie King and Queen. Punkies are lanterns traditionally made from a mangel-wurzel, a type of beet used to feed cattle.

https://www.youtube.com/watch?v=xvJ2_jKQsZw&t=4s

Colchester Oyster Feast

At Colchester, the oyster fishery dates back to Roman days and was granted a charter by Richard I in 1189. Each year, on the last Friday of October, there is an oyster feast to celebrate this produce.

Bristol St Mary Redcliffe Pipe Walk

On a Saturday in late October, there is the Bristol St Mary Redcliffe Pipe Walk. With a history stretching back over 800 years, this is one of the longest-established customs in the calendar. In the twelfth century, Robert de Berkeley donated a water supply and conduit to the church, and during the annual walk this is inspected for faults, in a ceremony rather like beating the bounds.

King Alfred Commemoration

Near to 26 October, King Alfred the Great is remembered at Winchester, the seat of his realm. He died on this day in 899. A service is given at Saint Bartholomew Church and from there, a procession heads to

Hyde Abbey Gardens, where flowers are laid on his grave and on the graves of his wife and son. The church was built on the old abbey, but some of its ruins still survive.

Halloween
Halloween is a corruption of All Hallows' Eve, the beginning of the three-day period of remembering saints, souls and the departed.

All Souls' Day
On All Souls' Day, or Galoshins as it is known in Scotland, mummers (people in disguise) would knock on doors and ask for soul cakes made for the poor in return for their prayers. These days, soul caking is still a popular venture in Cheshire. In many places, especially in England and Wales, mummers parade with a dressed horse skull, decorated with ribbons and bells, cavorting round the town centre.

The Mallard Song is an ancient tradition of All Souls' College, Oxford. It is sung every year at the Bursar's Dinner in March and the college's Gaudy in November. It is also sung in a separate special ceremony once a century.

In this ceremony, fellows parade around the college with flaming torches, led by a 'Lord Mallard' who is carried in a chair, in search of a giant mallard that reportedly flew out of the foundations of the college when it was being built in 1437. The procession is led by an individual carrying a wooden mallard tied to the end of a pole.

All Souls' Day is a 1,000-year-old festival to commemorate the dead. The particular dead after which the Oxford college is named were those who fell in the opening battles of the Hundred Years War, a war which started in 1337 with Edward III of England trying to enforce his claim to the French throne and ended in 1453, with England losing all her continental territory except Calais.

The procession was revived in 1801, repeated in 1901 and again in 2001, with someone named Lord Mallard for the night being carried about the quad shoulder-high by fellows roaring out the song.

Samhain

Pronounced 'SAW-win', this is a Celtic festival marking the end of summer – 'Samhain' meaning summer's end – and the beginning of the Celtic New Year, celebrated from 31 October to 1 November. This is considered the origin of modern Halloween and the Equinox Viking Boat Burn, with events like the burning of the Wicker Man and story-telling experiences. The event held at Glastonbury includes a procession of dragons, representing the seasons.

Souling

Around October/November time, Souling takes place. This is where children visit homes on All Souls' Day (2 November) to offer prayers for the dead in exchange for small treats like soul cakes. A notable one is at Halton in Cheshire. The plot of the Halton Souling play involves the revival of a combatant by the doctor but with the addition of a wild hobby horse. Their script follows the original one from the 1880s and includes the singing of 'Poor Old Horse'. Their characters include the Old Woman, Turkish Champion, little Jerry Dout, Beelzebub and, of course, brave St George, the doctor and the Cheshire Old Horse with three legs and his driver. A collection is made for the local hospice.

THE POOR OLD HORSE SONG

https://www.youtube.com/watch?v=IFk-RjKgDMI

A highlight of the Cheshire play is the dramatic entrance of the horse and its driver towards the end of the performance. The Cheshire horse is especially notable for its real skull and three legs.

The Winter Droving

At Penrith, Cumbria, from later in the month through to mid-November, the Winter Droving takes place. This is a comparatively new festival, designed to celebrate rural heritage. It includes parades, the torchlit procession, a masquerade and rural-themed sports. These events include agricultural activities such as hay-bale racing, where participants race to carry and stack hay bales, with the winner being the first to complete the stack within a set time.

NOVEMBER

Ottery St Mary Tar Barrels

Held on Bonfire Night but with different origins, the people of Ottery St Mary get together to carry around flaming tar barrels above their heads. Local pubs sponsor a barrel each, which is soaked in tar and lit. The barrels are then carried through the town by locals known as 'barrel rollers', who are togged up in flameproof clothing and dodge crowds and obstacles. Notwithstanding, many are still singed by the process.

Like Cooper's Hill, safety is a longstanding concern, which seems only to enhance the enthusiasm for the event. The tradition is hundreds of years old and its origins are unknown. Some say it was about the fumigation of cottages, others that it was a warning of the approach of the Spanish Armada. The West Country has a history of torchlight processions and burning barrels in general, but Ottery is the only town in the country carrying full-sized lighted tar barrels through the streets.

The traditional day for the Tar Barrels is 5 November and this only changes when the 5th falls on a Sunday. The procession and fireworks are normally on the Saturday before 5 November.

https://www.youtube.com/watch?v=QRYh-Sq5IlM

The Bonfire Societies of Lewes

The country town in Sussex has one of the world's biggest celebrations on the night of 5 November (unless it falls on a Sunday). Apart from celebrating the death of Guy Fawkes, it also commemorates the seventeen Protestant martyrs from the town burned at the stake for their faith. This was under the reign of the zealous Catholic queen Mary Tudor (Bloody Mary), who burned 280 Protestant martyrs at the stake. She was succeeded by Elizabeth I.

It features more than thirty processions from seven separate societies through the town's ancient streets. Each society has its own traditions, costumes, bonfires and fireworks. Cliffe is the joint oldest with Lewes Borough. The latter claims to be older, but the former continues to maintain the true bonfire traditions. People dress up in Viking, French Revolution and fire brigade costumes.

There are other societies too. The Commercial Square Bonfire Society was inspired by a protest, when some members visited America and saw the treatment of Native Americans. South Street was originally a children's society but now has members of all ages. Waterloo is an adult society that some say is more family-orientated. In 1969 it introduced a costume of the savage tartar of the Mongolian Empire,

Genghis Khan. Finally, the Nevill Juvenile Bonfire Society is one specifically for children.

The Lewes Bonfire Society is famous for its enemies. It has had enemies in the past, including the police, the courts, the *Sussex Advertiser* and local councillors. Those councillors who have tried to limit the celebrations have been paraded in effigy. Home Secretaries who have tried to make political capital out of criticising Bonfire Night have had the same treatment.

The Cliffe Bonfire Society was banned from the Bonfire Council for refusing to stop carrying a 'no popery' banner. Ian Paisley, the notoriously Protestant Northern Irish politician, handed out anti-Catholic pamphlets in Lewes, which backfired and led to him being burned in effigy the following year. Confused? Yes. Me, too.

'Visit Lewes' urges people not to travel to the town for Bonfire Night, saying that the 'combination of dense crowds, flaming torches and firecrackers can be dangerous'. This is a recurrent theme of many British traditions. It's why they go.

Mick Symes is known locally as 'Mr Bonfire'. He got involved in a local bonfire society for social reasons. Although the Lewes bonfires involve a few days of celebration, bonfire season lasts for three months. Members of a bonfire society will tour their local region. In Mick's case, this means the area of East Sussex. They'll go and socialise with other societies in their local pub. Each society, of which there are seven in Lewes, has its own local. It is where their committee generally meets. It is also the meeting point the night before Bonfire Night, where they gather to pay their annual subs. This allows them to 'have it large' on the streets of the town the following night. Some societies have moved to social clubs to allow under-eighteens to be part of the revelry. But the actual night itself is built around a pub crawl.

People will meet at a pub. Then they will walk to another pub. They may pick up additional torches along the way and set off on a march around the town, finishing at the bonfire site. Mick's society meets at the top of the town, near the racecourse. Sometimes, historical rivalry results in fisticuffs. Carrying of truncheons used to be encouraged to stop these fights. More recently, common courtesies have been encouraged between the societies. Mick's society, the Borough, meets on the High Street Bridge, with the Cliffe society joining their march. There is an exchange of keys and pleasantries. Inevitably when the keys are handed back later that night, they have been defaced in some way. Usually, they're returned with the rivals' colours. It's all part of the fun.

From 1921, following the First Word War, an element of remembrance was introduced to the proceedings. During the war, full bonfire societies kept in touch with their bonfire boys who were sent to the front. They sent them letters and parcels and remained in close contact. One of the smaller societies lost fifty men. It was such a devastating number that they were unable to re-form for many years after. Today, the procession starts in darkness and heads to the War Memorial, where wreaths are laid and poems read. After they've paid their respects, the night can start and the torches are lit.

During the Second World War, all but a nod to the bonfire traditions was stopped. Lewes being so close to the coast resulted in movements being restricted to up to ten miles north of the town. Mick describes how in 1944 enormous numbers of overseas troops, particularly Canadians and Americans, boarded locally. Older bonfire boys and those who had disabilities – some, of course, from the First World War – still met during this time, largely to keep morale up. They held dances and raised money for good causes but also better times. They would meet and make torches in enormous numbers, which they stockpiled so that when victory arrived, they could celebrate in style. Victory in Europe Day in 1945 was when they were deployed in a truly amazing spectacle. Mick and his team commemorated that event on VE Day 2025, eighty years on.

In the early days of this bonfire tradition, there was a bit of a divide between the posh bit of Lewes and those from the rougher end of town. Those from the wrong side of the river would roll barrels of tar down through the streets to the river. Things got so rowdy, the Riot Act was read one year. As a result, law enforcement moved the bonfire events to outside of Lewes town. King James I encouraged such commemorations. It was an Act of Parliament that compelled people to give thanks that the Gunpowder Plot had been uncovered. So, in 1850 it was decided to let the bonfire boys have their fun back in the town centre. In 1851, records show that the commemorations had become a procession. In 1853, Mick's society took its first subs.

Today, there are about 5,000 torches and several bonfire sites involved in the evening's proceedings. Each bonfire society also has a tableau known as a 'tab'. These are figures that will be burned on the bonfire. Each group has a 'captain' in charge of various aspects of the proceedings and one captain is responsible for creating the tab. What they create is entirely at their discretion and it is kept secret from the rest of the society until the day of the bonfire. There is no coordination between societies. Mick describes their choice as not overtly political. The tab is there to poke fun, not cause offence. It strikes me as a very British way of going about things. The tab is strapped to something like an old caravan that's been stripped down to its chassis. Set pieces and other bits of social commentary are created and assembled at the bonfire site, but these are not part of the march.

Fireworks are also a big part of the proceedings. Different towns had their own special type of bang. The Lewes Rouser was legendary. It consisted of a broom handle wrapped with paper to form a cartridge. This was loaded with black powder, which was readily available from the local chemist. A good measure of iron filings was also added, sourced from the three foundries that surrounded the town. The Rouser was designed not to be launched vertically but to terrify horizontally. It would whizz around the streets until it hit a wall, which would launch it airborne. The Rouser was banned following two serious fires on the lath and plaster of properties in the town centre.

Mick decided to move the bonfire society to a more family-friendly club that could include his grandchildren. Most societies these days are built around the family. In the 1960s, the first juvenile societies were formed. Since the late 1800s, women have been involved and in 1890, the women of one society dressed as pink flamingos. This caused quite a stir. It was the first time that anyone's legs had ever been on show. Mick explains that Lewes folk 'don't really need much excuse to dress up'.

Flamingos were not the only costume controversy. Lewes was a cosmopolitan town: it had two large papers produced there, the *East Surrey News* and the *Sussex Herald*, also known as the *Advertiser* and *Gazette*. As a consequence, the town had an international outlook and many local people would read about international events. The Zulu nation was much revered. Mick said that one bonfire society had honoured the Zulus by dressing up as them for many years. He added that this was way before Michael Caine ever got in on the action. This costume soon fell out of favour, in part because it was deemed politically incorrect. Furthermore, the ostrich-feather headdresses had become so enormous that people were unable to see over the top of them. Zulu battle dress was replaced by Celtic warrior attire. Mick was sorry not to see the Zulu tradition maintained. However, in 2017, he managed to persuade an actual Zulu dance troupe to come to the streets of Lewes and take part in Bonfire Night. It was deemed a massive success but not repeated. The Zulu dance troupe appreciated the difficulty and commented that in their neighbouring village there was a morris dancer troupe who were having similar difficulties because they had blackened their faces.

Head out on Bonfire Night in Lewes and those Celtic warriors are joined by smugglers, Mongolian hordes, Vikings and Native Americans. These traditions stem back to the mid-1800s.

Political correctness has not stopped the bonfires. Although originally introduced to commemorate the foiling of the Gunpowder Plot, Lewes is also linked to the seventeen martyrs of the Marian persecutions, which took place between 1555 and 1557. In 1899, it was decided that they would commemorate those martyrs as well as celebrate the end of Guy Fawkes. Although some societies still focus on those martyrs and carry seventeen crosses on their Bonfire Night, the religious aspects are downplayed.

Legislation hasn't stopped the bonfires either. The societies have kept ahead of health and safety officers by making sensible changes to their revelry. Mick said cost is the only thing that will kill off the tradition. The societies pride themselves in never taking a penny from the public purse. All costs are raised by membership subs and donations from local traders.

There are four or five generations in one society. It brings people together; it makes those bonds between generations stronger. Today, Mick says: 'I sent out some birthday congratulations to one of our members who is seventy-three today and this year is his seventy-third year in the society. It's a rite of passage for people in our town. It's who we are.'

https://www.youtube.com/watch?v=C_7i3JyMlRA&t=12s

On this busy night, when most of the nation is involved in some kind of pyrotechnics, the villagers of Shebbear in Devon are doing something a bit different. They launch an assault on a large rock on the village green in order to turn it over. If they fail to complete their mission, bad luck will follow. The boulder is known as the Devil's Stone. Legend has it that St Michael dropped it on the devil himself and thus prevented him from doing evil.

THE DEVIL'S STONE OF SHEBBEAR, DEVON

https://www.youtube.com/watch?v=taDQDq-pXqU

Armistice Day

Armistice Day is on 11 November, commemorating those who gave their lives during the First and Second World Wars and all conflicts since. Across the whole nation, we mark this solemn moment with two minutes' silence on the eleventh hour of the eleventh day of the eleventh month.

Meanwhile, there are other traditions that take place on 11 November. Close to the 11th, the village of Trefin in Pembrokeshire holds an election for a Mock Mayor as part of its St Martin's Fair. The event is a revival, but its basis was a medieval fair.

In Fenny Stratford, a commemorative event is held in memory of Dr Thomas Willis, a seventeenth-century anatomist, neurologist and psychiatrist. Among his discoveries was what's now known as the Circle of Willis, the circulatory system that supplies blood to the brain and surrounding areas in reptiles, birds and mammals. The tradition was started by his grandson Brown Willis. He built St Martin's Church in Fenny Stratford in honour of Thomas, who died on 11 November 1675. The custom involves the firing of six small cannons, known as the Fenny Poppers.

THE FENNY POPPERS

https://www.youtube.com/watch?v=sfUA-2Le5Ec

Wroth Silver

At Knightlow Hill near Ryton-on-Dunsmore, Warwickshire, a ceremony has been performed on this day for hundreds of years. In order for commoners to drive their cattle over the Duke of Buccleuch's estates, dues must be paid. The duke's agent reads a charter at dawn and then calls each of the local parishes to come forward to make their payment. Proceedings are followed by a slap-up breakfast at a nearby pub, known as the 'Wroth Silver' breakfast.

Bridgwater Guy Fawkes Carnival

Another early November event can be found at Bridgwater, Somerset, which holds a Guy Fawkes Carnival. There is a huge procession of floats leading to the lighting of 'squibs' (fireworks on top of long poles). It is the largest illuminated carnival in Europe.

London to Brighton Veteran Car Run

On the first Sunday of the month, the Royal Automobile Club organises its vintage car rally. The course starts at Hyde Park London and finishes on Brighton seafront. It commemorates the Emancipation Run of

1896, which celebrated the Locomotives on the Highway Act. The Act increased the speed limit to fourteen mph.

Soulcakers

The performance of mummers' plays continues throughout the month. Another early November event is put on by the Comberbach Soulcakers. The group performs mummers' plays to their village. Later in the month, the Warbuton Soulcakers and the Antrobus Soulcakers put on their productions. This latter group has gone one further than the usual hobby horse character with the introduction of the Wild Horse of Antrobus, who, by all accounts, is the equine equivalent of Rod Hull's Emu.

The Silent Ceremony

On the Friday before the second Sunday of the month, what is known as the Silent Ceremony takes place in London on the eve of the Lord Mayor's Show. It is the swearing-in ceremony for the Lord Mayor. It is carried out in complete silence except for the reading of the oath. There is a procession and regalia in the form of a sceptre, sword and badges.

The Lord Mayor's Show

The following day, the show itself takes place. It is the oldest civic procession in the world. The Lord Mayor travels from Mansion House to the Royal Courts of Justice to swear his allegiance to the Crown. There is a river pageant, a procession through London's streets and then fireworks. The band of the Grenadier Guards provides musical support. Legend has it that two stern but benevolent giants, Gog and Magog, are London's guardians and they too feature during the proceedings. Livery groups and other institutions and community groups are all part of the festivities.

Rye's Bonfire Society

Bringing up the rear of bonfire season is Rye's Bonfire Society. They choose to celebrate their day on a Saturday in the middle of November. Their performance features a burning boat and a fire-breathing dragon. Some customs relate to the Gunpowder Plot, but the boat is believed to be a nod to a victory over the French in the fourteenth century.

Hatherleigh Carnival

On the second Saturday of the month in Hatherleigh, a carnival takes place, another extension to the Guy Fawkes season. This event features a tractor-drawn parade of floats and 'barrel running'. Barrels are set alight and dragged through the town at speed on specially made sleighs.

Battle of Sheriffmuir Commemoration

On the Saturday nearest to 13 November, the Battle of Sheriffmuir is remembered. A wreath is laid at the monument to commemorate the events of that day in 1715 and all who fell during the Jacobite Uprising. There is then a procession to the gathering stone, a short distance away. Although the battle did not give a victory to either side, it marked the end of this period of Jacobite uprisings.

Lumiere Durham

Mid-month, Durham holds an arts festival featuring illuminations to brighten up the dark evenings. Late in the month, Sunderland also holds a substantial illuminations event. Going since the 1930s, except for a lapse of a decade in the 1990s, Sunderland's illuminations are accompanied by displays of tableaux in Roker Park.

Across the country, the first Christmas carols can be heard. In Yorkshire, several villages start singing carol services now and continue through to New Year – the venue is as likely to be a local pub as the village church. At Cotehele, their National Trust medieval manor house is hung with an enormous and elaborate garland of dried flowers.

World's Biggest Liar Competition

Over in the parish of Wasdale in the middle of the month, an intriguing contest of the telling of tall tales takes place. In memory of a local publican who used to tell hilarious and far-fetched stories, a competition is held to hear the best tale told in under five minutes. Those from professions considered to have an advantage in telling fibs (politicians chief among them) are barred from entering.

Oasby Baboon Night

In Culverthorpe, Lincolnshire, at this time of year you will find a man in a monkey suit being chased around the village. He is barred entry to the local pub until someone manages to throw a toy monkey over the roof. This commemorates an unfortunate incident in the eighteenth century when the infant heir to Culverthorpe Hall was thrown from a window by the family's pet monkey.

https://www.youtube.com/watch?v=cU99pnKaKPs

Real Ale Wobble

The Real Ale Wobble is the Marathon des Sables of pub crawls. Over thirty miles long, over the hilly terrain of Llanwrtyd Wells, it is not for the faint-hearted. It coincides with the Mid Wales Beer Festival that takes place mid-month.

Clovelly Herring Festival

On the third Sunday of November, the fishing village of Clovelly in North Devon hosts a herring festival. Sea shanties are sung and bloaters consumed.

Wareham Court Leet

Late in the month, Wareham holds a Court Leet, where the local produce is tested for both quality and quantity. Local officials tour the town testing and tasting bread, meat and ale. The cleanliness and the state of the chimneys are also examined in each premises. This has its origins in medieval times.

Thanksgiving

On the fourth Thursday of November, the US celebrates Thanksgiving, harking back to the Pilgrim Fathers thanking God for their deliverance. Thanksgiving dinners are offered in many places across the UK.

St Edmund's Day

The feast day of St Edmund, patron saint of Suffolk, is on 20 November. At Southwold, they celebrate by giving sticky buns to local schoolchildren.

St Clement's Day

23 November is St Clement's Day, the patron saint of blacksmiths. On this day at the Finch Foundry near Okehampton, blacksmiths meet to demonstrate their skills and to test the strength of their anvils by detonating gunpowder on them.

St Catherine's Day

The feast day of St Catherine is on 25 November. In Hastings, they hold an event to mark both St Clement's and St Catherine's days. A pub crawl starting at St Clement's Church takes place, during which they light Catherine wheels en route. This recreates an old custom of touring hostelries to gather beer and apples to mark these feast days. Cattern cakes are often baked at this time too. These are biscuits spiced with cinnamon, mixed spice and carraway. The lacemakers of Nottingham would bake these cakes to honour their patron saint. The cakes are also associated with Katherine of Aragon, who deliberately destroyed her lacework in order to commission more work, on hearing lacemakers were facing hard times.

St Andrew's Day

30 November is St Andrew's Day, patron saint of Scotland. His martyrdom is shown on the Saltire flag. He was crucified on an X-shaped diagonal cross, as he felt he wasn't worthy to die on the same shape of cross as Jesus. Events are held across the UK and particularly in Scotland. Glasgow, for example, holds a large torchlit procession in his honour. In the village of Athelstaneford in Scotland, they remember the events of the ninth century, which gave rise to the creation of the Saltire. As King Angus prepared to lead his forces into battle, he prayed and saw the white cross of St Andrew in the sky, an omen of the victory he went on to secure. These events are commemorated at the village year-round, with a memorial flying the Saltire in the churchyard. Near to St Andrew's Day, a service is held to hoist the flag up for another year.

The Eton College Wall Game

The Eton College Wall Game is another variation on rugby, played on a strip of ground called the Furrow next to a brick wall built in 1717. The annual St Andrew's Day match features one team climbing over the wall, after throwing their caps over in defiance of the other. Players engage in what is known as a 'bully' (like a rugby scrum against the wall). The goal is for the attacking team to move the ball along the wall to score points while the defenders try to halt their progress. The ball needs to be held against the wall and the goals are a door at one end and a tree at the other.

https://www.youtube.com/watch?v=UhG4829Opn8&t=9s

Advent

At the end of November, on the Sunday nearest the 30th, Advent starts and so do the preparations for Christmas. Across the UK, on a Sunday late in the month, 'Stir-up Sunday' is held. This is traditionally the day when Christmas puddings were mixed in order that they would have time to steep before being consumed. On this Sunday, the service includes the line: 'Stir up, we beseech thee O Lord.' The divine and the culinary have become linked. In Newport, a fun run is held for anyone prepared to dress as Father Christmas. Christmas lights are turned on in most towns and villages, wherever there is a high street, from mid-month onwards. Some have spectacular ceremonies involving either celebrities or, in the case of South Shields, three real camels. Christmas tree festivals have also sprung up across the country in the last few years as a way of bringing people together.

L ooking at the traditions at the start of a new year, they are all geared around chasing the winter blues away and enjoying life.

Pantomime

The Christmas-season pantomimes feature at every theatre across the UK. This popular form of theatre typically takes place during the festive period, with its origins in eighteenth-century Italian theatre. However, pantomime has become so thoroughly British that many would consider the UK the prototype 'panto nation'. In addition to professional productions, amateur shows can be found in almost every church hall and community theatre. Audience participation is compulsory. Pantomimes usually feature well-known children's stories such as *Peter Pan*, *Aladdin*, *Cinderella* and *Sleeping Beauty*. Interlaced with these are adult themes and jokes. The concept often baffles Americans – much like Jack Black's admission in *School of Rock*: 'I've been touched by your kids and I'm pretty sure I've touched them.'

https://www.youtube.com/watch?v=2FoMaM_EuJw

There is no set script for pantomimes, because they are usually updated with contemporary songs, dances, slapstick jokes and especially audience participation. Traditional phrases like 'Oh no it isn't!', 'Behind you!' and enthusiastic booing and hissing at villains are all part of the fun. Cross-dressing has long been a theme. So have pantomime animals, usually featuring two people playing the front and back of a horse. This great tradition has even been referenced in feature films.

For instance, in Blake Edwards's *The Pink Panther*, a French sergeant in a pantomime zebra suit is caught drinking the punch at a costume party. Inspector Clouseau upbraids the sergeant, saying: 'I'll have your stripes for that.' This illustrates yet another pantomime tradition: the double entendre. Pantomime is famous for its suggestive humour, embodied in the peculiarly British word 'saucy' – for example: 'She wanted a double entendre, so I gave her one.'

https://www.youtube.com/watch?v=kEsfYG_bF-E

In real life, the *Shameless* actress Tina Malone was arrested and cautioned for possession of cocaine after a performance in the pantomime *Sleeping Beauty* in Barrow-in-Furness. Only a panto enthusiast would point out: 'She had no difficulty remembering her lines.'

DECEMBER

As winter starts to bite and the shortest day of the year comes and goes, December has feasting, fire and festivities. Traditions such as mumming, soulcaking and vigorous sporting activities help burn off the calories.

Advent begins at the end of November and finishes on Christmas Eve. In churches across the country, candles are lit and wreaths hung. Advent calendars are opened, starting on 1 December. In some towns, a tradition of Advent windows has also been established, where windows are illuminated to display scenes from the Nativity or other festive images. Each day of Advent, a new window is revealed. This custom received a boost during Covid, as it provided a safe way for people to come together, at least metaphorically.

On the nearest Saturday to 1 December, Tenbury Wells holds a Mistletoe Festival. With traditions rooted in druid heritage, mistletoe is blessed with beer and apple juice before being cast into the River Teme. A Mistletoe Queen and a Holly King are elected and crowned. The day ends with a lantern parade.

MISTLETOE FESTIVAL, TENBURY WELLS

https://www.youtube.com/watch?v=Nh8eWi666LM&t=554s

Great Christmas Pudding Race

On the first Saturday of December, the Great Christmas Pudding Race takes place in London's Covent Garden. This is a relay race with obstacles and trials, where teams must get a tray of puddings around the course unscathed.

Krampus Run

On the first Saturday of the month in Whitby, there is the Krampus Run. The Krampus is a horrible creature and Saint Nick's sidekick, deployed if children are naughty and accompanying the saint on his present-giving mission. Krampus first made an appearance in the UK in 2015 but has been making children cry across Europe and in America for many years.

Bonnie Prince Charlie Weekend

That same weekend in Derbyshire, Bonnie Prince Charlie is celebrated both in the town and at Swarkestone Bridge on the River Trent. The prince reached this point in early December 1745. It was as far as he got. The festivities include reenactments and pipe bands.

Choosing Day

On the first Monday of December, it is Choosing Day at Brightlingsea, when the local mayor selects his deputy. This tradition dates back to the early sixteenth century. The Freemen of the town are also elected on this day, with oaths sworn and beer consumed.

The Rochester Dickens Festival

Early in the month, Rochester holds its second Dickens Festival of the year.

Winter Watch

In Chester, on a Thursday early in the month, the Winter Watch takes place after sunset. The Watch has its origins in medieval times and marks the turn of the year. The city is known for its historic parades, and this one features spectacular costumes and pyrotechnics. Like many such events, it is organised by local businesses and takes place over two nights. The parade has even included a nod to the Roman traditions associated with Saturnalia, which falls at the same time.

Saturnalia

Saturnalia is a midwinter festival celebrating the Roman god Saturn. He was the god of agriculture and honouring him was believed to help ensure a good harvest the following year. As well as eating, drinking and general merrymaking, the festival included a tradition of role reversal, where masters and servants would swap roles.

In York, which was a major centre during Roman times, Saturnalia is marked with a huge torchlit procession led by a Roman legion through the city's streets, stopping at several alehouses along the route. By all accounts, things get rather rowdy.

https://www.youtube.com/watch?v=rLk7tNBMyiA&t=241s

Another UK-wide tradition that has become established in recent years is the tractor or truck convoy. The vehicles are often decorated and usually accompanied by a fundraising initiative for local good causes. These convoys are growing in number and can now be found in almost every part of Britain. Some have even evolved into races.

St Nicholas Day

The feast day of St Nicholas is on 6 December. In Alcester, the day is celebrated with a parade featuring a child bishop, as St Nicholas is the patron saint of children. In Durham, lanterns are carried by children up to the cathedral to mark the occasion.

Saint Nicholas is one of those saints who multitasks. As well as being the patron saint of children, he is also the patron saint of sailors. On the Sunday nearest 6 December, a service in his honour takes place at Canterbury, recognising all his responsibilities.

In Salisbury, St Nicholas's feast day is honoured by choosing a Boy Bishop. This custom was once widespread in many churches during the Advent period. Most of these practices ceased at the Reformation, but the tradition was revived in Salisbury and is based on medieval customs. The Boy Bishop's duties on that day include delivering their own sermon. Ripon also follows this practice, electing a Child Bishop, who may be a boy or a girl.

Richmond Christmas Dole

Mid-December in Richmond, Yorkshire, specially minted coins

are distributed. This tradition dates back to the sixteenth century, when provision was made for the town's elderly and poor. Permission for this charitable act was granted in a charter by Queen Elizabeth I, allowing funds to be given to those in need in the run-up to Christmas.

St Lucy's Day

Close to 13 December, Scandinavian traditions are observed in several places around the UK. This day is the feast of Saint Lucy, who was martyred in the fourth century. She is associated with bringing light and events focus on a candlelit procession led by a girl dressed in white robes and wearing a crown of candles.

Glastonbury Thorn Cutting Ceremony

Mid-month in Glastonbury, there is the Thorn Cutting Ceremony. According to legend, the thorn tree was said to have sprung from the staff of Joseph of Arimathea and flowers at this time of year. Each year, a cutting is taken and sent to the monarch to decorate the table on Christmas Day. In modern times, local schoolchildren are involved in the ceremony.

World Pie-Eating Championships

If you need to get some practice in before tackling Christmas dinner, head over to Wigan for the World Pie-Eating Championships. Taking place in the middle of the month, the emphasis is on speed rather than volume. The challenge is to consume a beef and potato-filled pie in the fastest time possible. This is one event that seems to have succumbed to political correctness. It used to be that the winner was the person who ate the most pies in an allotted time. The rule change was introduced in response to healthy-eating guidelines.

https://www.youtube.com/watch?v=NtYiR2vM6p0

Tin Can Band

On a Sunday after 12 December in Broughton, Northamptonshire, an event takes place that would challenge even the most lenient environmental health officers. The objective is to make as much noise as possible using ordinary household items or anything else you happen to have to hand. The Tin Can Band is said to drive away evil spirits and at the same time, allows the village to mark its boundaries. To maximise the annoyance, it all takes place in the dead of night, just after midnight. After a brief walkabout to ensure everyone is fully awake, there is a chorus of 'Auld Lang Syne' before everyone heads home to bed.

Pantomime Horse Race

On a Sunday in the middle of the month, London hosts the Pantomime Horse Race. The course winds through the streets of Greenwich and after the steeds have been paraded, they set off on a gruelling route. There are several distinct differences that set this event apart from Cheltenham, Ascot or Goodwood. Firstly, the horses are allowed to stop at the pub if they get a bit thirsty. Secondly, in addition to horses, you can expect to see cows, unicorns and possibly other creatures. This is all perfectly within the rules. Thirdly, alongside the usual hedges and fences, there are other obstacles to overcome. For example, the final stretch requires participants to mount and bounce on a space hopper over the finish line.

https://www.youtube.com/watch?v=3pnU1_AG-DM

Burning the Clocks Festival

On 21 December, many events take place across the country to mark the middle of winter. In Brighton, the Burning the Clocks Festival is held to honour the winter solstice, with bonfires and lanterns lit on the beach.

Montol Festival

In Penzance, there is the Montol Festival, which means 'turning point of the year'. In addition to the usual lanterns, hobby horses and mummers, there are some more sinister traditions as well. The event culminates with the Chalking of the Mock (a yule log) by drawing a stick man on it before it is burned.

BOSCASTLE CHALKING OF THE MOCK

https://www.youtube.com/watch?v=UbJGdSocl5I

Sheriff's Riding

In York, on 21 December at dusk, the Sheriff's Riding takes place, now combined with another festive tradition called Yulegirthol. The sheriff's traditional ride has been downgraded to a brisk walk around the city streets. The event begins with a proclamation at Micklegate Bar, declaring the old-world equivalent of a Club 18–30 holiday. It welcomes 'whores, thieves, dice-players and other unthrifty folk' to revel in the city for the twelve days of Christmas. The sheriff then tours the town, accompanied by his Waits and Guards in beautiful livery.

Winter Solstice

On 21 and 22 December, events take place across the country to mark the Winter Solstice, but nowhere more notably than at Stonehenge. Here, druids perform a sister ceremony to their summer solstice ritual.

A modern tradition of tree dressing has been taking place across the UK for about thirty years, encouraging people to appreciate trees and celebrate our heritage.

Crying Christmas

Around 21 December, a procession takes place through the streets of Lincoln. This is a tradition that dates back to the sixteenth century. Today's custom is a modern revival of this ancient service. Known as Crying Christmas, proclamations are read out at various points in the city by people representing the Magi. The city's civic leaders and dignitaries also join the procession.

Carols at the Cross, Ryton

On the Tuesday before Christmas Eve, a spectacular carol service takes place in the village of Ryton, Tyne and Wear. Carols are accompanied by a brass band, mummers and sword dancers. After the service at Holy Cross Church, villagers head to Ye Olde Cross pub for more singing.

https://www.youtube.com/watch?v=BYSO4gleATM

Tom Bawcock's Eve

On 23 December in Mousehole, it's Tom Bawcock's Eve. Bawcock is celebrated for an act of heroism in the sixteenth century, when the village faced famine due to repeated storms that prevented the fishing fleet from putting to sea. He braved the waves to bring home a fine catch. The custom features an enactment of his heroism, lanterns are lit and a pie with whole fish in it is shared. The dish is known as starry-gazey pie, as the fishes' heads poke out of the pastry crust.

Christmas Eve

In a few country pubs, the practice of 'burning a bundle of withies', known as faggots, takes place on this night. The custom is known as Ashen Faggot. As each stick cracks, a sip of drink is taken. At Axmouth, Devon, the faggot is a massive six-feet-long.

In Yorkshire on this night, the Poor Old Hoss of Richmond can be found. Known locally as the T'Owd 'Oss, he is a hobby horse fashioned from an actual horse's skull. He is joined by mummers dressed as huntsmen, who perform around the town. The custom dates back to the seventeenth century and is performed to bring good luck.

Kimberley Poor 'Owd 'Oss

Late in December at Kimberley, Nottingham, you can find a traditional mumming play on a similar theme: the Poor 'Owd 'Oss. He appears for one night of the year, with the sole purpose of creating absolute chaos for anyone he encounters. This custom used to be quite common but is less so now and has largely been kept going by morris dancers. The 'Oss and their supporting cast tour the pubs around the Kimberley area to perform the duties.

Hoodening

Another event on the theme of horses is Hoodening, a custom that takes place in Kent. The tradition originally began with a hobby horse visiting houses and community buildings to perform and collect a fee. In modern times, the custom is largely staged at pubs and has been enjoying something of a revival. One of the most established Hoodenings takes place at St Nicholas-at-Wade.

Christmas Day

Bucks Green on 25 December sounds like the start of a bad joke: a horse walks into a bar before Christmas lunch is served. Again, no one is sure exactly why. The horse receives treats for its trouble.

As Christmas Day approaches, bells can be heard across the UK. In Dewsbury, they go the extra mile: bellringers toll one bell for every year since Christ's birth, with the final peal sounding dead on midnight. Quite why this takes place is not fully understood.

While Christmas is a religious festival, many elements of it are adopted from ancient traditions. Churches and homes are festooned with evergreens as symbols of eternal life and lights represent Christ as the light of the world. The Christmas tree is a comparatively modern tradition, introduced in the nineteenth century. Predating this custom is the hanging of mistletoe. The custom of leaving a stocking out to be filled by St Nicholas (also known as Father Christmas) appears to have started in America, with records dating back to 1823.

Many take part in Midnight Mass on Christmas Eve. There are carols and more mummers' plays. Parlour games are also popular at this time of year. At 3 p.m. on Christmas Day, the monarch delivers a televised speech. This is a tradition that began in 1932 when King George V delivered the first broadcast via wireless. It now forms a neat dividing line between lunch and tea.

At Ripon on Christmas Day, choristers distribute red apples to the congregation. The origins of this tradition date back to medieval times, with the apples said to represent life. They were accompanied by rosemary, symbolising the Virgin Mary.

At Sherborne Castle, more goodies are distributed to children in the form of chocolate and coins.

Boxing Day

26 December, known as Boxing Day, is also the feast day of St Stephen. It got its name from the custom of 'boxing' up gifts and leftover food for servants. Boxing Day was traditionally a day for hunting and many still meet to ride or walk a trail. It is also a day for mummers and morris dancers to perform. On Boxing Day in Bedford, the local dancers perform the Boar's Head Ceremony: a boar's head is paraded in a local hostelry while a special song is sung. A cake is balanced aloft on a large sword and dished out to soak up the large quantities of alcohol.

Sword Dancing

At Flamborough, sword dancing with a fishing theme takes place, with dance moves that mimic the threading of nets. In Redcar, a tradition of sword dancing on Boxing Day has been going on for hundreds of years. Although it lapsed for a time, it was revived five decades ago. The dancers perform outside Greatham Hospital, wearing red coats.

At Grenoside, sword dancing has been a tradition for at least 150 years, with the dancers wearing distinctive clogs. In Handsworth, the dancers carry very long swords, as is traditional in the north of England. They interlock their swords in complex patterns and finish with their lead dancer holding the star of locked swords aloft.

GRENOSIDE SWORD DANCERS

https://www.youtube.com/watch?v=qhGAnIvoarw

Cutty Wren

On Boxing Day in Suffolk, the Cutty Wren tradition takes place. Wren hunts used to be held on this day, during which the poor bird was killed and paraded about as part of a house-visiting custom. Today, the tradition has been revived, but thankfully no actual wrens are sacrificed. Instead, a carved wooden replica is processed through the town streets to a local pub. There is dancing and singing and a story is told about how the tiniest bird became the king of the avian world.

The Hunting of the Wren was a Celtic custom that has been revived at Silsoe on Boxing Day. Again, no real birds have to suffer for the village's entertainment.

Derby Ram

Over in Derby, the Old Tup or Derby Ram takes place. It is a mumming play based on a house-visiting custom. The Ram is a puppet, paraded to the song 'The Derby Ram', which is a merry tale about butchery and all things ovis-related.

Geddington Boxing Day Squirt

The wonderfully named Geddington Boxing Day Squirt does not disappoint. It's a water fight between Geddington and Kettering Fire Stations. The teams take up positions on either side of the River Ise in Northamptonshire, with the task of propelling a barrel of water over the river using their hoses. If they accidentally hit the other team on the opposite bank, that's just a bonus.

More sports involving barrels of booze can be found at Grantchester in Cambridgeshire. Whisky barrels apparently perform like wonky supermarket trolleys.

At Knaresborough in Yorkshire, their Boxing Day sport is tug of war. However, they too have embraced cold water: the rope spans the icy waters of the River Nidd. The sides are formed by the patrons of two pubs, the Half Moon and the Mother Shipton. A similar event takes place in Ludlow, where the teams are also pub-based: The Feathers v. The Bull.

At Matlock, they at least give their townsfolk a fighting chance of not getting wet. The Matlock Raft Race, which takes place on Boxing Day, started in the 1960s. Homemade rafts race along the River Derwent.

At Pagham, Sussex, their sport stays firmly on land. The Pagham Pram Race was started by returning Second World War veterans to raise spirits and funds. It is serious stuff, with a three-mile course and a strict set of rules. The route takes in various hostelries and pairs of contestants (one pushing, one riding in the pram) must consume at least three pints over the course. Windlesham has also opted for a pram race, complete with drinking rules.

The fishermen and firemen theme continues at Scarborough with a Boxing Day football match between the professions. This is followed by a raft race organised by the Aqua-Lung Club. Everyone involved in both events ends up in the sea.

Waltham Cross also holds a football match and has done for at least a century. This time, it is between bakers and chimney sweeps. In addition to unusually large balls, what marks this match out is that the players are also armed with flour and soot. It is an ideal opportunity for a soap powder company in search of a sponsorship opportunity.

The good burghers of Winchelsea have opted for something a bit more provocative: a ball game using a Frenchman's head – facsimile, not actual. The town was on the front line of defence against the French in the fourteenth century.

On 27 December at the Cathedral Church of St Peter and St Paul in Sheffield, a special service for silversmiths is held. The service, along with a charitable legacy, was founded by Mary Parsons in 1817 in memory of her brother, who was a notable figure in the trade.

Battle of Wakefield Commemoration

On 30 December 1460, the Duke of York was killed near Sandal Castle, Wakefield, setting back the Yorkist cause. The encounter that led to his death is commemorated on this day with the laying of a white rose wreath and a minute's silence by his statue near the castle. They also commemorate Edmund, the duke's second son, who was slain on the same day.

New Year's Eve

On the last day of the year, Allendale lights tar barrels and carries them aloft through the streets to welcome the New Year. A First Footing event is also held.

https://www.youtube.com/watch?v=nqWsVoQnQyg

At Barlaston, Staffordshire, on New Year's Eve, a wassailing tradition was founded a mere twenty years ago. A mummers' play is performed featuring characters from the village's history, including the founding father, Beowulf. The evening commemorates the area's Anglo-Saxon heritage. Banners with Saxon themes are carried for each month of the year and verses to the Angles are read. In recent years, a longboat is also burned.

Hogmanay

Pyrotechnics can also be seen in Comrie on New Year's Eve. As part of its Hogmanay celebrations, the village holds the Flambeaux Procession. This is a custom originally intended to rid the village of evil spirits. Standard bearers carry ten-foot poles with sacking wrapped around the top. To welcome the New Year, these are set alight and paraded through the streets before being thrown into the River Earn. Edinburgh, too, hosts a torchlit procession, fireworks and a huge party. Scotland's capital city is a focal point on New Year's Eve, not just for our nation but for many around the world.

Flamborough Fire Festival

At Flamborough, there is a fire festival with a Viking theme at this time of year. The event usually features a huge torchlit procession, a longboat and Viking sports to test strength and skill. The finale is a spectacular fireworks display.

https://www.youtube.com/watch?v=X8K6tpvtmSg

Stonehaven Fireballs

Over at Stonehaven, a procession of residents swirl fireballs around their heads to see in the New Year. The balls are attached to long wires, enabling this spectacular display. Their efforts are meant to encourage the sun to return. The whirling infernos, which are lit at midnight, are finally extinguished by being hurled into the sea.

https://www.youtube.com/watch?v=_b2HxWEsCSA

At Stromness, their chosen sport is the log pull, another revival of an old tradition. It is a tug of war with a twist. A large tree trunk is placed in the centre of the rope. The winning team is the one that pulls the trunk over the line. It is as gruelling as it sounds.

Around Christmas and New Year in Llangynwyd and Chepstow, the Mari Lwyd takes place. This is a house-visiting custom featuring the central character of a Grey Mare, which takes the form of a hobby horse made from a decorated horse's skull. A number of road-running races also take place in South Wales to celebrate local athlete Guto Nyth Brân.

Newburgh Oddfellows Parade

In Newburgh, Fife, there is the Oddfellows Parade and torchlit procession, which has been established for more than a century. This is led by a rider facing backwards on a horse, wearing a mask on both sides of their head to symbolise the old and new year. The rider is accompanied by a rather unpleasant crowd of disturbing folk, who cause mischief and abuse the crowd to the tune of a brass band. The Oddfellows groups were early pension and insurance societies.

https://www.youtube.com/watch?v=2MlYjtRNLRE

Germanic in origin, Christingle services take place throughout the Christmas period, but largely in December. Sweet kebabs are impaled onto an orange, stuck with a candle and wrapped with a red ribbon. The sweets represent the seasons, the orange the world and the red Christ's blood. It is considered an acceptable form of bribery to get small children to endure mass. The upside in church outreach more than makes up for the inevitable cocktail-stick stabbings and occasional immolation.

In Keele, they have found a good use for redundant and surplus Christmas trees: a new game called Christmas-tree throwing. It is not complicated. Performance is measured by distance and height.

Nativity plays are a widespread and much-loved custom. Parents get creative with costumes, using tea towels for shepherds and tinsel for angels. Some productions go above and beyond: real animals are occasionally involved and the story is told at different locations around the village. One production that definitely channels Cecil B. DeMille is the Astbury Live Nativity. The play travels through several locations, accompanied by torchlight, from the church to the local inn, across fields and finally ending in a stable. There are plenty of sheep but not yet camels.

JANUARY

New Year's Day
After the New Year's Eve celebrations, New Year's Day traditions seem

to centre around courage and fortitude, as well as a lot of good luck. It is, of course, a bank holiday – the first of the year. Bank holidays were dreamed up by Sir John Lubbock, MP for Maidstone, to give bank workers the chance to watch a day's cricket and were established by the Bank Holidays Act of 1871.[1]

As an island nation, it should be no surprise that taking a dip in our freezing coastal waters is a cheap day out after the excesses of the Christmas season. Whether it's salt or fresh water, the consistent theme is the colder, the better. These are modern traditions – one guess is that they're in part due to improved medical care if someone does slip into hypothermia. Such events also take place at Christmas and Boxing Day.

The Serpentine Swimming Club in Hyde Park was established in 1864, has its own (somewhat spartan) changing facilities. Members are permitted by the Royal Parks to swim in the lake every morning from 5 a.m. to 9.30 a.m. The Serpentine swimmers do their stuff on Christmas Day as well as New Year's Day.

THE SERPENTINE SWIMMERS

https://www.youtube.com/watch?v=8VRw8F4kXNs

The Haxey Hood

The Haxey Hood is played on 6 January, the Twelfth Day of Christmas (unless the 6th falls on a Sunday, in which case the event is held on the Saturday). It takes place in Haxey, North Lincolnshire. It's basically a large rugby scrum (the 'sway') that pushes a leather tube (the 'hood') to one of four pubs in the town, where it is kept until the following year.

Haxey is in an area known as the Isle of Axholme. The story goes that in the fourteenth century, Lady de Mowbray, wife of local land-owner John de Mowbray, was out riding when her silk riding hood was blown away by the wind. Workers in the field rushed to help and chased the hood all over the field. It was caught by one of them, but being too shy to hand it back himself, he gave it to another to return to her. She thanked the farm worker who had returned the hood, saying he had acted like a lord, whereas the worker who had caught the hood was a fool. So amused was she by the chase and this act of chivalry that she donated thirteen acres of land on the condition that the chase for the hood would be reenacted each year.

At around noon on the day, the Lord of the Hood and his eleven 'Boggins' begin a tour of the four public houses in the parish: the Carpenters Arms, the Duke William, the Loco and the Kings Arms, all in Haxey. They sing traditional songs, including 'John Barleycorn', 'Drink England Dry' and 'The Farmer's Boy'. They then gather at the front of St Nicholas Parish Church, where the Fool makes a speech of welcome. During this speech, a fire is lit behind him with damp straw and the smoke rises around him. This ritual is known as 'smoking the Fool'. It is, in fact, a modified version of an earlier custom in which a large fire was lit and the Fool was suspended over it, only being cut down when he was on the point of suffocation. The Fool ends his speech with the traditional words: 'Hoose agen hoose, toon agen toon, if a man meets a man knock 'im doon, but doan't 'ot 'im.' The crowd chant along with him.

At this point, everyone moves to nearby Upperthorpe Hill, where, after some preliminaries for the benefit of the children, the main game is played with a 'hood'. This is made from a two-foot length of leather, this being the nearest modern equivalent that can be used in place of the original hood, which was allegedly a freshly slaughtered bullock's head.

There are no official teams. All the participants simply join in and attempt to move the hood towards their favoured pub. The Lord acts as referee as best he can and the Boggins round up any stragglers and protect property. The game is rather like a large rugby scrum, in which the hood is pushed or pulled in the desired direction. No one is allowed to run with or throw the hood.

The thirteen characters from the original story are represented as follows: the Lord, the Fool and eleven Boggins, one of whom is the chief Boggin.

The Lord and chief Boggin are dressed in hunting pink (red) coats and top hats decorated with flowers and badges. The Lord also carries his wand of office. This is a staff made from twelve willow wands with one more placed upside down in the centre. These are bound together thirteen times with willow twigs and finished with a red ribbon at the top. The thirteen willow wands are said to represent the twelve apostles, with the upside-down one symbolising Judas.

The Fool wears multi-coloured strips of material attached to his trousers and top. He sports a feathered hat decorated with flowers and rags and his face is smeared with soot and red ochre. He carries a whip and a sock filled with bran, which he uses to belabour anyone who comes within reach.

The remaining ten Boggins wear red jumpers. The game is played by locals, although anyone is welcome to join in.

The hood, which cannot be thrown or run with, is moved slowly by 'swaying'. That is, by pushing and pulling the hood and the people within the Sway towards their chosen pub. The Sway makes very slow progress, often snaking around and stopping when it collapses, so that crushed participants can be pulled out of the mud. Safety is a prime concern and the entire event is supervised by the Boggins. The Lord acts as referee, ensuring the game is played fairly.

At any one time, there are usually around 200 people in the Sway, with about 1,000 spectators watching. Games can last from a couple of hours to well into the night. Everything in the path of the Sway goes down before it, including hedges and walls, so another of the Boggins's jobs is to prevent the Sway from destroying everything in its path.

Nobody parks on the roads where the Sway may go and with good reason. In 2002, a couple of drivers parked opposite the Duke William. The Sway headed straight for them, pushing one of the cars ten feet down the road and into the other.

The game ends when the hood arrives at one of the pubs and is touched by the landlord from his front step. The landlord then takes charge of the hood for the year and is supposed to give everyone a free drink. The winning pub pours beer over the hood and then hangs it behind the bar. Each pub has two hooks especially for this purpose. According to legend, it used to be roasted on a spit over the pub fire after being doused with ale, which was then drunk by those present.

This has similarities to other village combats, such as Ashbourne's Royal Shrovetide Football, the Shrove Tuesday Football Games in Sedgefield (Durham) and Alnwick (Northumberland) and the Hallaton Bottle Kicking contest in Leicestershire.

THE HAXEY HOOD

https://www.youtube.com/watch?v=P3kDirthDRg

The 'Loony Dook'

The 'Loony Dook' is an annual New Year's Day tradition in which people take a cold-water swim in the Firth of Forth at South Queensferry, near

Edinburgh, Scotland. Participants often wear fancy dress and the event raises money for charity.

https://www.youtube.com/watch?v=173ECNYaBiA

The Kirkwall Ba' game

The Uppies and Doonies are the two teams in the Kirkwall Ba' game, a traditional street football match played in Kirkwall, Orkney, on Christmas Day and New Year's Day. The teams compete to get a leather ball to their respective goals, which are scattered across the town with one of them being the harbour. Whether you are an Uppie or a Doonie depends on where you were born.

Instead of a conventional football or basketball, the Kirkwall Ba' is extremely heavy. It would definitely spoil your day if you were smacked in the face with it! Records show the game was being played as early as 1684. Today, it can involve up to 300 players and can last all day.

https://www.youtube.com/watch?v=VlQYxz6p4eU

If being smacked in the face with a seventeenth-century bowling ball is too pedestrian for you, you might wish to head to Mappleton. Okeover

Bridge spans the River Dove, where locals chase away any lingering hangover by jumping thirty feet into its icy waters. After swimming to the finishing post, they are rewarded with prizes.

If you really don't fancy getting wet, then perhaps the Ponteland Wheelbarrow Race is the event for you. In true plucky British fashion, this takes place in all weathers, including deep snow. The dubious origins of this malarkey allegedly stem from a landowner asking his tenants to forage for food.

Like many curious adventures in this book, the main aim is for local communities to raise funds for good causes. New Year's Day was once a time when homes were given out to the needy and there are many local charities dedicated to that aim, whether they involve feats of derring-do or not.

Plough Sunday and Monday

Plough Sunday and Plough Monday are traditional celebrations marking the start of the English agricultural year. Plough Sunday, which falls on the Sunday after Epiphany, involves a church service to bless the ploughs and pray for a good harvest. Plough Monday, the first Monday after Epiphany, marks the return to work in the fields.

The first recorded Plough Sunday event took place in 1413 in Durham. Today's celebrations commemorate those early traditions. In Durham, the plough is drawn through the streets and received by the dean of the cathedral, who pays those who pulled it for their efforts.

Plough Monday was the day farm workers resumed their duties. Many would go to the villages to raise funds, accompanied by mumming plays and straw effigies. They often dressed up and blackened their faces with soot to disguise themselves. The Hinckley Bullockers from Leicestershire stand out, as they choose to paint their faces with red raddle, which is usually used on narrowboats.

Morris dancers, especially Rattlejag morris dancers and mummers, are also associated with this festival.

THE HINCKLEY BULLOCKERS

https://www.youtube.com/watch?v=bxoQHrPmN44

There are an enormous number of mummers' events across the UK, but the Calverton Real Ale and Plough Play Preservation Society (CRAPPPS) deserves special mention, not least for their name. They have been performing their mummers' play on three consecutive evenings for over three decades. These celebrations were most common in the East Midlands and East Anglia, as they are today.

Church services also took place on these plough days and some churches still continue these traditions, such as Exeter Cathedral. The also wonderfully named Muskham Pinkies have been carrying on a tradition dating back to the nineteenth century.

THE MUSKHAM PINKIES

https://www.youtube.com/watch?v=graKaSq-SOU

These traditional folk plays are performed by groups of actors known as mummers, who visit homes, pubs or streets to put on their performances. The plays often feature a hero, such as St George, who is killed in a fight but is then brought back to life by a doctor.

The tradition of mumming has its origins in primitive ceremonies marking the stages of the agricultural calendar. The term 'mummer' is related to the German word *mumme*, meaning mask. Mumming plays are still performed in some villages in England and Northern Ireland.

Mumming plays are a type of drama performed by locals at specific times of the year, typically on Boxing Day, Easter or Halloween. In the eighteenth and nineteenth centuries, mumming plays were part of a wider range of activities centred around 'cadging'. The verb 'cadge' described someone who acted like a peddler but was actually more like a beggar.

A group of friends or family dress in disguise and visit homes during the Christmas season. The mummers perform for the hosts, who try to guess their identities before offering them food and drink. To make identification more difficult, the mummers may cross-dress, speak while inhaling or stuff their costumes.

You can still see the Old Mumming Play in the village of Headington Quarry, Oxford, on Boxing Day. The play, based on the story of St George and the Turkish Knight, usually starts at the Crown and Thistle pub.

https://www.youtube.com/watch?v=_7VJ5JS5ZdM

Whittlesea Straw Bear Festival

Whittlesey is a market town in the Fenland district of Cambridgeshire. Whittlesea (the original spelling) has a custom, observed on the Tuesday following Plough Monday (the first Monday after Twelfth Night), of dressing one of their own as a 'Straw Bear'. This tradition marks the start of the English agricultural year. The bear is taken around the town to 'entertain by his frantic and clumsy gestures the good folk who had on the previous day subscribed to the rustics, a spread of beer, tobacco and beef'. (Beef again!)

The bear is described as

> having great lengths of tightly twisted straw bands prepared and wound up the arms, legs and body of the man or boy who was unfortunate enough to have been chosen. Two sticks fastened to his shoulders met a point over his head and the straw wound round upon them to form a cone above the bear's head. The face was quite covered and he could hardly see. A tail was provided and a strong chain fastened around the armpits. He was made to dance in front of houses and gifts of money or of beer and food for later consumption was expected.

It seems the tradition fell into decline at the end of the nineteenth century, with the last sighting recorded in 1909. Apparently, an overzealous policeman had forbidden 'Straw Bears' as a form of cadging.

https://www.youtube.com/watch?v=iAwvPzDSHQ8

The Hubberholme Parliament is an annual auction held at this time of year, letting sixteen acres of church land. A candle is lit and the bidding begins; when the candle burns out, the highest bidder wins. The event takes place, like many others, at the local pub, which was once the vicarage. When the reverend was at home, he would indicate this by placing a candle in his window. Today, the pub does the same during opening hours. These days, the proceeds from the auction are used to support local charities.

Faggot Burning

If, on 5 January, you've been discharged from hospital and survived any adventures undertaken on New Year's Day, then the customs surrounding the Ashen Faggot might be of interest. This tradition is, essentially, another excuse for a booze-up. A large log, wrapped with willow sticks or withies, is burned in the hearth. Each time a withy breaks in the fire, onlookers are required to drink.

Food production also has its own traditions and lore. Wassailing still takes place in orchards. The word has its origins in the Old English toast *waes hael*, meaning good health. Ceremonies are rife in cider-producing counties.

St Nicholas at Wade Wassail

In addition to the usual festivities, many events feature special attractions. At the Bell Inn in St Nicholas-at-Wade, Kent, several volleys are fired by the reenactment group 3rd East Kent Regiment.

In Herefordshire, the ceremony includes the Burning of the Bush and the Apostle fires. Given climate change, these practices sound rather risky around precious apple trees.

At Curry Rivel in Somerset, the locals are very efficient and combine wassailing and faggot burning.

The rise of community orchards has also led to new wassailing events springing up, even in towns and cities. The event at the Community Orchard in Ovingham, Northumberland, is one such example. Apple Howling is another variant on traditional wassailing.

Water Blessings

Margate is the setting for the Blessing of the Seas on 6 January, a tradition that is part of the Greek Orthodox calendar and marks the baptism of Christ. Since the mid-twentieth century, Margate has been home to a large Greek Cypriot community and has become a focal point for this custom. After a church service, there is a procession to Marine Sands and the beach, where doves are released and a cross is thrown into the waters. Unlike other sea blessings, which leave a wreath on the surface, the cross is retrieved by a diver and handed back to the archbishop.

Another water blessing takes place on this day in the middle of the River Thames. The parishes of Southwark and St Magnus the Martyr meet in the middle of London Bridge to pray and cast a wooden cross into the river. This service was established around the same time as Margate's and also has its origins in the Orthodox Church.

Twelfth Night

Slightly further down the river from the Thames blessing is Bankside, where a Twelfth Night celebration has taken place for the last twenty-five years. The holy man arrives over the Millennium Bridge with wassailers and mummers, whose play is based on the theme of St George. Cakes are handed out, some concealing a dried bean or pea; if you're lucky enough to find one, you're crowned King or Queen for the day. As usual, the merriment ends down the boozer, a pub on Borough High Street. Similar celebrations across the UK draw on local themes.

Baddeley Cake

On this day, a performance also takes place at Drury Lane Theatre, away from public gaze. Robert Baddeley (1733–94), a well-travelled actor famous for his glamorous wife, uncanny accents and for fighting a duel, left a bequest in 1794 for cake and wine to be provided each Twelfth Night in the Green Room of the theatre for impoverished actors. The charity is still provided to this day for those working in the theatre after the last performance of the night. The service is known as Baddeley Cake.

If you can stand even more wassailing, both Bodmin's and Guildford's Twelfth Night parties will be taking place this evening, as will more faggot burning at the Squirrel Inn in Laymore, a village near Chard, Dorset. The ceremony at the pub was revived in the 1970s and continues a tradition that once involved a roasted boar's head.

Burning of the Clavie

More pyrotechnics, this time at Burghead. The burning of a peat- and wood-stuffed herring barrel, called a Clavie, is another fire custom held every 11 January, which used to be New Year's Eve before the Gregorian calendar was introduced. The Clavie is carried through the village by a Clavie King, who dispenses good luck and smouldering embers. The festivities culminate with the lighting of a large bonfire.

Falkirk Battle Commemoration

The Second Battle of Falkirk was fought on 17 January 1746 and was the last victory for the Jacobites under Bonnie Prince Charlie. It is commemorated on the nearest Saturday to the anniversary, with wreaths laid at the obelisk marking the centre of the battle. The 1745 Association also organises battlefield tours.

Carhampton Wassail

More wassailing can be found at Carhampton, Somerset, on 18 January, which is one of the few original events still taking place. Along with the usual booze and singing, shotguns are also fired – just to be sure the tree spirits have been properly woken up.

Calan Hen

Around the middle of the month, Calan Hen is staged at Llandysul, Ceredigion. This a tradition that has been held for 200 years. There is a special service at St Tysul's Church with readings from the Welsh Bible, contributed by all the local churches. Once the service is finished, children visit houses, singing in return for sweets and money, and in the evening, the whole community gathers for food and a knees-up.

Salmon Procession

Over in Horncliffe, on the River Tweed in Northumberland, the annual Salmon Procession takes place. Salmon fishing is a vital part of the local economy and the mighty fish is honoured with a procession of fish lanterns, accompanied by music and morris men. The landlord at the Fishers Arms proposes a toast to the salmon, after which the lanterns are burned.

Goathland Plough Stots

The Goathland Plough Stots are a traditional longsword dance team, with a history stretching back at least a couple of hundred years. They have six dances, each with its own tune, and are accompanied by a fool and musicians. Expect to see them lock swords in the traditional way. Every January, they host their Day of Dance, starting with a parade from the Reading Room and performing throughout the day at various locations around the village. The name 'Plough Stots' comes from the ancient practice of performing on Plough Monday. Nowadays, they perform on the Saturday following Plough Monday, which falls around the middle of the month.

Selkirk Haggis Hunt

A week before Burns Night, a haggis hunt is held. Locals, in search of something suitable for next week's supper, make their way onto Selkirk Hill armed only with sticks and nets. The wild haggis is depicted as a creature with unique characteristics, such as the ability to jump six feet in the air and a thick black coat. To date, no haggis have ever been caught.

Burns Night

Celebrations take place all over the world on 25 January to mark the birthday of the famous Scottish poet Robert Burns, but they are naturally especially popular in Scotland. Formal Burns Suppers often feature recitations of Burns's 'Selkirk Grace' and other verses, the 'piping in' of the haggis with bagpipes and often a ceilidh to follow. The traditional fare is haggis and neeps (turnips or swede for us Sassenachs).

Nantwich Holly Day

Fifty years ago, the Nantwich History Society decided to commemorate the lifting of the Siege of Nantwich during the English Civil War on 25 January 1644. Holly wreaths are laid and locals join in by wearing sprigs in their hats. Today, the event is marked with a large battle re-enactment. The town is warned of its commencement by a church bell tolling, just as it did in 1644 to sound the alarm.

Katherine of Aragon Festival

In Peterborough, an annual festival is held on 29 January in memory of Katherine of Aragon. Alongside a Catholic service, someone takes on the role of the queen and reenacts her by speaking the words of her last letter to King Henry VIII.

Annual Commemoration of Charles I

Two events mark the execution of Charles I, both taking place in London. On 30 January he was beheaded outside the Banqueting Hall in Whitehall. The Society of King Charles the Martyr organises an event each year. The English Civil War Society also organises a parade to Whitehall to mark the anniversary which is held on a Sunday near to 30 January. In full Civil War dress, they solemnly march up The Mall to the sound of muffled drums. A drumhead service is held at Horse Guards, where a wreath is laid under the archway, close to the King's bust. A second wreath is also laid at his statue at Charing Cross.

Trial of the Pyx

Other events that take place in January include the Pyx Trial at Goldsmiths' Hall in London. Since the time of Henry III, sample coins from the Royal Mint have been placed in the pyx throughout the year. Each year, the Freemen of the Goldsmiths' Company choose a convenient date to check that the coins are of the correct quality and weight. The ceremony used to take place at Westminster Hall, but it was moved to the City in 1870.

Driffield Penny Scramble

There are also events to mark the first trading day of the year. In Driffield, Yorkshire, the children of the town are treated to sweets by local traders. This is a tradition that is now centuries old and originally involved small coins. Some reports even mention the coins being heated to make it more challenging for the urchins to collect them. Great efforts have been made to keep the custom alive.

The Queen's College Needle & Thread Gaudy

This is another centuries-old tradition. Members of the Oxford college are each given a needle and silk thread to mend their academic hoods.

Up Helly Aa Day

This is a relatively recent tradition (by British standards), established in the 1880s. Up Helly Aa is a Viking fire festival that takes place on the last Tuesday of January in Lerwick, in the Shetland Islands. Around 1,000 torchbearers, many dressed as Vikings, form different 'squads' and drag a replica galley to the burning site. Another group surrounds the galley with torches and throws them in, creating a dramatic Viking pyre. Afterwards, there is traditional Shetland music, dancing and drinking. Unsurprisingly, the day after is a public holiday.

https://www.shetland.org/videos/culture/up-helly-aa-fire-season

The leaders of these squads are known as Guisers, a word that also gave rise to the English term 'geezer'. The term originates from the Middle English word *gysar*, which comes from the verb *gysen* and the suffixes -ar and -er. In Scotland, a guiser is someone in disguise, often a mummer. The tradition of 'guising' involves dressing up in costumes and going door to door on Halloween night. It's similar to what is known as Trick or Treat in America. Participants typically perform a song, dance or tell a joke in exchange for sweets or money.

Lunar New Year

Many major cities in the UK celebrate Lunar New Year, also known as Chinese New Year, with vibrant festivities that draw large crowds. The festivities typically include lively parades featuring traditional lion and dragon dances, which are believed to bring good luck and drive away evil spirits. Food plays a central role in the celebrations. Noodles are served to symbolise long life, while spring rolls represent wealth due to their resemblance to gold bars. Tea eggs, oranges and tangerines are offered as symbols of good fortune and abundance. Lettuce is often included in lion dances, as the Chinese word for lettuce sounds like 'rising fortune', and the lions 'eat' the lettuce and then spit it out to spread prosperity to the crowd.

FEBRUARY

Saint Brigid's Day

Saint Brigid's Day, also known as Lá Fhéile Bríde, is celebrated on 1

February and marks the beginning of the pastoral year and the coming of spring in Ireland. The day honours St Brigid, one of Ireland's three patron saints, alongside St Patrick and St Columcille. In the pagan calendar, this time of year is known as Imbolc, marking the start of spring, and is celebrated across the UK as well.

At Butser Hill in Hampshire, there is a reconstructed Iron Age village that on this day hosts blessings around the Roundhouse. Other traditional commemorations include making corn doll images of the saint and holding services involving fire and water.

Marsden Imbolc Fire Festival

In Marsden, the turning of the year is celebrated with dancing, stilt walking, lanterns and fire. The outgoing winter is represented by Jack Frost and the incoming spring by the Green Man. A symbolic fight between the two ensues.

A Blessing of the Salmon Fishing

On 1 February in Norham, there is a blessing of the salmon fishery. This ceremony used to take place at midnight later in the month, with the vicar of Berwick performing the blessing from a boat on the River Tweed. Along with prayers, a line is cast into the waters – the first of the fishing season. Whisky and shortbread are then shared.

Carlow's Charity Bread Dole

Carlow's Charity, based in Woodbridge, Suffolk, traditionally handed out bread to the needy on 2 February. Although the custom lapsed for a time, it was revived in 2020. Similar charitable bread doles were once common across the country, though many have now sadly disappeared.

Ripon Candlemas Festival

On the same day, the Christian festival of Candlemas is celebrated across the country. It commemorates the presentation of Jesus at the temple and marks the end of the Christmas season. The festivities in Ripon are perhaps the most spectacular, with the cathedral illuminated by 5,000 candles.

Rocking Ceremony

On the closest Sunday to 2 February, the Nottinghamshire parish of Blidworth holds its traditional Rocking Ceremony. The baby born nearest to Christmas Day is baptised during the morning service and in the afternoon is rocked, hopefully to sleep, by the vicar in a flower-decorated cradle at a special candlelit service. This custom is hundreds of years old and all the babies who have been honoured in this way are listed at the back of the church.

The Blessing of the Throats

At St Etheldreda's Church in Holborn, London, the Blessing of the Throats service takes place on the same day. Parishioners are blessed as they kneel, with two candles held to their throat.

Feast of Saint Blaise

At Saint Blazey in Cornwall, Saint Blaise events were revived a couple of decades ago. Drawing inspiration from former Imbolc celebrations, the centrepiece is an illuminated ram, which, accompanied by lanterns, is paraded through the dark streets, led by the Bishop of Truro. A blessing of the throats follows, along with a bit of wassailing and the local speciality bake: saffron buns.

On the closest Sunday to 3 February in Frampton on Severn, Saint Blaise is honoured by the sharing of pancakes, apple juice and cider.

Clown Service

On the first Sunday of February in Hackney, London, All Saints Church hosts a Clown Service. It is to celebrate the life of Joseph Grimaldi, the father of clowns. The congregation dresses in full clown regalia and unicycling is encouraged.

Shaftesbury Snowdrop Festival

In Shaftesbury, Dorset, a flower festival takes place early in the month. This recent tradition was established as part of a vision to create the UK's first 'Snowdrop town'. Mass plantings of snowdrops, begun to celebrate the Diamond Jubilee of Queen Elizabeth II, have created famous snowdrop walks. During the festival weekend, evening parades feature young children carrying lanterns shaped like snowdrops, as the town welcomes spring. Local legend tells of a dragon that grew from a bulb planted during the reign of King Alfred the Great. Each year, a special verse is chanted to entice the dragon to emerge from his resting place beneath a local hill. The dragon so far remains asleep.

Boar's Head Ceremony

Around this time, the new Lord Mayor of London is presented with a boar's head by the Worshipful Company of Butchers. This tradition harks back to the days when butchers needed the mayor's permission to wash their meat in the River Thames. The offering is paraded through Cheapside to the drums of the Royal Logistic Corps.

Cornish Hurling

Cornish hurling, also known as Hyrlîan in Cornish, is a traditional team sport played on different days in various towns across Cornwall. In St Columb Major, it's played on Shrove Tuesday and the following Saturday; in St Ives, it takes place on Feast Day, the first Monday after 3 February. Two teams, usually 'town' versus 'country', compete to carry and throw a ball made of applewood, covered in silver and inscribed with the words: 'Town and country do your best.' The game is somewhat similar to rugby. The aim is to get the ball into the goal or across the parish boundary. The winner returns the ball to the market square and visits every pub in town, dipping the ball in pints and sharing the drink with patrons. There are few other rules: you can't use vehicles and you must surrender the ball if instructed. The game is played through the streets and even on private property, including gardens, fields, houses and pubs.

https://www.youtube.com/watch?v=RXDJLbjLsaI&t=7s

Massacre of Glencoe Commemoration

The Massacre at Glencoe took place on 13 February 1692. The Clan Macdonald were brutally murdered by guests who turned out to be the Earl of Argyle's soldiers, punishment for not swearing allegiance to King William III. Today, church services and wreath laying commemorates those dark events.

Valentine's Day

In Suffolk and Norfolk, there is a tradition of leaving presents on people's doorsteps on Valentine's Eve, supposedly delivered by Jack Valentine or, in some cases, by Father or Mother Valentine.

Penny and Bun Day

On 14 February, or the nearest school day, in Suffolk, Penny and Bun Day is celebrated with a private service at Somerleyton Hall, Lowestoft. The owners are entertained by children from the local primary school, who each receive a penny and a bun for their efforts. This tradition has been carried on for over a century.

Jorvik Viking Festival

The City of York has a rich Viking heritage and each year in mid-February, it celebrates all things Norse. Alongside the festivities, there's the serious business of a beard competition and a battle reenactment, complete with pyrotechnics. Sadly, due to the conscientiousness of York's health and safety officers, the traditional boat-burning aspect of the Jorvik Viking Festival is no more.

Radcliffe Commemoration at Langley

On 24 February 1716, James Radcliffe was executed for his part in the Jacobite uprising of 1715. Langley, Northumberland, is home to one of two monuments to him and Charles Radcliffe, who was executed after the 1745 uprising. The Northumbrian Jacobite Society commemorates James's death on a Friday near to the anniversary by pinning a wreath to the memorial cross and lunching at Langley Castle.

The Slaithwaite Moonraking Festival

This festival, held in late February, celebrates the exploits of the smuggler gangs that once operated in the area. The highlight is a lantern parade, which features a giant moon.

Rhubarb Festival

On the last weekend of the month, Wakefield in Yorkshire holds its Rhubarb Festival. The fruit has been grown in the area for over 150 years.

The Spital Sermon

In late February, or sometimes early March, an endowed sermon is preached at the church of St Lawrence Jewry. It's a tradition that has taken place since the fourteenth century. Originally, the sermon was intended to raise funds for the local alms houses. Today, the great and the good of the City of London are in attendance.

29 February, Leap Year
Leap Day is traditionally the only day on which women propose marriage to men.

———————————✦———————————

So much of national life is built around local traditions and customs. Not only do they add a sense of fun and occasion, but they also make a valuable contribution to local economies. Even though these are local British events, they often have global reach, attracting participants and families from around the world. Viewed through 'progressive' eyes, some traditions may seem outdated, but only the most humourless and po-faced could deny themselves a smile at the antics of the Lewes Bonfire Societies.

———————————✦———————————

THE DAILY RITUALS

When?	Name	URL
Daily from Michaelmas (29 September) to Shrove Tuesday	Bainbridge Hornblowing	https://calendarcustoms.com/articles/bainbridge-hornblowing/
Daily	Berwick Curfew	https://calendarcustoms.com/articles/berwick-curfew/
Daily	Buckingham Palace, London, Changing of the Guard	https://calendarcustoms.com/articles/buckingham-palace-changing-the-guard/
Daily from 11 October to 21 March	Burgh le Marsh Curfew	https://calendarcustoms.com/articles/burgh-le-marsh-curfew/
Daily	Canterbury Curfew	https://calendarcustoms.com/articles/canterbury-curfew/
Weekdays from Michaelmas (29 September) to Lady Day (25 March)	Chertsey Curfew Bell	https://calendarcustoms.com/articles/chertsey-curfew-bell/
Daily except Sundays	Edinburgh One O'Clock Gun	https://calendarcustoms.com/articles/edinburgh-one-oclock-gun/
Daily	Lincoln Curfew	https://calendarcustoms.com/articles/lincoln-curfew/
Daily	London Lincoln's Inn Curfew	https://calendarcustoms.com/articles/lincolns-inn-curfew/
Daily	Morpeth Curfew	https://calendarcustoms.com/articles/morpeth-curfew/
Daily	Oxford Curfew	https://calendarcustoms.com/articles/oxford-curfew/
Twice daily	Presteigne Curfew	https://calendarcustoms.com/articles/presteigne-curfew/
Twice daily	Richmond Curfew	https://calendarcustoms.com/articles/richmond-curfew/
Daily	Ripon Hornblowing	https://calendarcustoms.com/articles/ripon-hornblowing/

When?	Name	URL
Daily except Sundays and Christmas and Boxing Days (usually)	Sandwich Curfew Bell	https://calendarcustoms.com/articles/sandwich-curfew-bell/
Daily for three weeks both before and after Christmas	Scarcliffe Curfew	https://calendarcustoms.com/articles/scarcliffe-curfew/
Daily	Tower of London Ceremony of the Keys	https://calendarcustoms.com/articles/tower-of-london-ceremony-of-the-keys/
Daily (usually)	Wallingford Curfew	https://calendarcustoms.com/articles/wallingford-curfew/
Daily	Winchester Wayfarers' Dole	https://calendarcustoms.com/articles/wayfarers-dole/
Wednesdays and Saturdays from Easter to end of October	Walsingham Pilgrimages	https://calendarcustoms.com/articles/walsingham-pilgrimages/
Monthly, on the 23rd of the month	London Southwark Crossbones Vigil	https://calendarcustoms.com/articles/london-southwark-crossbones-vigil/

In certain parts of the country, there are daily rituals. Some are of national edicts that have died out in most places. Others are location specific.

Some can take place at any hour, such as the Winchester Wayfarer's Dole. This is assistance given to any traveller who asks for it at the Porter's Lodge at the Hospital of St Cross and Alms House of Noble Poverty. It is one of the oldest charitable institutions in the UK and dates back to the early twelfth century.

Other traditions are highly time specific. If you could fly across the British Isles to witness them all, this is how your day might look.

7.20 a.m.

The first curfew bell of the day rings out in Presteigne, Powys, signalling that it is time to rise. Curfew bells were usually sounded to tell communities it was time to turn in for the night. A few places also sounded them to tell people it was time to get to work.

8 a.m.

The bell at Richmond's Holy Trinity Chapel is rung to rouse the apprentices.

The bell is also rung at 11.55 a.m. on Shrove Tuesday to remind everyone to make their pancakes.

9 a.m.

The Bell Harry Tower at Canterbury, named after the prior and donor of its first bell, rings its curfew bell to announce morning services.

11 a.m.

The Changing of the Guard at Buckingham Palace is a ceremonial event in which guards from the regiments of the Foot Guards march from St James's Palace to Buckingham Palace to collect the keys and relieve the outgoing shift.

The guards at Horse Guards are also changed daily at 11 a.m. (10 a.m. on Sundays). Horse Guards serves as the official gatehouse to both St James's and Buckingham Palace. The site was originally the courtyard of Henry VIII's palace at Whitehall.

Between 11.30 a.m. and 2.30 p.m.

The time of the Speaker's Procession varies depending on the parliamentary day, but during these hours, whenever the House of Commons is sitting, its Speaker processes from their rooms into the Chamber. Prayers are then said in private before the session begins. The House of Lords holds a similar ceremony.

1 p.m.

Every day except Sundays, the Edinburgh Gun is fired at 1 p.m. sharp. This practice was originally introduced as a shipping aid, allowing chronometers to be calibrated accurately. The gun used is a twenty-pound howitzer.

5.45 p.m.

The curfew bell of the day rings from the Tower of London.

6–7 p.m.

St Leonard's Church at Scarcliffe sounds its curfew bell during the shortest days of the year – the weeks preceding and immediately following Christmas. Legend has it that the bells had a patron in Lady Constantia, who is buried in the church. Their sound once guided her and her child to safety when they became lost in the forest.

In Southwark, London, on the 23rd day of the month at 7 p.m., there is a regular service to commemorate the outcast dead. The Crossbones Graveyard, where many of London's paupers are buried, contains the graves of the 'Winchester Geese'. These were sex workers licensed by the Bishop of Winchester. From 1996 to 2019, John Constable and Katie Nicholls worked to reclaim the graveyard as a sacred place and sanctuary. In 2004, they founded the Friends of Crossbones and the vigil started on 23 June of that year.

7.30 p.m.

The curfew bell at Presteigne is sounded to signal the settlement to retire for the night.

8 p.m.

At 8 p.m. on Wednesdays and Saturdays, from Easter until the end of October, the procession of Our Lady of Walsingham takes place. A statue of the Virgin Mary is carried to the Shrine Church, accompanied by candlelight and flowers. This tradition was established by Lady Richeldis, after she experienced a vision of the Blessed Virgin instructing her to build a Holy House. The shrine is particularly associated with prayers for motherhood and fertility. The original priory was dissolved in the sixteenth century.

8 p.m. is the traditional time when most curfew bells ring out. At

8 p.m. in Berwick-upon-Tweed, a bell is rung to mark the start of curfew – a tradition said to be unbroken since Norman times. Each July, locals attempt to complete a mile-long race around the town's walls within the duration of the bell's chimes.

Chertsey also maintains this custom, which is believed to have originated in 1235 after a serious fire damaged the abbey. In Lincoln, the twin bells of the north-eastern St Mary's Tower ring at the cathedral's close, following a curious formula: the first bell tolls 101 times minus the date of the month and the second bell tolls for the remainder.

The bells at Richmond's Holy Trinity Chapel are sounded for a second time each day at this hour. In Morpeth, the oldest civic peal of bells in the country continues the tradition as well.

Sandwich once had two bells: the 'pigbell', which signalled when to put animals out for the night, and the 'goosebell', rung at 5 a.m. – presumably to indicate that it was safe from foxes after their nocturnal hunt.

At Burgh le Marsh, a custom recently discontinued, the longevity of the curfew bell tradition was attributed to the legacy of a sea captain. He believed the curfew bells had saved his ship from disaster while navigating the coastline, so he left funds to purchase a silk bell rope, to ensure the bells would continue to ring.

9 p.m.
At Wallingford, the curfew bell rings out just before 9 p.m. every night. Wallingford received a special extension of an hour from Norman times as a reward for cooperating in the post-Conquest castle-building programme, thus earning the approval of the King.

At Lincoln's Inn Chapel, Christchurch College, Oxford, the 'Great Tom' bell chimes its curfew every day at this time.

Over in Ripon, the Wakeman blows his horn at this hour. This usually happens in the marketplace, but on days when the Mayor is away, it also happens at the town hall. Hundreds of years ago, his position was created by the church to keep the order.

MUSIC TO ACCOMPANY *POMP & CIRCUMSTANCE*

DEAR LORD AND FATHER OF MANKIND

https://www.youtube.com/watch?app=desktop&v=b1MN3chW1Hk

OH GOD OUR HELP IN AGES PAST

https://www.youtube.com/watch?v=rsHIwXTjAOU

FANTASIA ON A THEME BY THOMAS TALLIS

https://www.youtube.com/watch?v=0U6sWqfrnTs

ABIDE WITH ME

https://www.youtube.com/watch?v=NTT5HGSaO-Y

I VOW TO THEE MY COUNTRY AT THE FESTIVAL OF REMEMBRANCE

https://www.youtube.com/watch?v=bvouc8Qs_MI

ENIGMA VARIATIONS, OP.36: IX (NIMROD)

https://www.youtube.com/watch?v=7iM5dymBBI4

BRITTEN – FOUR SEA INTERLUDES FROM PETER GRIMES, OP 33A (ORAMO)

https://www.youtube.com/watch?v=ht9mQE6X0C0

LARK ASCENDING

https://www.youtube.com/watch?v=ZR2JlDnT2l8

NOTES

PREFACE

1   https://www.newyorker.com/culture/cultural-comment/richard-rortys-philosophical-argument-for-national-pride

CHAPTER ONE: THE END OF AN ERA

1   Noël Coward, *This Happy Breed*, 1939
2   https://www.kiplingsociety.co.uk/poem/poems_englishflag.htm
3   https://www.thetimes.com/comment/columnists/article/populists-jd-vance-law-migration-gl5bcgl97
4   https://www.bbc.co.uk/iplayer/episode/m000mv1h/the-romantics-and-us-with-simon-schama-series-1-3-tribes
5   https://aeon.co/essays/why-is-english-so-weirdly-different-from-other-languages
6   https://www.youtube.com/watch?v=5bFWQ16BuSQ

CHAPTER TWO: CHANGE AND DECAY

1   https://www.thetimes.com/uk/society/article/one-third-of-babies-born-to-overseas-mothers-8zvdco2nf
2   https://www.nbcnews.com/id/wbna32156155
3   https://researchbriefings.files.parliament.uk/documents/SN03339/SN03339.pdf
4   https://www.bbc.com/news/articles/cly37mexj5lo
5   https://hansard.parliament.uk/Lords/2024-10-09/debates/60F7EDDD-3EC4-4BF6-82FE-1AEC24F3B52D/IllegalMigrants
6   https://www.statista.com/statistics/1107572/covid-19-value-g20-stimulus-packages-share-gdp/
7   https://committees.parliament.uk/publications/7872/documents/81760/default/
8   https://www.thetimes.co.uk/article/spectre-hits-forecourts-as-rolls-royce-sales-set-new-records-ppq899zfz
9   https://www.reuters.com/business/pandemic-boosts-super-rich-share-global-wealth-2021-12-07/
10 https://commonslibrary.parliament.uk/research-briefings/cbp-9428/
11 https://www.ons.gov.uk/peoplepopulationandcommunity/wellbeing/articles/worriesaboutclimatechangegreatbritain/septembertooctober2022
12 https://www.statista.com/statistics/284752/bbc-tv-reach-by-channel-in-the-uk/
13 https://www.bbc.com/news/uk-politics-49278729
14 https://theanalyst.com/2023/05/premier-league-sackings-in-2022-23-managers
15 https://www.bbc.com/sport/football/40704646
16 https://www.bma.org.uk/advice-and-support/nhs-delivery-and-workforce/pressures/nhs-backlog-data-analysis
17 https://www.statista.com/statistics/751605/average-house-price-in-the-uk/

18 https://www.statista.com/statistics/863276/violent-crime-in-london/

19 Chris Lewis and Pippa Malmgren, *The Leadership Lab: Understanding leadership in the 21st century*, Kogan Page, 2018

20 http://fortune.com/2017/11/06/apple-tax-avoidance-jersey/

21 https://www.reuters.com/article/us-deutschebank-libor-settlement/deutsche-bank-fined-record-2-5-billion-over-rate-rigging-idUSKBN0NE12U20150423

22 http://www.bbc.com/news/business-31248913

23 https://www.theguardian.com/business/2012/jul/17/hsbc-executive-resigns-senate

24 https://www.forbes.com/forbes/welcome/?toURL=https://www.forbes.com/sites/kenrapoza/2017/09/15/tax-haven-cash-rising-now-equal-to-at-least-10-of-world-gdp/&refURL=https://www.google.co.uk/&referrer=https://www.google.co.uk/

25 https://www.theguardian.com/business/2016/nov/08/rbs-facing-400m-bill-to-compensate-small-business-customers

26 https://www.ft.com/content/87f72e9e-bafb-11e7-9bfb-4a9c83ffa852

27 https://www.theguardian.com/business/2008/dec/28/markets-credit-crunch-banking-2008

28 http://www.businessinsider.com/how-bernie-madoffs-ponzi-scheme-worked-2014-7

29 https://www.forbes.com/sites/greatspeculations/2019/05/03/20-years-since-the-uks-massive-gold-sales-heres-the-big-lesson-for-gold-investors/#51fb3a932ac6

30 https://www.cnn.com/2017/06/29/world/timeline-catholic-church-sexual-abuse-scandals/index.html

31 http://www.bbc.co.uk/news/uk-43121833

32 http://www.bbc.com/news/education-11621391

33 https://www.telegraph.co.uk/news/newstopics/mps-expenses/5357568/MPs-expenses-Sir-Peter-Viggers-claimed-for-1600-floating-duck-island.html

34 http://www.foxnews.com/politics/2017/12/25/7-biggest-political-scandals-2017.html

35 https://www.militarytimes.com/news/your-military/2016/09/12/report-wars-in-iraq-afghanistan-cost-almost-5-trillion-so-far/

36 http://www.nbcnews.com/id/22794451/ns/world_news-mideast_n_africa/t/study-bush-led-us-war-false-pretenses/

37 https://www.standard.co.uk/news/politics/damn-eu-referendum-result-shocks-world-leaders-as-britain-backs-brexit-a3280031.html

38 https://www.theguardian.com/education/2018/feb/11/thousands-of-teachers-caught-cheating-to-boost-exam-results

39 https://www.huffingtonpost.com/topic/teacher-sex-scandal

40 http://www.independent.co.uk/news/business/news/bae-systems-pays-400m-to-settle-bribery-charges-1891027.html

41 PWC Success Study 2018

42 https://www.bbc.co.uk/news/business-34324772

43 https://www.theguardian.com/environment/2015/oct/09/mercedes-honda-mazda-mitsubishi-diesel-emissions-row

44 https://edition.cnn.com/2019/12/30/business/carlos-ghosn-lebanon/index.html

45 https://www.bbc.com/news/business-48755329

46 http://www.bbc.co.uk/news/entertainment-arts-41594672

47 https://www.theguardian.com/media/greenslade/2014/feb/19/newsnight-lord-mcalpine

48 https://www.telegraph.co.uk/news/uknews/crime/jimmy-savile/12172773/Jimmy-Savile-sex-abuse-report-to-be-published-live.html

49 http://www.bbc.co.uk/sport/athletics/43301116

50 https://www.theguardian.com/society/2013/feb/06/mid-staffs-hospital-scandal-guide

51 https://www.theguardian.com/law/2017/feb/02/iraq-human-rights-lawyer-phil-shiner-disqualified-for-professional-misconduct

52 https://www.theguardian.com/us-news/2018/aug/22/how-many-of-trumps-close-advisers-have-been-convicted-and-who-are-they
53 https://www.bostonglobe.com/ideas/20/01/20/trillions-dollars-have-sloshed-into-offshore-tax-havens-here-how-get-back/2wQAzH5DGRwomFHoYPqKZJ/story.html
54 https://www.visualcapitalist.com/80-trillion-world-economy-one-chart/
55 https://www.forbes.com/sites/adigaskell/2022/08/11/covid-saw-an-exodus-of-over-50s-from-the-workforce/?sh=5d82e10758f5
56 https://www.businessinsider.com/gen-z-does-not-want-kids-will-get-married-2023-12

CHAPTER THREE: THIS HAPPY BREED?

1   https://www.ipsos.com/en-uk/what-makes-us-proud-be-british
2   https://www.dailymail.co.uk/travel/article-12006961/The-things-make-Brits-proud-British-revealed-Fish-chips-No-1.html
3   https://yougov.co.uk/society/articles/50248-what-has-five-years-of-measuring-britains-mood-weekly-shown
4   https://www.gallup.com/analytics/349280/gallup-global-emotions-report.aspx
5   https://www.instituteofcustomerservice.com/employees-facing-increased-customer-hostility-as-lockdown-eases/
6   https://www.statista.com/statistics/864736/knife-crime-in-london/
7   https://www.ons.gov.uk/peoplepopulationandcommunity/housing/bulletins/housingenglandandwales/census2021
8   https://www.ofcom.org.uk/siteassets/resources/documents/tv-radio-and-on-demand/bbc/bbc-news-review/research-documents/bbc-news-review-content-analysis-summary-report.pdf?v=324316
9   https://www.bbc.co.uk/aboutthebbc/documents/bbc-annual-plan-2024-2025.pdf
10 https://www.lgcplus.com/politics/workforce/exclusive-surge-in-first-time-chiefs-10-10-2024/
11 https://www.telegraph.co.uk/news/2024/01/19/older-people-special-police-volunteers-recruitment/
12 https://www.nationalworld.com/lifestyle/family-and-parenting/brits-only-live-25-miles-from-their-birthplace-on-average-4786911#:~:text=The%20average%20UK%20adult%20now%20lives%2025,released%20by%20leading%20family%20history%20website%20Findmypast.
13 https://lwbooks.co.uk/product/the-broken-promise-of-infrastructure
14 https://www.amazon.com/Road-Somewhere-Populist-Revolt-Politics/dp/1849047995
15 https://commonslibrary.parliament.uk/political-disengagement-in-britain-demographics-and-constituencies/
16 https://www.england.nhs.uk/2020/03/250000-nhs-volunteers/
17 https://greatergood.berkeley.edu/article/item/the_right_way_to_get_angry
18 https://www.bbc.com/news/uk-england-36863861
19 https://www.thetimes.com/life-style/property-home/article/the-uks-exodus-of-millionaires-is-not-good-for-the-country-t7tvtjxp2
20 https://www.lse.ac.uk/research/research-for-the-world/economics/how-much-tax-do-the-rich-really-pay
21 https://www.ukonward.com/data/how-often-do-you-feel-lonely/
22 https://www.urban.org/sites/default/files/2022-08/Solitary%20Confinement%20in%20the%20US.pdf
23 https://commonslibrary.parliament.uk/research-briefings/cbp-7749/
24 https://www.campaigntoendloneliness.org/facts-and-statistics/
25 https://www.mentalhealth.org.uk/our-work/public-engagement/unlock-loneliness/loneliness-young-people-research-briefing

26 https://www.latimes.com/opinion/story/2024-03-21/loneliness-epidemic-work-from-home-remote-guestrooms-airbnb-couchsurfing

27 https://www.centreforsocialjustice.org.uk/library/lost-boys

28 https://aibm.org/commentary/gen-zs-romance-gap-why-nearly-half-of-young-men-arent-dating/

29 https://www.samaritans.org/about-samaritans/research-policy/suicide-facts-and-figures/latest-suicide-data/

30 https://www.cnn.com/2020/12/17/economy/job-losses-women-pandemic/index.html

31 https://cawp.rutgers.edu/blog/gender-differences-2024-presidential-vote

32 https://www.bbc.co.uk/learningenglish/features/6-minute-english_2024/ep-240523

33 https://publications.parliament.uk/pa/ld201617/ldselect/ldlicact/146/14611.htm

34 https://www.aiforg.com/blog-database/gc9fpavl8fi3b5vn6vosd2pcbod6qc

35 https://www.ons.gov.uk/visualisations/censusareachanges/E08000032

36 https://x.com/RobertJenrick/status/1903138449491656916?lang=en

37 https://hansard.parliament.uk/commons/2025-06-09/debates/27E94862-93C7-4D29-B0DA-F77F92D14161/Non-StunSlaughterOfAnimals

38 https://www.theguardian.com/society/2025/feb/06/gen-z-authoritarianism-populism-democracy-uk-research

39 https://lgiu.org/resources/local-government-facts-and-figures/local-government-facts-and-figures-england/#section-4

40 https://www.statista.com/statistics/1050929/voter-turnout-in-the-uk/

CHAPTER FOUR: WHO WE ARE

1   https://assets.publishing.service.gov.uk/media/662692cd1cbbb3400ba7e601/business-and-trade-facts-and-figures.pdf

2   https://www.thetimes.com/business-money/energy/article/down-the-37-mile-tunnel-built-to-keep-londons-lights-on-9r2wvnndv

3   https://www.worldsbestcities.com/rankings/worlds-best-cities/

4   https://www.statista.com/chart/16417/share-of-people-who-donated-money-to-charity/

5   https://keywordtool.io/blog/most-spoken-languages-in-the-world/

6   https://www.archbishopofcanterbury.org/about/anglican-communio

7   https://www.amazon.com/History-Hit-Story-England-Making-ebook/dp/B0CXJPNHDG

8   https://en.wikipedia.org/wiki/List_of_countries_by_past_military_expenditure

9   https://www.royalnavy.mod.uk/equipment/submarine/astute-class

10 https://committees.parliament.uk/committee/111/national-security-strategy-joint-committee/news/204906/how-vulnerable-is-the-uk-to-undersea-cable-attacks/

11 https://www.quora.com/What-are-the-some-of-the-most-weird-football-clubs-traditions

12 https://www.liverpoolfc.com/news/lfc-most-watched-club-premier-league-global-audience-471-million-last-seasonliver

13 https://www.sportspro.com/news/premier-league-viewership-tv-ratings-2023-2024-sky-nbc-peacock/

14 https://www.premierleague.com/news/4016793

15 In *The Story of Dr Doolittle*, created by English American engineer turned children's writer Hugh Lofting: https://en.wikipedia.org/wiki/Hugh_Lofting

16 https://www.amazon.com/Peaceably-Because-Violence-Sticker-Tumblers/dp/B09V7F61YF

CHAPTER FIVE: GOD SAVE THE KING!

1   John Pudney, 'For Johnny', *For Johnny: Poems of World War II*, Shepheard-Walwyn (Publishers) Ltd, 1976; https://www.poetryfoundation.org/poets/john-pudney

2   https://allpoetry.com/poem/8479523-Love-by-Sir-Walter-Scott

3   https://www.kiplingsociety.co.uk/poem/poems_englands_answer.htm

4 https://poets.org/poem/work-4
5 https://www.bbc.com/news/uk-politics-23548094

CHAPTER SEVEN: DEFENCE OF THE REALM
1 https://www.dailymail.co.uk/news/article-12933727/Defence-memorial-Navy-slave-trade-Alan-West-Penny-Mordaunt.html
2 https://responsiblestatecraft.org/silicon-valley/
3 https://www.mqup.ca/understanding-military-culture-products-9780773527157.php
4 https://www.gov.uk/government/publications/uk-defence-doctrine-jdp-0-01
5 https://thedockyard.co.uk/wp-content/uploads/2020/12/The-history-of-the-Jolly-Roger-.pdf

CHAPTER EIGHT: WHY BRITAIN'S TRADITIONS MATTER
1 https://ojin.nursingworld.org/table-of-contents/volume-28-2023/number-3-september-2023/articles-on-previously-published-topics/gratitude-practice-to-decrease-stress
2 https://www.england.nhs.uk/2020/03/250000-nhs-volunteers/
3 https://yougov.co.uk/politics/articles/47473-public-services-are-in-bad-shape-across-the-board-say-britons
4 https://yougov.co.uk/politics/articles/47473-public-services-are-in-bad-shape-across-the-board-say-britons
5 https://www.morningadvertiser.co.uk/Article/2016/01/27/Multi-purpose-pubs-maximise-property-with-post-office-and-shop/
6 https://www.positive.news/society/the-colourful-rise-of-community-owned-local-pubs/
7 https://www.amazon.co.uk/How-England-Made-English-Neighbours/dp/0670919144
8 https://englishbreakfastsociety.com/about-us.html

CALENDAR OF OUR CUSTOMS
1 https://www.nationaltrust.org.uk/visit/cornwall/cotehele/our-work-coteheles-orchards

SPRING
1 https://www.bbc.com/news/uk-scotland-highlands-islands-60125288

SUMMER
1 https://www.bbc.co.uk/news/articles/c7711yjj6130
2 https://www.nottinghampost.com/news/local-news/mp-blocks-selston-park-boulder-4442438
3 https://www.theguardian.com/environment/article/2024/aug/01/eyemouth-herring-queen-fishing-industry-change-women-scottish-town

WINTER
1 https://www.amazon.co.uk/How-England-Made-English-Neighbours/dp/0670919144

INDEX